"In an era of breathtaking change, *Future-Focused Church* provides leaders with a compass as well as guardrails for navigating our way forward. Practical insight combined with a hopeful vision for the church make this an essential resource for all of us."

Andy Stanley, North Point Ministries

"I am a firm believer that the best days for the church are ahead of us, not behind us. *Future-Focused Church* should be required reading for every pastor and leader. It provides the insights and practical tools needed to navigate through current realities and move into the hope-filled future that awaits. We have a generation to reach and a mandate to fulfill. This book shows us how."

Christine Caine, founder of A21 and Propel Women

"The experience and research in this book combine to deliver a compelling resource for a new breed of leaders. It's no secret that future-focused leaders need practical gifting and skills to lead diverse communities. In your hands are the words that will transform you into a most effective generational leader."

Rev. Dr. Charlie Dates, senior pastor, Progressive Baptist Church and Salem Baptist Church

"By drawing from their varied experiences and expertise, the authors of *Future-Focused Church* have done the extraordinary. This team has given us a map with compelling destinations and clear directions, while simultaneously making room for God's Spirit to take us on detours of God's design. Reflections from Scripture are made concrete with real-life stories of churches in process and research from social science. This book will equip your church to get to the future, not with resigned reluctance but joyful anticipation."

Walter Kim, president, National Association of Evangelicals

"If I could summarize the purpose of *Future-Focused Church*, it's this quote: 'We don't want your church to go the way of Blockbuster.' Using a wealth of data from in-depth interviews, church training cohorts, and decades of hard-won personal experience, Powell, Mulder, and Chang provide a process for church leaders to think concretely about not only where their congregation will be in a decade but also how to take tangible action now to move closer to that goal."

Ryan Burge, author of *The Nones* and *The Great Dechurching*

"In a world of constant change and uncertainty, *Future-Focused Church* is a must-have for church leaders looking to foster a vibrant and thriving church or ministry. Packed with valuable insights and practical strategies, this book provides a step-by-step roadmap for transformational change across all faith traditions, with a particular emphasis on empowering young people. It will inspire you to embrace adaptive thinking and confidently believe that the best days of ministry are yet to come."

Christina Lamas, executive director, National Federation for Catholic Youth Ministry

"Against the pull of the past and the temptation to remain in a static present, the story of Jesus and the church is that of pressing forward into the future. In *Future-Focused Church*, Kara Powell, Jake Mulder, and Raymond Chang not only remind us of this call and its *why* but also show us the *what* and *how* of being future-focused. They help us navigate the tensions of change, recognize that the 'next generation' should be seen as the 'now generation,' and embrace the diverse tapestry of the church to be reflective of the kingdom we anticipate inhabiting. In doing so, we are encouraged to know that the best days of the church are in front of us."

Bishop Claude Alexander, pastor of The Park Church and author of *Becoming the Church*

"The future is brighter than we think. Many significant books have been written about the challenges faced by the church today, and we need this insight into our current reality. In this text, Powell, Mulder, and Chang offer a thoughtful analysis but even more so point us toward a potential positive prognosis. This prognosis is not based upon speculation, hyper-negativity, or ideology but upon thorough research and theologically thoughtful response. We need this book for such a time as this."

"Most church renewal guidebooks are very big on vision or are very narrowly prescriptive; neither works very well on the ground. *Future-Focused Church* is wonderfully grounded in a wide and deep foundation of evidence and experience. It offers sound, comprehensive advice for churches seeking to thrive in their ministry and mission, packaged for easy adaptation in a wide variety of contexts. In our Latino/a churches, which are typically already vital and growing, *Future-Focused Church* is so helpful in understanding and navigating intergenerational tensions (one of the greatest challenges we face at this historic moment). I would recommend this book to anyone seeking to ensure that their congregation becomes increasingly relevant as we move into the future."

"Powell, Mulder, and Chang collaborate in *Future-Focused Church* to translate years of wisdom, research, and experience into a guide for any congregation that wants to discern God's leading and discover new life. Faith and wisdom are threaded through this clear, accessible approach to church leadership that will help any congregation chart a path forward."

FUTURE-FOCUSED CHURCH

PREVIOUS BOOKS BY AUTHORS

Growing Young
    by Kara Powell, Jake Mulder, and Brad M. Griffin

Growing With
    by Kara Powell and Steven Argue

3 Big Questions That Change Every Teenager
    by Kara Powell and Brad M. Griffin

3 Big Questions That Shape Your Future
    by Kara Powell, Kristel Acevedo, and Brad M. Griffin

Faith Beyond Youth Group
    by Kara Powell, Jen Bradbury, and Brad M. Griffin

FUTURE-FOCUSED CHURCH

LEADING THROUGH CHANGE,
ENGAGING THE NEXT GENERATION,
and BUILDING A MORE DIVERSE TOMORROW

KARA POWELL, JAKE MULDER,
and RAYMOND CHANG

BakerBooks

a division of Baker Publishing Group
Grand Rapids, Michigan

Published by Baker Books
a division of Baker Publishing Group
Grand Rapids, Michigan
BakerBooks.com

Printed in the United States of America

Library of Congress Cataloging-in-Publication Data
Names: Powell, Kara Eckmann, 1970– author.
Title: Future-focused church : leading through change, engaging the next generation,
    and building a more diverse tomorrow / Kara Powell, Jake Mulder, and Raymond
    Chang.
Description: Grand Rapids, Michigan : Baker Books, a division of Baker Publishing
    Group, [2025] | Includes bibliographical references.
Identifiers: LCCN 2024024993 | ISBN 9780801093395 (cloth) | ISBN 9781493449149
    (ebook)
Subjects: LCSH: Church work with youth—United States. | Christian leadership—
    United States.
Classification: LCC BV4447 .P65253 2025 | DDC 253—dc23/eng/20240822
LC record available at https://lccn.loc.gov/2024024993

Cover design by John Kwok, TENx10 Collaboration

Authors are represented by WordServe Literary Group (www.wordserveliterary.com).

Baker Publishing Group publications use paper produced from sustainable forestry practices and postconsumer waste whenever possible.

25 26 27 28 29 30 31   7 6 5 4 3 2 1

To all young people,
starting with our own amazing children:
Nathan, Krista, and Jessica Powell;
Will and Theo Mulder;
and Sophia Chang.

You are the present
and future of the church,
and you inspire us
to prayerfully work toward a world
that reflects Jesus in truth,
love, mercy, and grace.

CONTENTS

ZONE III
THERE—Where God Is Leading 155

ZONE IV
HOW—Navigating the Journey Together 197

ACKNOWLEDGMENTS

Leading change faithfully and effectively in a congregation or ministry requires a team. So does conducting research and writing a book on the topic. While the three of us are this book's authors, its insights are drawn from over a decade of experience and the contributions of a world-class group of scholars and leaders.

This book wouldn't exist without the marvelous teams of the Fuller Youth Institute (FYI) and the TENx10 Collaboration. For over a decade, FYI has provided innovative yearlong cohort training to church teams, which functioned as a learning lab for our early research (and initial hunches) about leading change. Special thanks to Zach Ellis, Brad Griffin, Chuck Hunt, and Andy Jung for their stellar leadership in training congregations and leaders.

The qualitative interviews on congregational change were designed in part by Tyler Greenway and conducted thanks to the faithful help of Jane Hong-Guzmán de León and Patrick Jacques. We're grateful to other remarkable FYI staff (past and present) who read interview transcripts and shared their wisdom during a two-day, in-person research summit, including Jen Bradbury, Jennifer Guerra Aldana, Yulee Lee, LaTasha Nesbitt, Caleb Roose, Ahren Samuel, and Hannah Struwe.

We're grateful for support in launching this book into the world and supporting ministry leaders in untold ways by others on the

Fuller Youth Institute team, including Steve Argue, Macy Davis, Rachel Dodd, Nica Halula, Jen Hananouchi, Roslyn Hernández, Issac Kim, and Giovanny Panginda.

The capable and visionary team of the TENx10 Collaboration encourages us that a brighter future for the church is indeed ahead, and we're excited about how this book's contents might better support faith communities through the work of team members Kate Amaya, Charissa Dornbush, Abbigail Fraser, Lisette Fraser, Vanesa Zuleta Goldberg, Cory Hendrickson, John Kwok, Everidis Mendez Fontanez, Paul Matsushima, Sarah Roop, Shannon Schmidt, Jason Shafer, and Jason Villegas.

We're continually encouraged and sharpened by our colleagues in the Leadership Formation Division at Fuller Seminary, as well as the team at FULLER Equip.

Our highly respected faculty and staff colleagues in Fuller Seminary's School of Mission and Theology and School of Psychology & Marriage and Family Therapy have influenced our thinking, scholarship, and leadership in countless ways we're aware of and probably even more of which we're unaware. Frequent references throughout the book to our colleague Scott Cormode highlight how much his scholarship, language, and friendship have influenced us. We're grateful for his wisdom and mentoring, as well as his role as Jake's doctoral supervisor on congregational leadership and change.

Every line in the book was made better by an invested group of conversation partners and prereaders, including John Jay Alvaro, Jonathan Banks, Jim Candy, Cass Curry, Jeff Fernandez, Ernie Hinojosa, Phil Hirsch, John Kim, Steven Kim, Kristen Lashua, Seth Martin, Aqueelah Ligonde, Brett Talley, and Kim Zovak.

In addition to Brad Griffin's role in making the research and cohort training, his copyediting skills and review of the final manuscript made all chapters better.

Funding for the qualitative interviews was provided through Lilly Endowment Inc.'s generous support of a larger project on innovation and developing new approaches to ministry with young people. As always, we're honored by their visionary financial investment and partnership.

Baker Books has been a fantastic publisher, and we greatly appreciate the wisdom, hard work, and spirit of partnership their whole team consistently provides. Greg Johnson of WordServe Literary has continued to demonstrate incredible backing and faithful shepherding of this entire process.

Last, but definitely not least, our families have provided the ongoing support that made this book a reality. That has included prayer, encouragement, sharpening conversations about the content, and flexibility in schedules (for late nights, early mornings, and out-of-state travel). Our spouses, Dave Powell, Lauren Mulder, and Jessica Min Chang, help all of our work and our lives make sense. We also can't imagine life, leadership, or authoring this book without our kids, who remind us every day of the hope and possibility of this generation and have served as inspiration and conversation partners on the content.

Introducing the Future-Focused Church

Mapping the Journey
of a Future-Focused Church

The best days of the church are ahead.

Really.

Don't get us wrong. We are under no illusion that churches have it easy in this season. These days the church can feel . . .

So fractured.

So distracted.

So divided and politicized.

So exhausting.

So hard to lead.

Like everything is an uphill battle.

You may remember a simpler season. When people of all generations seemed less busy and showed up every week—or more frequently—to church worship and gatherings. Or when mental health concerns didn't seem so prevalent. Or technological interruptions so pervasive. Or young people's journeys so complex.

Or perhaps you're starting out in your leadership journey. You have big dreams. You're ready to roll up your sleeves and try new things, but others around you seem resistant or are moving too slowly.

We've led through these challenges. We feel them too.

But nonetheless, we believe the future of the church will be brighter than the past.

In fact, we believe the best days of *your church* are ahead.

But the question is, What do you think?

When you consider your church five months, five years, or five decades from now, what does the future look like? Brighter than the past? Or, if you're being honest, a little dim?

In answering those questions, leaders like you are all over the map. There's a mix of hope and heartache.

While the three of us have been in church and ministry leadership collectively for nearly seventy-five years, in this last decade we've encountered more church and ministry leaders who are trying harder yet seeing diminishing results. Who are often doing more work while seeing less fruit. The data paints a picture of US Christian leaders who are *dedicated yet drained*. Two-thirds of pastors in one study named 2020 (the first year of the pandemic in the US) as their toughest year in ministry ever.[1] According to 2023 data from the Exploring the Pandemic Impact on Congregations (EPIC) multiyear study, 53 percent of religious leaders have seriously considered leaving pastoral ministry, up from an already astonishing 37 percent in 2020.[2] Pastors who are younger, female, part-time, or bi-vocational are most likely to consider quitting.[3]

Weary leaders like these often oversee churches or parishes that are shrinking in size, as median worship has declined from 137

FIGURE 1.1

Percentage of Religious Leaders Considering Leaving Ministry

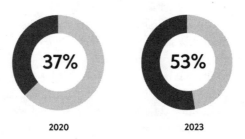

2020   2023

FIGURE 1.2

Percentage of US Adult Population That Is Christian

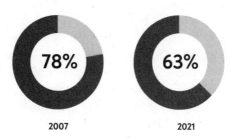

2007   2021

people in 2000 to 75 in 2023.[4] The decline in the number of Christians in the US is equally apparent. In 2007, 78 percent of the US adult population identified as Christian. That figure dropped to 63 percent in 2021[5] and is projected by the Pew Research Center to drop below 50 percent by 2070.[6]

Between 2007 and 2021, the number of adults who identify as religious "nones" (meaning they profess to be atheist, agnostic, or believe "nothing in particular") has grown from 16 percent to 29 percent. So, almost one in three US adults identify as religiously unaffiliated, compared with one in twenty in 1972.[7]

In addition to the "nones," we are intrigued by the rise of the "umms," described as those who take their faith seriously, are fond of the church in general (and usually even their last local congregation), and were actively involved in congregations in the past but no longer participate.[8] While this group has yet to be specifically

FIGURE 1.3

Portion of US Adults Who Identify as "Religiously Unaffiliated"

quantified, we think that across generations, and especially with a significant number of teenagers and young adults, this category accurately describes those who haven't "left" the church; they've more just "stopped being part."

With statistics like these, it's no wonder the future of the church feels less than bright for many leaders.

We know leaders like Vince, a senior pastor of a small rural congregation in the Mainline tradition, who shared, "I know God has called me to this work and this church. But I honestly don't know that our discipleship efforts in the last decade have made a tangible difference. People seem more divided than ever. Maybe it's time for me to get out of the way and let someone younger and more relevant take over."

Or Marissa, a youth leader in a large, innovative parachurch ministry, who lamented, "I'm the only person of color leading at my level in our area, and my organization seems to expect me alone to guide us into a more diverse future. I believe in where we're going, but I'm mentally and physically exhausted."

Or Luis, a board member of a midsized, highly diverse urban congregation, who reflected, "I want to help our pastors and church leadership move forward, but I'm not always sure the best way to help. In my day job, we'd simply fire people who aren't on board with the future. But our church has so many people who like the way things have been and don't seem to want to change."

The Challenge of Leading Change for the Future

Are you old enough to remember the thrill of walking through a physical video store like Blockbuster? You could spend hours debating which movie to watch only to be disappointed when your particular movie was "sold out" because all the physical copies had been rented. Those were the days—until a little start-up named Netflix came along. Just like that, you could order movies to come by mail, and now it's become the go-to destination for streaming. Blockbuster had every advantage of history, size, funding, and experienced staff. But today, Blockbuster is nearly out of business. (At the time of writing, one still remains in Bend, Oregon.) But Netflix? It's a multibillion-dollar company. Why? Because, at the end of the day, Blockbuster failed to adapt. They couldn't change with the times; they couldn't move forward to the future.

We don't want your church to go the way of Blockbuster.

Leading change in organizations, including churches, is not for the faint of heart. As a classic *Harvard Business Review* article "Cracking the Code of Change" explains, "Despite some individual successes . . . change remains difficult to pull off, and few companies manage the process as well as they would like . . . the brutal fact is that about 70 percent of all change initiatives fail."[9]

The good news? This resistance to change is normal. It's something even Jesus experienced!

In Mark 8, we glimpse one noteworthy exchange related to change when Jesus asks his disciples, "Who do you say I am?" Peter replies, "You are the Messiah" (Mark 8:29). The future is looking pretty good for Peter at this point. His confession and confidence make sense, given Jesus has recently healed many people, walked on water, and miraculously fed over five thousand people.

Then the story takes a turn in the wrong direction (for Peter at least). Jesus shares with his disciples that he will suffer, be rejected, be killed, and rise again.

What is Peter's response?

Peter takes Jesus aside and begins to rebuke him. While Peter has left everything to follow Jesus and declared Jesus is the Messiah, when Jesus tries to alter Peter's understanding and expectation beyond his comfort level, Peter resists and rejects.

In other words, Peter doesn't want things to change.

And if we're honest, we can probably relate. Whether you're trying to lead complex change in a large church or ministry or trying to shift the entrenched mindset of one person, you know leading change can be unpredictable and elusive. If you're going to be effective, you need help making sense of and navigating the challenges ahead.

You need help facing the future.

Churches Remain Hopeful but Wonder How to Change for the Future

Despite the formidable task of helping churches change, we remain unwavering in our conviction that the expiration date for the church is not drawing near. These difficult days are a wake-up call—an opportunity for transformation. And we are not alone in this hope.

We have the honor of leading a movement called the TENx10 Collaboration, whose mission is to help faith matter for ten million teenagers in the next ten years in the spirit of the abundant life Jesus describes in John 10:10. We recently gathered nearly 250 church and national ministry leaders from over one hundred organizations who hunger to work together to respond to the heartbreaking reality that one million US young people leave the Christian faith every year.[10] Those assembled represented the widest and most diverse movement of Protestant, Catholic, and Orthodox leaders who care about young people that we know of, including those from prominent parachurch ministries, dozens of denominations and networks, foundations, training and resource organizations, ministries that specifically serve people of color, megachurches, church plants, new and historic congregations, and many more.

> To find out more about the vision, mission, resources, and amazing organizations involved in the TENx10 Collaboration, please visit TENx10.org.

We spent three days discussing how the church (and younger people's experience of it) *must* and *can* be different. We explored reasons young people are drifting from faith as well as both the barriers to and opportunities for change. Several leaders shared the pain of their own teenage and adult children who had given up on the Christian faith altogether. Others, including Ray and Jake, shared hope that their young children would experience faith communities where their identity in Jesus Christ will be shaped through deep belonging and relationship.

At one point, an experienced denominational leader who has been actively involved with a national parachurch ministry voiced,

"I've dedicated my career to helping people discover God's best for their life and building up the church. The question is not *if* we need change. It's *how* that change can take place in local faith communities and across the country. This is world-changing work, and I am *all in* for it."

This leader's perspective was echoed throughout the room and ministries nationwide. You might be both surprised and encouraged to realize that across a broad spectrum of denominations, 82 percent of those who attend church services are optimistic about the future of *their* church (note it's *their* church, not necessarily *the* church).[11] That optimism is mirrored by churches' openness to change. When asked if they were "willing to change to meet new challenges," 73 percent of denominationally and ethnically diverse churches affirmed this willingness. (For those who are cynical about this high percentage, we recognize that expressing willingness to change is very different from actually changing.)[12]

Many leaders we've encountered in the last decade know *what* they want to see change but struggle with the process and path for *how* to bring about those desired revisions. They long to lead a church that is more like the one they see throughout the pages of Scripture—a courageous and compassionate church, a just and diverse church, a loving and generous church, and a faithful and vibrant church. But they don't always know how to get from where they are today to where they feel the Scriptures are calling them to be tomorrow.

Given our opening statements that we believe the best days of *the church*, and more specifically, *your church*, can be ahead, we're clearly optimistic about the potential for change and the future of both *the* church and *your* church. Not because we're ignorant of the challenges churches face but because we believe God is bigger than those challenges. And our big God invites us to be a people of hope. Hope that is grounded in the fact that God is a God of resurrection who makes things new, brings life out of death, and shines light in darkness.

Consider this: What if we're not merely in the midst of a decline but also an era of reimagining and renewal? While the gospel *message* never changes, the specific *methods* we utilize deserve our ongoing reimagination.[13]

To be honest, we don't see an easy option, fast path, magic wand, or quick fix that immediately enables churches to move forward. We believe this is a season in which leaders need to attend to what the Holy Spirit is doing in new ways and in local contexts and to develop skills and systems for ongoing adaptation. While change and moving into the future aren't *easy* in this reality, there are insights and lessons that can make them *easier*. That can save you from spinning your wheels and make it more likely you'll be effective.

That can help you lead a Future-Focused Church.

So, What Exactly Is a Future-Focused Church?

Our collective research and experience yield a definition of a Future-Focused Church as *a group of Jesus followers who seek God's direction together—especially in relationally discipling young people, modeling kingdom diversity, and tangibly loving our neighbors.*

Let's take a second to break this down into its five key components.

- *A group of Jesus followers.* At its most basic level, we understand a church to be not merely a building but a *people* who regularly gather in Jesus' name (Matt. 18:20).
- *Who seek God's direction together.* While we encourage you to listen to good research and think strategically about the future of the church, this is ultimately about following where God is leading.

We should pause here to make an important distinction. The rest of our Future-Focused Church definition highlights the 3 Checkpoints. By Checkpoints, we mean *intentional points on your journey that you need to pass through on the way to your future THERE.* We believe these 3 Checkpoints reflect values outlined in Scripture, offer the best hope for your church culture, are grounded in recent research, and have disproportionate importance given the dynamics of US churches and our world today.

That being said, let's unpack the rest of what it means to be a Future-Focused Church.

- *Relationally discipling young people* (Checkpoint #1): As you focus on the future, the faith formation of young people does not need to be the *only* priority or the *top* priority, but we contend it needs to be *one of your top priorities*. Research and experience consistently demonstrate that we can best form the faith of young people through a supportive journey, incorporating empathetic peer and intergenerational relationships, that meets young people's significant need for identity, belonging, and purpose.

- *Modeling kingdom diversity* (Checkpoint #2): God's kingdom is inherently diverse (Rev. 7:9). In fact, this was one of the shocking hallmarks of the early church (Acts 2:5–11; 10:34–35; 13:1–3). The gospel broke through dividing lines to turn strangers and enemies into friends and family, including those set in opposition to each other along ethnic and cultural lines. Outsiders noted the diversity and were both appalled by and drawn toward it. Today's young people are the most ethnically diverse generation ever, and the US is more culturally diverse than at any other previous time, and yet many of our churches do not currently reflect this diversity. We think churches can and should be the premier examples of the vibrant variety God intends.

- *Tangibly loving our neighbors* (Checkpoint #3): People from diverse ages and cultures want to know how the church is responding to the deepest needs in our world—with particular attention on those who are marginalized. We believe

As explained in *3 Big Questions That Change Every Teenager* and *3 Big Questions That Shape Your Future*, we believe that all people, and especially young people, are wrestling with 3 big questions:

1. Identity: Who am I?
2. Belonging: Where do I fit?
3. Purpose: What difference can I make?

churches are at their best when all generations are focused on how to tangibly love their neighbors (near and far) by seeking reconciliation, righteousness, and shalom.

While we won't provide a full theological analysis of the Future-Focused Church (though we could!), here we'll stick to two compelling examples from Jesus' life and ministry.

First, when Jesus teaches in the Lord's Prayer, "Your kingdom come, your will be done, on earth as it is in heaven" (Matt. 6:10), he is offering a future-focused prayer. When we pray these words as a church, we're engaging in the future-focused work of inviting more of God's way of life to come to earth through us—for the future of our community and our world to be better and more faithful than our present.

Second, after Jesus' resurrection, when the disciples witness his ascension and stand looking upward, two angels appear and ask, "Why do you stand here looking into the sky? This same Jesus, who has been taken from you into heaven, will come back in the same way you have seen him go into heaven" (Acts 1:11). As followers of Jesus, we also wait and work with hope and expectation for Jesus' future second coming.

Living into this future-focused orientation of the church shouldn't leave us disconnected from our past, disengaged from our present, or disillusioned about our church's future. Instead, it should enliven and empower us through the Holy Spirit to roll up our sleeves and partner with what God is up to in our world here and now.

Given the pain and possibility of church leadership in today's complex and fast-changing world, inviting God's kingdom to come and God's will to be done on earth requires prayerful focus on the

▶ *Shalom* is a Hebrew word that occurs throughout Scripture. While it can be translated as "peace," it has a rich history of meaning and interpretation including completeness, wholeness, prosperity, safety, flourishing, and harmony. Overall, it emphasizes a state where things are made right.

greatest areas of need and opportunity. Being future-focused is not optional or just a good suggestion for *some* churches but rather an affirmation of what is central for *all* churches to be healthy, vibrant, and vital.

A Future-Focused Church in Action

We encountered one exemplary church in our research that gives us hope. If we said this church's name, we are certain you would have heard of it. It was started by a few young adults with limited ministry experience. As a brand-new church plant, it drew an ethnically diverse group of several thousand on its first day.

From there, it continued to grow quickly. Large groups of people were baptized. The teaching was Spirit-filled and powerful. People were praying fervently, worshiping passionately, and giving generously. While its members gathered for large group experiences and worship, they also connected in smaller groups—sharing meals and their lives. The church was generous to all who needed food and shelter, providing a countercultural example of love and unity in a world that was selfishly segmented. In addition, miraculous healings were witnessed and reported. It was clear something new and unique was happening in this community.

It didn't take long for news about this church to spread. Many leaders of more established faith communities in their city didn't love the new work and growth taking place and questioned the validity of the leadership of these less experienced upstarts. Despite the wider skepticism and resistance, the new church continued to grow and transform lives as people were invited to follow Jesus. The church received a significant boost when several people chose to sell their property and all they owned and use the proceeds to meet the needs of those inside and outside of the church.

While much was going well, not everything was perfect in the early life of this congregation. At one point, a financial scandal involving two members of the church rocked the community. Another member of the church's leadership experienced legal trouble and was arrested, though released shortly after. The church experienced big obstacles to unity in the midst of its significant cultural and ethnic diversity, including intense disagreements from top leaders about their most important values. On another occasion, one group complained to the leadership that they weren't receiving the same level of congregational care and support as another group. In the middle of these challenges, the church made the needed adjustments and retained its focus on Jesus as the hope and truth, even when it was tempting to chase after other (usually good) distractions.

In the years that followed, this new church faced more challenges, but its members didn't give up. They continued to pray, worship, love their neighbors, give to those in need, share time and meals together, train up future leaders, and do their best to model the way of Jesus. People took notice. Their ministry flowed beyond the four walls of any building. Many were sent out as missionaries to share the good news of Jesus with those who had not yet heard. Several of these leaders went on to start vibrant new churches.

You don't need to Google "fastest growing churches" to know what church we're talking about here. We're referring to the early church described in the book of Acts. The church that comes together in Acts 2 and goes on to grow and eventually transform the world with the gospel is one of the best examples of what it means to be a Future-Focused Church.

The story of the early church in the book of Acts isn't just a story from a different, disconnected time and place. It is *our story*. It's about our foundation, our identity, and our narrative of who we are and where we come from. If you are part of a faith community today, you inherit and continue the story of a group of people who experienced uncertainty, instability, resistance, and conflict—but also great hope, clarity, joy, and excitement about what God *has done* and what God *will do*. Being *future-focused* means living into and building on your past, while looking ahead to the future where God is leading.

Myths about Future-Focused Churches

Collectively, along with the team at Fuller Youth Institute (FYI), we have guided over a thousand local churches through a comprehensive (often yearlong) change process to become more vibrant and vital in the future. We have gathered data along the way through congregational surveys and evaluations, as well as in-depth interviews with forty-five leaders from twenty-three of those congregations, which were then analyzed for themes and insights. We have spent time in person with many of these congregations, and in some cases, we have walked with them for over ten years.

In the midst of this rich research, work, and conversation with churches and Christian leaders, we've run into several myths and erroneous assumptions about Future-Focused Churches, including that they:

- Focus only on young people and leave older generations behind.
- Forget their church's history and neglect the past.
- Water down or de-emphasize the good news of Jesus Christ.
- Make drastic and sweeping changes quickly.
- Miss out on what's happening in the *present* because they only live in the *future*.
- Lose their denominational or cultural identity.
- Abandon traditional worship styles in favor of more contemporary styles.
- Want to become megachurches or multisite churches.
- Are monocultural and homogeneous.
- Are led by a single visionary pastor or have a vision that shifts significantly every year.

However, the reality is quite different. In the research and work that led to this book, we've learned from numerous churches who are trying to be more future-focused, are embracing the 3 Checkpoints, and demonstrate many of the five components mentioned above. These are examples of what a Future-Focused Church actually looks like:

- A church plant in California integrating spiritual formation, justice, and community development.

- A Black, multisite megachurch with a hundred-year history that presses toward holistic discipleship.
- A small, rural, predominantly White congregation in the Pacific Northwest that meets for Sabbath on Saturday and is growing quickly in its engagement of young adults.
- A midsized, multiethnic, Mainline, urban congregation on the East Coast with a rich history of national and global influence.
- A predominantly Chinese-immigrant church learning new ways to engage with and serve the surrounding neighborhood.
- A nondenominational church in the Midwest that pioneered and trained thousands of other churches in innovative approaches to ministry.
- A fast-growing, bilingual, Latina/o congregation in the South that emphasizes the importance of church as family.

No two Future-Focused Churches look the same. They represent a wide variety of locations, sizes, theological and denominational backgrounds, racial and ethnic makeups, and much more. That means that any congregation or parish—including yours—can become future-focused.

Mapping the Journey to Your Church's Future

As you and your church seek to be future-focused, be encouraged that Jesus is the most effective change leader who ever lived. He has brought, and continues to bring, transformation to individuals (including the three of us), families (including ours), communities, organizations, and societies. In fact, we contend that leading change in the church is fundamentally about inviting people to trust and follow Jesus.

While this book will draw on the example of Jesus along with the experience of many churches, there is also much that can be learned from research on organizational change. Organizational change experts Charles O'Reilly and Michael Tushman state that, at a basic level, "Managing change involves moving an organization from its current state to its desired future state through a transition period."[14]

In other words, change involves people journeying from HERE to THERE.

FIGURE 1.4

Mapping the Journey

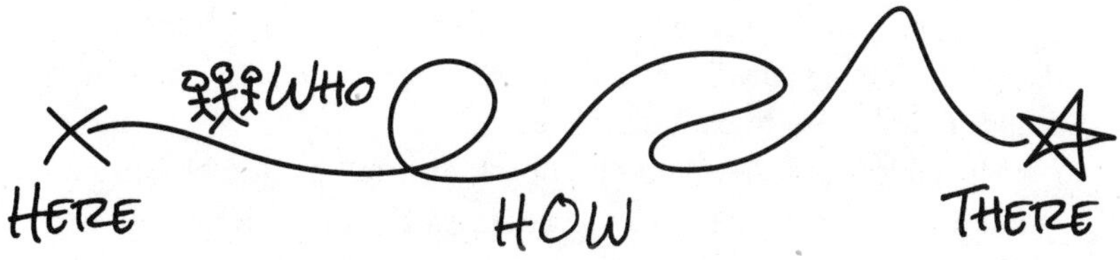

HERE represents where your church is now. This includes your physical location as well as other elements that make up the current reality of your church—your people, culture, current sense of life and vitality, resources, infrastructure, programs, and more.

THERE represents your desired future reality or destination. If you were to picture your church six months, six years, or sixty years from now, this is what you want your church to be doing or what you might want it to look like.

WHO represents the people who will be part of the journey. In most churches, this encompasses your overall congregation, your key leaders (such as a board, staff, or elders), attendees across generations and at various levels of congregational leadership, as well as people who are not yet part of the church but whom you hope to engage.

HOW is the path to navigate between where you are now and where you hope to be in the future.

Together, these four zones construct your *map of change*.[15]

You probably use a map to navigate frequently in your daily life. To arrive at an unfamiliar destination, you rely on a GPS or digital map (or if you're really old school, paper maps) to anticipate the terrain and know when to make a turn. Having a map makes it much more likely you'll arrive at your desired destination. While simply having the map doesn't immediately solve your problems, constructing the map allows you to invest your limited time in the right places to increase the likelihood of change.

Notice we said *constructing the map*. You—and the team you will build—are the cartographers for your church. While we will be your companions for this journey, we cannot offer you a finished map. No one can. Nor can you simply imitate the map of another church. The map for your community is unique to your context. By engaging in experimentation and exploration and embracing the guidance of the Holy Spirit, you will get your bearings and be able to lead your church forward with confidence and hope.

Throughout this book, we'll unpack in detail how to construct such a map for change in your congregation as well as how to navigate the journey ahead. For now, we offer several important considerations:

- In this journey, Christian leaders are both guides and fellow travelers. In some cases, you may know the way and be able to share wisdom about the path ahead. In others, you will be leading along a path with which you're unfamiliar. The zones can be explored through guiding questions.
  - HERE: Where are we now, and why are we here?
  - THERE: Where is God leading us?
  - WHO: Who are the people in our congregation (or ministry) and wider community whose unique perspectives and gifts must shape this effort?
  - HOW: What is our next faithful step, and how might we move into a more faithful future?[16]
- You need to be clear about both where you are starting from and where you are headed before you chart your course. We are often surprised by how frequently church leaders engage in the HOW without being mindful about their HERE or THERE.

FIGURE 1.5

Mapping the Journey with Questions

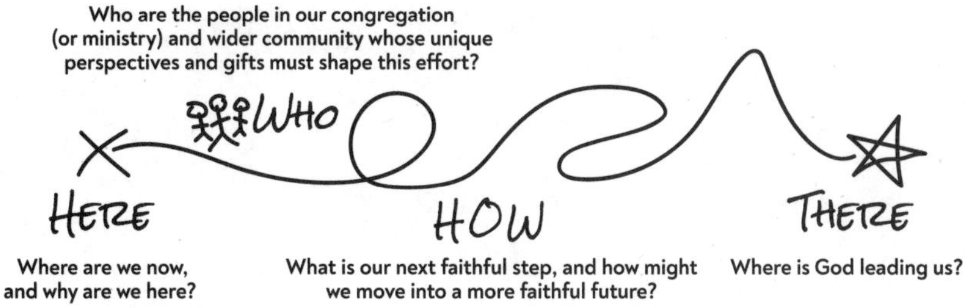

Who are the people in our congregation
(or ministry) and wider community whose unique
perspectives and gifts must shape this effort?

HERE

HOW

THERE

Where are we now,
and why are we here?

What is our next faithful step, and how might
we move into a more faithful future?

Where is God leading us?

- If you take time to clarify your HERE and THERE, God often illuminates HOW you'll navigate the journey.

- While it's our responsibility as Christian leaders to make wise plans, God is the one who ultimately establishes (or changes) those plans through the power of the Holy Spirit.

- Change would be tough enough if you were making decisions on your own, but you also need to be clear about WHO is on the journey with you. Taking into account your unique people, community, history, and culture means no two church journeys will be exactly the same.

- Rather than following a formula or engaging in well-ordered and consistent steps, we find the image of the map helpful because leading complex change often involves engaging in both/and thinking rather than either/or thinking. Throughout the book, you may notice several dichotomies future-focused leaders must hold together. This is because the work of leading culture change in the church is often not about finding just the right solution—but about managing tensions.

One last caveat we will offer on this map: if you have been leading for any amount of time, you know that change isn't as simple as moving from one static starting point to one static future destination. Our world and church leadership are dynamic, and there

FIGURE 1.6

Mapping the Journey—Multiple There

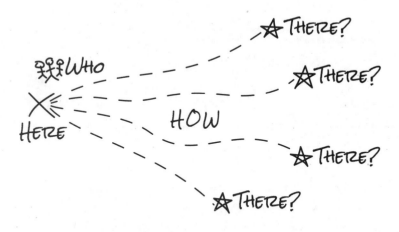

could be multiple potential future realities for your church. That's why the path has highs, lows, and multiple twists and turns. That is also why we've added this second diagram. As a cartographer for your community, you need to prepare for, and be able to pivot into, more than one potential future.

For some leaders, simply seeing this revised visual might be enough to raise your blood pressure and make you want to throw in the towel. Yes, the tools we'll offer you in this book are research-based and rooted in Scripture, but they won't make change easy. Or pain-free. As leaders who have guided change in churches and other organizations, we've personally experienced how much this work can cost. We carry the stories and scars and can show you our therapy and coaching bills as proof.

It's not an accident that respected organizational change scholar Ronald Heifetz spends a significant portion of his book on adaptive leadership addressing the personal side of change leadership.[17] It's also not an accident that Scripture is filled with examples of the costs and dangers of change leadership, such as the Old Testament prophets being persecuted, Jesus being crucified, the disciples being arrested, or Paul being shipwrecked, beaten, and stoned. As you get deeper into the content of this book, and especially if you begin to feel overwhelmed, we encourage you to take a step back, pray, and remember many other leaders have struggled or felt similarly. We urge you to surround yourself with the personal and relational support required to take your next faithful step and trust that God will guide your church's journey.

How This Book Can Help Your Church Realize Your Future

We've written this book with a wide variety of roles and types of leaders in mind. You might be a senior leader in your congregation, such as a lead pastor, priest, executive pastor, elder, or board member. Or you might carry responsibility for, or volunteer with, a particular age or area, such as ministry with children, youth, young adults, women, small groups, senior adults, missions, worship, or more! While our research and examples will focus on faith communities, we also hope to equip leaders in parachurch organizations, nonprofit leadership, education, and the marketplace.

Whatever your role and calling, we hope you experience this book as both a source for key insights and data and a practical field guide. Even if you are reading this book on your own now, we recommend you find at least one person, or ideally a small team of volunteers or other leaders and staff, and read alongside them at a later date.

While some books (such as novels) are meant to be read as quickly as you have time to consume the content, we encourage you to take this book a bit slower. It is not meant to be a sprint but to be digested, discussed, and deployed during the various stages of your change journey. Even if you choose to read it through from start to finish in a short period of time, the various chapters and practical tools are designed to be your conversation partners in upcoming years and months as you encounter ongoing challenges and opportunities.[18]

As you read on, we hope you'll join us in the hope-filled belief that the best days of your church and *the* church can be ahead. Not because all is sweetness and light in church leadership these days or because all of the answers are in this book. But because, while you may be dedicated yet drained, we pray you will live out of the hope you inherit and continue the Acts 2 narrative of Jesus followers who experienced difficulty and exhaustion yet discovered profound hope and joy that sparked a movement for millions.

Our prayer is that, instead of being depleted, you and your church will be empowered and guided by God's grace. Your church's fresh future-focused journey can begin now. Let's write the next chapter together.

REFLECTION QUESTIONS

Given our definition of a Future-Focused Church (a group of Jesus followers who seek God's direction together—especially in relationally discipling young people, modeling kingdom diversity, and tangibly loving our neighbors), on a scale of 1–5 (with 1 being "not at all" and 5 being "very"), how future-focused is your church?

Do you believe the best days of your church are ahead? Why or why not?

What lessons or insights from the story of the early church in Acts seem most important for your church?

Of the four zones of the change map (HERE, THERE, WHO, HOW), which feels particularly clear for your church? Which feels the murkiest? Why?

What is your biggest prayer for how God will work through you and your team to help your church become a Future-Focused Church?

3 Checkpoints That Shape Your Church's Culture

What do you do when your once fast-growing church plant begins to plateau? When your reputation as a go-to destination for young people in your community shifts, and your average age begins to increase? When your previous palpable sense of vibrancy and vitality now feels . . . distant?

These were the pressing questions faced in a nondenominational church founded a few decades ago by a Gen X pastor with a cutting-edge approach to ministry and dynamic gospel-centered teaching.

While the church actively championed all 3 Checkpoints of a Future-Focused Church, as the years passed and the original young adult membership aged into their later forties and fifties, some of the original magic began to wane. The church certainly wasn't in decline, but for perhaps the first time, leaders started to use words like *stagnant* and *stalled*, and their team began to search for answers.

One month into the process of prayerfully discerning their future, a group of young adult leaders had a lightbulb moment. While the church's founding DNA was based on engaging diverse younger people, many of whom were skeptical of church and passionate about changing their neighborhood and world, their senior leadership team had lost that focus. As the church and its senior leadership aged, they continued to prioritize the (now older) age cohort who had founded the church and had lost sight of what mattered most to *today's* young people.

For the next year, the senior leadership of the congregation gave the young adult leadership team some freedom to explore potential future-focused changes. These young adults engaged in significant listening—to both congregants and unchurched neighbors across generations.

As the young adult leadership team continued to listen and reflect, they concluded they needed to reemphasize some of the powerful DNA from which the church plant was born. First, they would need to place greater priority on understanding and investing in today's teenagers and young adults. Second, the church should double down on their commitment to ethnic and cultural diversity. Third, the congregation would need to pursue biblical justice and love their local and global neighbors in ways that were more relevant to all generations—especially young people.

When the young adult leadership team presented their insights to senior leaders, they felt the senior leaders were interested but not ready to take action. The young adult leaders were given permission and responsibility to try some initiatives within young adult ministries but no authority to enact changes across the congregation. As a result, there was no sustained churchwide action or culture change.

When we recently crossed paths with one of the young adult leaders, he summarized where they were on the journey, saying, "We have a diverse team of young and committed leaders who know *what* we want to see, but *how* to make that change happen and change our church culture is unclear and seems out of reach."

We've written this book for leaders like this young adult pastor, their church's senior leadership team, and so many others. Leaders who are asking the right questions about *what* they should focus on as they move into a brighter future as well as *how* they could move in that direction.

Perhaps leaders like you.

We want to explore the importance of church culture and the 3 Checkpoints we believe are key to *what* needs to change as your church moves forward toward your most faithful future. While these 3 Checkpoints don't cover everything your church needs to be healthy and transformational, we believe they are nonnegotiable for any church or ministry that wants a vibrant and vital future.

The Importance of Culture in Becoming Future-Focused

Culture eats strategy for breakfast.[1]

The journey of becoming a Future-Focused Church depends on changing your church's culture. Simply put, *culture* is what you repeatedly do and what is embraced as normal.[2]

Any future-focused map or strategy will ultimately fall short if you don't shift your church culture. The good news is there are tools to help you make these shifts. The first we find in Scripture, which offers us a narrative of how the early church shifted and cemented its culture.

Let's return to the early Acts church. Post-resurrection, Jesus charges his disciples to make disciples and teach people to obey everything he's commanded (Matt. 28:19–20). In essence, Jesus hands his disciples a compelling future THERE.

The challenge?

While people were excited to follow Jesus, those same people differed in what they embraced as normal. When the early church came together in Acts 2:42–47 for teaching, meals, fellowship, sharing possessions, and worship, its members were Jews who already lived out of a well-established culture and a deeply held history. But they also spoke different languages, operated under different laws and authorities, ate different types of food, and almost certainly had different expectations for how their new Christian community should function. It couldn't have been easy.

Although amazing miracles were happening and lives were being changed, the disciples probably had their hands full helping people understand how to more effectively live the way of Jesus. We wonder how much of that teaching and discussion was an echo of Jesus' common words of, "You have heard that it was said. . . . But I tell you . . ." (Matt. 5:21–48).[3] How often might the disciples have gathered together in a room, exhausted, lamenting with each other about some members of the church who were still unwilling to share their possessions? How often do you think they debated to decide which new disciple would have the next conversation with them? Or during one of the meal and fellowship times, might one of the twelve have had to pull an older member of the church aside for a heart-to-heart, perhaps because that member was frustrated with a few of the younger people who were eating unfamiliar food or talking too loudly near them?

The early church faced internal conflicts of Ananias and Sapphira being dishonest about giving their money to the church (Acts 5:1–11), the Hellenistic Jewish widows being overlooked in the distribution of food (6:1–7), and ongoing persecution (5:7–42). Still, the growing community of disciples held fast to the charge Jesus had given them and used the tools at their disposal to help new and old Jesus followers take on more and more of the way of Jesus. They had *a lot* of discussion about what cultural practices should be accepted as normal (such as the Council at Jerusalem in Acts 15:1–35), all while repeating regular practices over and over (such as staying sensitive to the guidance of the Holy Spirit in Acts 13:1–4).

Over time, what they repeatedly did and embraced as normal created a church that was Spirit-led, adaptable, generous, and radically focused on Jesus. As a result, many people became convinced that the ultimate truth, the full and abundant life, and the best way to God were found by being baptized in the name of Jesus and taking on Jesus' way.

As the church spread, so did its culture.

3 Essential Checkpoints for Your Church's Future

The truth is you'll make the best progress in a Future-Focused Church when you make the needed cultural shifts. As you map your journey, the 3 Checkpoints below offer some of the best potential to propel you toward God's best for your church in this way. Why? Because all 3 Checkpoints:

- Emerge from Scripture.
- Are part of holistic discipleship for all generations.
- Are confirmed as important by the best current empirical research.
- Play a central role in the church's compelling public witness to nonbelievers of all ages.
- Have been proven to bear fruit in a wide variety of churches both recently and throughout the centuries.

We're aware you or someone on your team might ask, "Are these the only areas of church culture that matter? The only ones a church needs to prioritize to be healthy?" Our short answer is no.

Our slightly longer answer is that there are many areas where your church (and most churches) is already doing pretty well. Here, we're less concerned with those *bright spots*. Instead, we believe God is inviting courageous leaders to reflect on church *bare spots*—which means understanding who is missing from our communities and why, reasons our churches may not resonate with those we need to serve, and how God might want to adjust our church culture moving forward.

These Checkpoints are some of the most important markers of the journey from HERE to THERE for Future-Focused Churches

FIGURE 2.1

Mapping the Journey—3 Checkpoints

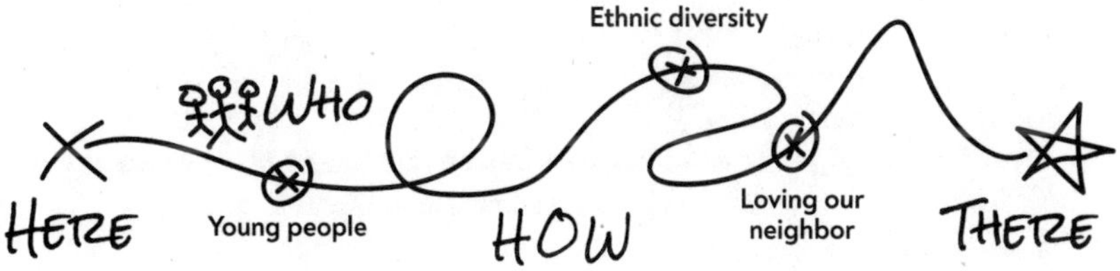

because they represent a generative intersection between the needs of our world today and the invitations and commands of Scripture. In future chapters, we'll focus on how to catalyze change, but first we want to highlight the key areas in which most churches want—or may need—to make changes.

Checkpoint #1: Prioritizing and Empathizing with Young People

While the invitation of the gospel is for all people (of every age, racial and ethnic background, gender, and culture), *we believe there is no question more pressing than how congregations and parishes will form the faith of young people.*

Unfortunately, much of the data about young people and faith feels more like bad news than good news. According to the Pinetops Foundation's data-driven projections, over one million US Christian young people are likely to disaffiliate from Christianity annually.[4] By 2050, between thirty-five and fifty million youth are projected to leave the Christian faith.

In addition, it's undeniable that churches are also *aging*. On average, one-third (33 percent) of congregants are 65 or older; that age group represents 17 percent of the general US population. Those ages 18–34 represent 14 percent of congregants and 23 percent of the US population. More encouragingly, those ages 13–17 represent 9 percent of churchgoers and 7 percent of the general population.[5]

> When we say "young people," we are primarily referring to teenagers and young adults. But if your church doesn't have many (or any) young people, you might consider what it means for your church to form the faith of *younger* people (meaning younger than the average age of your congregation now). By identifying teenagers and young adults, we aren't intentionally neglecting children's ministry. (We believe many of the concepts here and throughout the book will also apply or be reflected in children's ministry.) Given the difference in development between these age groups, we focus our analysis and advice on the areas where we have the greatest expertise (teenagers and young adults).

FIGURE 2.2

Congregational Participants Age Chart

The Ages of Congregational Participants Doesn't Parallel the US Population

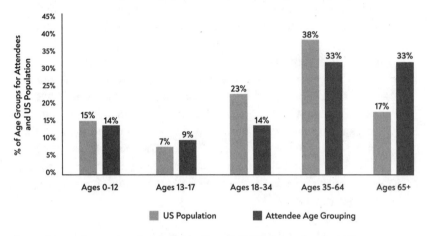

Comparison numbers are based on the Census Bureau's 2019 American Community Survey.
Source: 2020 Faith Communities Today survey. Hartford Institute for Religion Research.

Another challenge in reaching this generation? They're also experiencing historic mental health challenges. Clinical-level depression in teens and young adults more than doubled between 2011 and 2021; the teen suicide rate also more than doubled between 2007 and 2019.[6] That's part of why one of three adjectives used by the Fuller Youth Institute to describe today's young people is *anxious*.[7]

But that's not the full story.

Where there's bad news, there's still good news too. While there are plenty of depressing studies about today's young people, those need to be paired with uplifting data about young people and their role in the future of the church.

In addition to *anxious*, what are the other two adjectives used by FYI to summarize today's young people? *Adaptive* because of their amazing creativity, and *diverse* because of their great variety and their openness to those who are different from them.[8]

In addition, teenagers and young adults are open to relationships with caring, older adults. Encouragingly, coming out of the pandemic, 70 percent of thirteen- to twenty-five-year-olds reported valuing relationships even more now.[9] Churches with a future-focused culture don't believe the lie that young people don't want relationships with adults. Young people want to get to know older generations, but as we'll explore, our care needs to be authentic and our love unconditional.

Even better news: young people are not only open to relationships with warm adults but also open to Jesus. After studying twenty-five thousand teenagers globally, the Barna Group concludes, "It's rare that teens think poorly of Jesus. Most teenagers around the world have a positive perception of him." Five attributes of Jesus young people are especially likely to appreciate are that he offers hope, cares about people, is trustworthy, is generous, and makes a real difference in the world today.[10]

The good news is that this cultural Checkpoint is an area where Scripture and data overlap. Jesus' perspective on young people is clear as he tells his disciples, "Let the children come to me, and do not hinder them" (Luke 18:16), and he shares with others, "Unless you change and become like little children, you will never enter the kingdom of heaven" (Matt. 18:3). In 1 and 2 Timothy, Paul takes on an invested mentoring relationship with younger Timothy, his "true son in the faith" (1 Tim. 1:2).

Our experience is that future-focused senior leaders of churches and national and regional ministry organizations consistently call out engaging young people as one of their top three needs or

> One of our research-based books that has especially resonated with church leaders broadly is *Growing Young: Six Essential Strategies to Help Young People Discover and Love Your Church.* *Growing Young* studied 250 congregations thriving in their ministry with teenagers and young adults and profiled the innovative core commitments that help engage younger generations and breathe vitality, life, and energy into the whole church.

opportunities. Showcasing the need to prioritize young people, one wise senior pastor we interviewed for our *Growing Young* research stated, "Everyone in our church rises when we focus on young people."[11] Twenty years earlier, this senior pastor's church had decided to invest more resources in the discipleship of younger generations. There was initial pushback from some adults in the church who felt that would lead to fewer resources for others. It's similar to the old adage that if a group of people is sharing a pie, and one person receives a larger piece, there will be less pie for others.

What actually happened when young people received a "bigger piece of the pie" in the church? Consistently, and over multiple years, *the whole pie grew bigger*. Attendance and giving increased. Across all sectors of the church, ministries and leadership were stronger. Young people were stepping in and using their gifts. There was a sense of energy and life in the church that encouraged all generations.

Checkpoint #2: Modeling the Ethnic and Cultural Diversity of God's Kingdom

In addition to welcoming all generations, Future-Focused Churches pursue a culture that embraces all ethnicities and races. Some forms of prioritizing diversity are often perceived or presented as part of a "partisan" or "ideological" agenda. But Scripture shows us that pursuing

> In describing the ethnic diversity of the church and our world, the two primary terms we will use are "people of color" and "racialized minorities." As with many domains, including Christianity, language about race is constantly changing. While "people of color" is a commonly used phrase, it leaves the false assumption that race is a fixed and unchanging concept, it falls short in appreciating the variations among racial and ethnic groups, and it doesn't recognize that White people's experiences are also shaped by racialization. The advantages of the term "racialized minorities" are that it recognizes that race shapes our identities and experiences (including those who are racialized White) and how we navigate the world, and that racism leads to disparate opportunities and outcomes.[12]

loving relationships with those who look or experience the world differently than we do while working toward the flourishing of all is first and foremost a biblical mandate (Jer. 29:7; 1 Cor. 12:12–14; Eph. 2:11–22). In the midst of today's politicized and polarized culture, we celebrate our vibrant variety as part of God's agenda and the pursuit of a diverse and just community as a kingdom pursuit.

Aligning with the vision in Revelation 7:9 of the future church representing "every nation, tribe, people and language," faith communities that prioritize the future can take hope in the ethnic and racial diversity crisscrossing the US today. While about two-thirds of US adults are White, that percentage drops to half for those under eighteen. That means less than 50 percent of US young people today are White and over 50 percent are people of color.[13] Looking ahead a few decades, by 2055, there will be no single racial or ethnic majority in the US.[14] Currently about 98 percent of Americans live in a county with a growing Latina/o population, and 95 percent live in a county where the Asian population is increasing. Overall, in nineteen out of twenty US counties, ethnic diversity is on the rise.[15]

This increase in ethnic and cultural diversity of our country is only partially reflected in US churches. In 2000, 12 percent of US churches were multiracial, meaning at least 20 percent of the church was not part of that church's dominant racial community. By 2020, that percentage more than doubled to 25 percent.[16] Greater racial diversity in churches is correlated with a number of thriving qualities

> ▶ Even in those increasingly fewer geographic areas in the US that have little to no ethnic diversity, there are other forms of diversity, such as socioeconomic diversity, that display this cultural Checkpoint. One question you can ask is, Would those from the most economically disadvantaged backgrounds find themselves at home in our community? While we believe a commitment to modeling the diversity of God's kingdom should be a priority for every congregation, exactly what this looks like and how quickly your church moves in this direction will be shaped by your unique context.

including increased growth, spiritual vitality, a clearer sense of mission and purpose, more young adults, and increased new members.[17]

Reflecting on the available data, sociologist Michael O. Emerson observes four characteristics that correlate with a greater likelihood that a church is racially and ethnically diverse: (1) being Evangelical or Catholic; (2) prioritizing expressive worship; (3) having younger members; and (4) being located in the western US. Unfortunately, Emerson's data also indicates that once a multiracial church becomes less than 50 percent White, the White members often leave.[18]

Given some geographic regions are more diverse than others, when leaders ask us "How diverse should our church be?" our answer is that we hope the ethnic diversity of their members is moving toward the ethnic diversity of God's kingdom. This might initially involve strategic choices to reflect the ethnic diversity of your neighborhood, with a goal of outpacing that diversity and leading toward greater understanding, empathy, and Christian community.

While there are many hopeful signs in US churches, there are still great challenges. Despite some progress made in the past several decades, racism and fear of "the other" (meaning those who are different) remain. While de jure (or legally sanctioned) racial segregation no longer defines our society, voluntary de facto (in practice outside of the law) forms of segregation continue to shape our church experiences more than we might realize. The average church in the US is still more racially segregated than its neighborhood, and churches are more severely racially segregated today than schools were during the Civil Rights era in the late 1960s.[19]

Interestingly, churches that were described as multiracial twenty or more years ago haven't become significantly more ethnically diverse since then. Further, while there are some wonderful examples of White Christians joining multicultural churches, much of the diversity we see today is a result of people of color actively joining White churches, thereby making them more diverse.[20] This means that the burden of "diversification" within the church has been driven by, and often falls on, racialized minorities. In a recent interview, Emerson observes, "All the growth [in multiracial churches] has been people of color moving into White churches.

We have seen zero change in the percentage of Whites moving into churches of color."[21]

As more people of color become involved in White-dominant churches, we have often observed the perspectives of White leaders and White culture still functioning (sometimes intentionally, but more often unintentionally) as the norm against which other perspectives and cultures are measured. In this scenario, varying cultures and perspectives aren't simply viewed as different while also deserving value and respect. Instead, they are often labeled as inferior or "not the way we do things around here." As a result, important differences can be erased and people of color feel tokenized, instead of the whole community fully appreciating the diversity of Christian expressions.

In light of this trend, as well as the opportunity for your church to embrace this cultural Checkpoint, it's important to remember that compositional diversity (or numerical representation of people who are different) is a necessary but insufficient marker of reflecting the kingdom. It's possible to be a church with ethnically diverse members that remains culturally homogeneous, or only featuring distinctions that don't threaten the status quo. Future-Focused Churches do the hard work of elevating not only diverse faces and skin colors but also diverse voices and practices.[22]

While we hope to be able to share more stories in the future of churches making significant progress in reflecting the wonderful variety of our world, diversity is admittedly so complex that sometimes new communities need to be created to reflect God's diverse kingdom on earth. The leaders of an ethnically diverse campus of a predominantly White multisite church in California came to the realization that there were fundamental differences between their diversity priorities and those of the broader church. This became especially apparent when George Floyd was murdered in 2020 and the church's central leadership team prohibited this campus's leadership team from publicly expressing their longing for justice around this topic.

So, those longing to speak up made the difficult decision to branch off and become an independent congregation. This was not the path they preferred, but their commitment to be a multicultural, multiethnic community and declare and apply the good news of Jesus in all contexts led them to make the tough decision to separate from the multisite church that birthed them. As one of the co-lead pastors shared, "Our church campus had to deal with issues of race, justice, and reconciliation at a much more accelerated pace than the church we were a part of was able to and willing to. That's why our campus made a mutual, missional, and prayerful decision to go on our own."

Now with three co-lead pastors (two men and one woman) all from different racial backgrounds, they are a church of six thousand people (making them one of the largest multiethnic/multicultural churches in the US) with a racial makeup that is 35 percent White, 30 percent Black, 20 percent Latina/o, 10 percent Asian, and 5 percent Indigenous, multiethnic, or other. This church needed to launch out on their own in order to faithfully live into God's kingdom vision that they saw permeating the Word of God.

It's clear that the biblical vision for the church is a multiethnic one. While it would be ideal for all churches to pursue a multiethnic and multicultural vision, we also believe there are important reasons for racialized minority churches to exist so that people of color can express their faith in culturally distinct and authentic ways (e.g., by being

> A commitment to ethnic and racial diversity must be coupled with a commitment not only to celebrating, embracing, and integrating cultural distinctions but also to justice. Only then do we display the fullness of God's peaceable, just, multiethnic, and multicultural kingdom. A commitment to ethnic diversity without a commitment to embracing cultural diversity and justice falls short of God's kingdom. As the history of race is closely tied to economic interests, it is also important to attend to how economics shapes our realities. In other words, if our churches tend to drift toward favoring the wealthy and neglecting the poor or toward maintaining economic segregation and separation, we are falling short of true Christian discipleship.

part of Black churches, Latina/o parishes, Indigenous communities, or Asian American congregations). Immigrant and ethnic minority churches fulfill a unique role in the broader church landscape, including being one of the few spaces where racialized minority Christians can participate in a culturally authentic and faithfully integrated worship experience. As long as racism exists (especially among the people of God), we need Black churches, Asian American churches, Latina/o churches, and Indigenous churches so that Christian faith expressions can be displayed through the different communities.

Reflecting on these ongoing cultural dynamics within present and future American evangelicalism, our Fuller Seminary colleague and theologian Soong-Chan Rah recommends,

> The American church needs to face the inevitable and prepare for the next stage of her history—we are looking at a nonwhite majority, multiethnic American Christianity in the immediate future. Unfortunately, despite these drastic demographic changes, American evangelicalism remains enamored with an ecclesiology and a value system that reflect a dated and increasingly irrelevant cultural captivity and are disconnected from both a global and local reality.[23]

Checkpoint #3: Tangibly Loving Our Neighbors

As we prioritize and empathize with our unique, future-focused congregants, we're likely to encounter their passion to tangibly love their neighbors. A recent analysis by the Annie E. Casey Foundation found the social issues that matter most to Gen Z are health care, mental health, higher education, economic security, civic engagement, racial equality, and the environment.[24] In the 2023 Junior Voices Survey, eight- to fourteen-year-olds wished that elected officials would pay most attention to the following issues: (1) gun violence prevention, (2) reducing food insecurity, (3) managing inflation, (4) reducing climate change, (5) promoting educational equity, (6) increasing access to health care, and (7) civil rights for people of different races, genders, and backgrounds.[25]

In our *Growing Young* research on churches that are thriving with teenagers and young adults, a core commitment of outstanding churches is that they aim to *be the best neighbors* in their community—with congregants often echoing Jesus' language to love our neighbors. Data aside, our hope is that all generations in your church are committed to a culture that understands that serving God means serving others. We don't need to look far in Scripture to hear the Old Testament prophets' calls for justice, Jesus' statement that the greatest commandments are to love God and *to love your neighbor as yourself* (see Mark 12 or Matt. 22), or Paul's plea in 2 Corinthians 5 for all believers to carry out the ministry of reconciliation.

Further, in the oft-quoted John 3:16, we read that God so loved the world that God sent God's only Son. In the act of sending Jesus, God demonstrated that the work of ministry is one that is present, proximate, and actively sacrifices privilege (see Phil. 2:5–11). We are called to live as Jesus lived and to love as Jesus loved—and we believe we are not doing so unless we are moving toward the poor, the marginalized, and the oppressed. What we say about and do for those who are sick, impoverished, orphaned, widowed, unhoused, and sojourning (including immigrants and refugees) proclaims in word and deed what we believe about the Jesus we follow.

Many Christian traditions already have a rich history of financial generosity, promoting health and healing through hospitals and other forms of wellness as well as caring for those who are homeless or hungry. Jumping forward to today, almost three-quarters (74 percent) of churches in a recent study reported offering some form of community service or ministry.[26] Nearly two-thirds (61 percent) agree that they identified and embraced new ministry opportunities during the COVID-19 pandemic. When asked whether their church had "made permanent changes to its community outreach" following the pandemic, 45 percent of respondents agreed they had.

One church we encountered, The Dwelling, exemplifies mutuality in tangibly loving its neighbors. It grew out of a partnership with a local ecumenical nonprofit that provided meals and shelter to neighbors who were homeless during the winter months. Members from the unhoused community began asking for a church that looked like them, where they could be leaders and not just "guests."

In February 2020, The Dwelling officially launched. However, the pandemic quickly brought all dreams of a gathered community to a halt. With public spaces largely closed, including public restrooms and showers, The Dwelling purchased a mobile shower trailer, which demonstrated tangible support and thus increased trust. As a sense of community developed, anticipation built for the opportunity to resume meeting regularly for Sunday worship. As pandemic restrictions were relaxed, regular gatherings around donuts and Bible study led to an Easter worship service of fifty people.

This community is now a dynamic church plant that regularly gathers two hundred people for worship, many of whom are young professionals and young families who joined after serving a meal or were invited to worship by those who are unhoused. This diverse community, which serves over fifteen hundred people annually, is one of the fastest growing congregations in its denomination.

While we can't always anticipate pandemics and other social crises, we can be quick to respond when needs emerge. A church culture in which we love our neighbors invites us to step into spaces and engage people who may look, think, feel, live, vote, or love differently than we do. As many pockets of our nation get more politically polarized, this gets more challenging—and more crucial.

Two areas that are especially divisive in churches and denominations today, and also very important to young people, are sexual orientation and gender identity. We recognize there are a wide variety of theological and pastoral perspectives on these topics. Here, we will not offer a single theological position we invite all readers to follow. Instead, we encourage you to use the tools in this book, along with Scripture, your theological tradition, prayer, and the wisdom of your community, to respond in a way that tangibly *loves your neighbors*. Regardless of your doctrine, we believe we can stack hands on our shared convictions that all people are made in the image of God, are loved by God, and are worthy of love, dignity, and respect.

Just as we believe it's valuable for every church to ask whether you're treating all people as being made in God's image, here's a revealing question we recommend asking those in your neighborhood: Would anyone miss our church if it closed down?

If the answer is a gentle no, that's your sign that perhaps you need to make a future-focused shift to grow into a lasting, Future-Focused Church.

How to Shift Your Church's Culture to Reflect the Checkpoints

While we'll offer you lots of tools throughout the rest of the book that help you shift your culture, here are three tips we want to highlight early in your journey.

One, culture change takes time. Sometimes, the only strategy that can effectively change church culture (other than the power of the Holy Spirit!) is time.[27] In other words, for culture to ultimately change in your church, enough time needs to pass so people experience the change and agree that the new approach leads to desired results.

Practically, we recommend you don't measure success, or declare victory, after three weeks or three months. We find that for church culture to shift, the change typically needs to be sustained for two to three *years*—or more. Certainly you can find small wins to celebrate along the way, but shifting to a longer horizon will adjust the expectations of your leaders, key stakeholders, and the overall congregation.

Two, stories shape culture. Organizational scholars Kim Cameron and Robert Quinn point out, "Organizational culture is best communicated and illustrated by stories."[28] As well modeled by Jesus, one of the best ways to shift the culture of a church is through the disciplined and consistent telling of clear and compelling stories that invite a different culture and way of being. As you go, we'll help you identify and continue to listen for great stories and look for every chance to share them.

Three, budget for change. We find that our church budgets tend to reflect our priorities. If you're seeking culture change in your church, we'd encourage you and other leaders to put your money where your priorities are. Consider how and where small or large shifts in budget or spending might make a difference in moving your church's culture to align with the 3 Checkpoints and your other priorities.

We worked with one congregation that wanted to focus more on young people (Checkpoint #1) and tangibly loving their neighbors in the surrounding community (Checkpoint #3). While they were a well-funded church, they said they didn't have any funds to allocate toward these areas. We asked if we could conduct a high-level review of their budget, which revealed they were spending nearly 30 percent of their budget (which was a significant dollar amount!) to pay professional musicians to lead worship. It wasn't that the church did not have the money; it's that their culture prioritized other values.

Other Checkpoints on Your Journey to a Vibrant Future

Part of the beauty of the 3 Checkpoints is that they invite us to love, and to live with and near, those who are different from us. These Checkpoints summon us into community with those who might be marginalized or who are nearby but of whom we are unaware. When we pursue those relationships as Christ would, we steer clear of any temptation to degrade or tokenize those who are young, diverse, or not yet part of our church—instead loving them genuinely and unconditionally.

As powerful as these Checkpoints are, we do not believe the future of your church, or any church, should be limited to them. Returning to the "Mapping the Journey of Change" diagram, your church will need to consider many different areas and ministries as you hold the life, teaching, work, and good news of Jesus Christ at the center of all you do. While not an exhaustive list, we'd also encourage you to make a commitment to things like

holistic discipleship and spiritual formation,

extending hospitality to all people,

placing a strong focus on developing leaders, and

catalyzing an everyday faith (beyond just weekly worship or activities).

Let these be additional Checkpoints along your journey. We hope our HERE to THERE map helps you make progress in the three

FIGURE 2.3

Mapping the Journey—Other Important Checkpoints

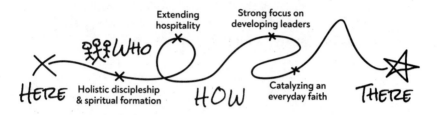

essential Checkpoints, as well as your church's other ministries and priorities.

You might be part of a church that was once fast-growing but has now hit a plateau. Maybe your church has been in slow decline for years. Perhaps your ministry has been relatively healthy, but you're looking for a better next step to unlock more effective discipleship and cultural vitality. Maybe you're a young adult leader with great ideas for the future but no traction or authority to make them happen. Or you're a founding senior leader who has led faithfully, and you now wonder what the next phase of your journey will look like.

No matter where you are on the journey, be encouraged that any step toward any one of these Checkpoints is a step in the right direction.

It's a step toward becoming a Future-Focused Church.

REFLECTION QUESTIONS

As you consider the 3 Checkpoints, on a scale of 1–5 (with 1 being "not at all well" and 5 being "very well"), how well would you say your church or ministry is doing on each Checkpoint?

How would you describe your church's current culture in three words or phrases? What words or phrases do you wish described your church's culture?

What is one next step (it could be small or large) you could take in the next week or month to prioritize and empathize with young people?

What is one next step you could take to model the ethnic diversity of God's kingdom?

What is one next step you could take to tangibly love your neighbors?

Beyond these three, what other Checkpoints seem especially important to incorporate in your church's journey from HERE to THERE?

ZONE 1

WHO

Partners
for the Journey

Plans fail for lack of counsel,
but with many advisers they succeed.

PROVERBS 15:22

Mapping the Journey—WHO

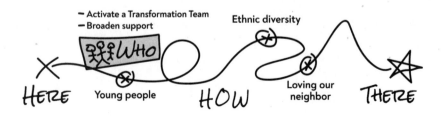

As you and your church navigate the four zones of your Future-Focused Church map, the two chapters in this section set you on the right trajectory to address WHO is central in your journey.

Your guiding question for this zone is:

> **WHO are the people in our church (or ministry) and wider community whose unique perspectives and gifts must shape this effort?**

We've intentionally placed WHO as the first section of the book so that you identify your WHO before you engage in the work of HOW or begin to move toward THERE. You also want to be sure WHO you've intentionally selected informs your work to understand your current HERE. Much of leading change (or really, any type of leadership) in local churches and ministry organizations is about being aware of and responsive to the daily realities of the people entrusted to your care.[1] As you read on, we encourage you to take an empathetic posture toward those with whom you share this journey. Since WHO takes into account your unique people, community, history, and culture, no two church journeys will be exactly the same.

EMOTIONS ON THE JOURNEY

Leading change is tough and will surface a wide range of feelings in you, your team, and those in your faith community who are affected by the change. At the start of every zone, a few reflection prompts like the ones below will invite you to check in with your emotions—either reflecting on your own or discussing with members of your team.

- As we start seeking all God has for our church in the future, I feel . . .
- Because of my past experience in trying to lead change, I'm anxious about . . .
- Journeying toward the future gets me most excited about . . .
- For the good of my own heart and soul, soon I should talk with someone I trust about . . .

PRAYER

Paul's powerful words "I planted the seed, Apollos watered it, but God has been making it grow. So neither the one who plants nor the one who waters is anything, but only God, who makes things grow" (1 Cor. 3:6–7) remind us that God is the initiator and guide of all change in our churches and ministries. So, we invite you (on your own or with your team) to pause and ask God to guide WHO to involve in change through these suggested prayer prompts:

- To guide you to the right members of your Transformation Team who, like Paul and Apollos, have important roles in God's work.
- To sense the right seeds to plant in these early stages of your future-focused change work.
- To rest in the peace that comes from knowing that God ultimately makes all things grow.

Activate a Transformation Team

You weren't meant to lead change alone.

In fact, you really shouldn't.

That certainly has been true of Loma Linda University Church (LLUC), a congregation whose leadership knew something needed to change. Despite its century of rich history, preeminence as the largest church in its denomination, and prime location on the campus of a major university, fewer young adults were calling LLUC home than in the past. The young adults the church attracted were mainly involved in a ministry targeted to their age group, and many rarely joined Sabbath worship services or activities. As is common nationwide, the disproportionately small young adult ministry functioned much like a separate congregation within the larger church.

While age-specific ministries can often be helpful, the leaders at LLUC knew the current approach was untenable long-term. Twenty-somethings were beginning to leave even the young adult ministry, and the broader congregation was missing out on the gifts, innovation, and passion of younger Christians. To be a future-focused, thriving, intergenerational church for generations to come, LLUC needed deeper connections among the diverse older and younger generations.

A better future required structural and cultural shifts in LLUC's staffing, ministry programming, and communication. These movements were beyond what any one staff member, even the senior pastor, could enact through a single sermon, meeting, or decision. While the church sensed God clearly leading them toward the goal of closer relationships, WHO would best bring about that needed transformation was anything but clear. The pastor we interviewed admitted, "As a congregation and leadership team, we were siloed and disconnected from one another. That bred miscommunication, sometimes even resentment, and misconceptions about each other. It led us not to see each other as part of one congregation or one team."

Widespread and systemic shifts required a coordinated and sustained team effort by congregants across every branch of the church. As part of a training facilitated by the Fuller Youth Institute, the church's leadership prayerfully discerned the right group for this work. Carefully and intentionally, they formed a cross-functional team that cut across several generations and ministries and built on momentum from related efforts already underway in the church.

Over a period of nearly two years, this team built trust, launched a variety of experiments, and tested several specific initiatives. While significant, their progress toward greater empathy and integration was not as linear or straightforward as they (or we!) might have hoped. In hindsight, as one of their pastors carefully reflected on what actually brought about the needed transformation, the top catalyst for positive change was the *indirect* and oftentimes *unintended* efforts of the Transformation Team.

▶ We define "Transformation Team" as a group dedicated to activating and advancing change.

As one example, perhaps counterintuitively, only a few members of the Transformation Team were involved in young adult ministry. Instead, the majority were congregational members who held influence in church life and leadership more broadly. LLUC took this approach because the majority of needed changes were not *within the young adult ministry*. Instead, most of the shifts required increased intersection and integration between young adults and other areas of the church.

In addition, instead of immediately launching new activities to strengthen the 3 Checkpoints, the team took the time to listen to the congregation and each other, forming a cohesive vision and common language. As they listened, they focused on identifying stories that could be shared in their meetings and throughout the church, as well as how they could deepen trust among Transformation Team members.

In other words, they didn't start their change effort with a focus on HOW to bring about change but by listening carefully to WHO was affected by the change.

Reflecting on the power of listening, the pastor commented, "Whenever we talked in staff meetings, board gatherings, Bible studies, or during sermons, the shared concepts and ideas we developed over time would emerge. They became part of our church culture. This wasn't due to any one program or experiment the team launched. Because of the people who were in that leadership group, the work spread organically, naturally, and honestly."

As a result of these strategic efforts and God's blessing, LLUC has made significant progress in increasing empathy among generations (Checkpoint #1) by shifting siloed staffing and structures to be more integrated and moving from being primarily program-driven to being discipleship-driven. While the journey hasn't always moved quickly or been straightforward, their future-focused progress stems from their careful reflection on WHO needed to be part of the change efforts and from the time they took to build a credible Transformation Team.

Scholars and Scripture Agree—Transformation Teams Best Lead Lasting Change

Like LLUC, your congregation, parish, or ministry has the best chance to achieve your future-focused goals and make progress in all three key Checkpoints if you don't try to implement changes on your own but rather enlist a team. The more complex the changes, or the more people involved in your ministry, the larger your team probably needs to be.

Research is clear about the importance of an effective team. John Kotter, widely regarded as a leading expert on organizational change, has developed a bestselling, research-based, eight-step change process. One of the earliest steps is to *build a guiding coalition* "of committed people . . . who guide, coordinate, and communicate" the change activities.[1]

In other words, the WHO shouldn't be just *you*.

While Kotter's research emerges largely from the business world, we find an equally strong intentionality about WHO leads in fields such as faith-based community organizing. In *Faith-Rooted Organizing: Mobilizing the Church in Service to the World*, Alexia Salvatierra (our faculty colleague at Fuller Seminary and academic dean for Fuller's Centro Latino) counters the stereotype of stand-alone corporate leaders driving change who "have 'take charge' personalities and boundless energy, confidence, optimism and charisma—with a pinch of ruthlessness when necessary."[2] Instead, she highlights the importance of a team approach by defining *faith-rooted organizing* as "the practice of bringing people together to create systemic change in their community."[3]

In our interviews with church leaders on moving from HERE to THERE, the top theme by far centered around the importance of cultivating an invested team. One leader commented, "I learned early on as a pastor that I can rarely tell people in our church what to do. While I can provide an initial spark for something and be an ongoing champion, I can't drive lasting change on my own. We've made the most progress on important initiatives when we get the right people together and take time to listen and learn and share responsibilities. While what *I* can do is limited, what *we* can do together is limitless!"

The Importance of Teams in Scripture

Just as scholars are clear on the need for a team to lead change, Scripture is similarly bursting with examples for inspiration and instruction. In Acts 1, when Jesus is taken up to heaven, the remaining eleven disciples gather regularly for prayer, along with Jesus' mother, Mary, other women, and Jesus' brothers (v. 14). They establish the qualifications for a new disciple to replace Judas: that person would have walked with Jesus for the duration of his earthly ministry, from John's baptism to witnessing his resurrection (vv. 21–22). The group chooses Matthias to be "added to the eleven apostles" (v. 26). They understand that it matters WHO will shape the early church.

Later, in Acts 6:1–4, the church faces the dilemma of some widows being overlooked in the daily distribution of food. The twelve disciples again gather to discuss and recommend a path forward, and they appoint deacons who were likely from the overlooked community themselves. The rest of Acts depicts multiple examples of teams coming together to discern the Holy Spirit's direction and guide major changes in the early church (such as Paul and Barnabas being sent on their missionary journey in Acts 13:1–3 or the decision that Gentiles need not be circumcised in Acts 15:1–21).

Other New Testament books outline the importance of WHO provides leadership, identifying overseers (or elders) and deacons as those who carry responsibility for guiding the direction of the church community. For instance, in 1 Timothy, Paul outlines qualifications for church leaders beginning with, "Here is a trustworthy saying: Whoever aspires to be an overseer desires a noble task" (3:1). When first-century leaders start new congregations, Acts 14:23 highlights that "Paul and Barnabas appointed elders for them in each church and, with prayer and fasting, committed them to the Lord, in whom they had put their trust." Furthermore, Acts 20:28 instructs, "Keep watch over yourselves and all the flock of which the Holy Spirit has made you overseers. Be shepherds of the church of God, which he bought with his own blood."

Additional moments throughout the Old and New Testaments when God works through a team include the scouts sent by Moses to explore the land of Canaan after the Israelites have left Egypt (Num. 13:1–33), those who build the wall of Jerusalem (Neh. 3:1–32), and the Pauline leadership roles of apostles, prophets, evangelists, pastors, and teachers responsible for building up the body of Christ (Eph. 4:11).

As you can see, this work was not designed to be done on your own.

▶ ## Lies Leaders Believe about Building a Team

We find many leaders don't take the time to build a team or don't fully utilize existing teams as they navigate toward the future because they've bought into (often subconsciously) one or more of the following leadership lies.

Lie: A team will slow me down.

Truth: It might take more time in the short-term, but you'll move faster and go farther in the medium- to long-term.

Lie: People will think I'm lazy or incompetent if I need help.

Truth: You'll accomplish *more* together. A team multiplies impact.

Lie: People only need to think they're shaping the process, but I'm really the one who pulls the strings.

Truth: You need people's full voice and contribution, not just their assent or the perception that they're contributing.

Lie: I was hired to do the work myself.

Truth: You weren't hired only to execute. You were hired to equip and empower others to carry out the work of God.

Lie: Others won't do as good of a job as I will.

Truth: The church is meant to be a body, and each part has a role to play (1 Cor. 12:4–11). Just because other members of the body do something differently doesn't mean it's inferior.

Lie: I should only invite those who agree with my idea or think like me.

Truth: It takes a significant amount of effort to include diverse, and even dissenting, voices, but it's worth it. More often than not, those multiple perspectives and positions address blind spots and curate greater creativity.

Lie: People don't have time or interest in this work.

Truth: People don't want to waste their time with busy or unimportant work, but they value finding deep purpose and making a difference.

Why Teams Are Vital to Leading Complex Change in Your Church

Building a team and being intentional about WHO is part of that team is vital because your church is a system. By definition, a *system* consists of many parts and can be broken down into even smaller parts and pieces. Those parts do not exist in isolation but connect to form something larger.

Take a moment to think about the various parts of your church that work together to comprise the whole. That might include the ultimate leadership body, the worship teams, various staff and volunteers, leaders who minister to a variety of ages and interests, teams that focus on outreach, small groups and Bible study groups, and much more. It is the intersection of all of those branches that makes up your entire church.

Systems thinking (considering both individual pieces and the larger whole) is important for changing your church culture because various areas interact with and affect each other. Making changes in one area often automatically and unintentionally results in changes in another area. For complex challenges related to change in the 3 Checkpoints, you can't focus on only one section or one ministry. You have to look at the whole.

As an example, imagine your church is short on volunteers for your local missions team. In an effort to become a more Future-Focused Church and emphasize Checkpoint #3 (loving our neighbors), you extend an impassioned plea for more participants to join that team. To your delight, five new people sign up that very day. However, the next week you find out that those people are actually already volunteering in other areas and are planning to drop out of their current responsibilities of setting up chairs, coordinating hospitality, or greeting at the entrances. Yes, you've recruited volunteers, but you've just encountered a systemic problem. In this case, recruiting volunteers requires intentionality to recruit new people rather than defaulting to the same group who always volunteers.

So, if you're encountering barriers or resistance to changes essential to becoming a Future-Focused Church, you may be encountering a bigger issue than you realize. You're likely encountering a systems problem.

The Importance of a Diverse Team

Diversity is also a must when it comes to building your Transformation Team. For your team members, we urge you to seek diversity in life stage, culture and ethnicity, gender, representation of a variety of ministry areas, socioeconomic level, and overall background and perspective (including skill sets, professional training and expertise, and relational networks in the church).

Why does diversity on your team matter? This is another area where Scripture and scholars agree. First and foremost, diversity reflects the body of Christ. In 1 Corinthians 12:12–31, Paul reminds us that one body is made up of many parts. The foot matters, the ear matters, the eye matters, and the nose matters. No one person in the church provides all of the gifts necessary for the church to thrive. If you're able to unite diverse perspectives together in a strong team, you're better positioned for your change effort.

The importance of bringing one's full self and establishing teams that include a wide variety of perspectives is reflected in a variety of fields—including theology and biblical studies. For example, Justo L. Gonzalez's classic *Santa Biblia: The Bible Through Hispanic Eyes* highlights how each of us brings a unique perspective when we interpret Scripture, shaped by our background and experiences. He explains, "Imagine that we are all looking at a landscape. The landscape itself is the same for all of us. Yet each one sees it from a different perspective, and will thus describe it differently."[4] Gonzalez unpacks how those who read the Bible from the perspective of marginalization or poverty will pick up on vital insights from Scripture that others will miss. As you assemble a Transformation Team to listen carefully, interpret Scripture, and determine the future vision of your church, we implore you to recruit diverse teammates to offer a well-rounded perspective and appreciate your full landscape.

A growing body of organizational research affirms that diverse teams are particularly well-suited for leading complex change efforts. One recent study from the Boston Consulting Group found "that increasing the diversity of leadership teams leads to more and better innovation."[5] After surveying multiple data sets, other researchers report in a *Harvard Business Review* article, "Nonhomogeneous teams are simply smarter. Working with people who are different from you may challenge your brain to overcome its stale ways of thinking and sharpen its performance."[6] Another study suggests that when groups consist of members with cognitive diversity, which means differences in perspectives, they tend to solve problems more quickly.[7]

The findings in these studies are reflected in the work of Alexia Salvatierra, whose scholarship on faith-rooted organizing we mentioned earlier. When Salvatierra outlines WHO needs to participate, she highlights the need to not only involve those in positions of power but also include the poor or undervalued. She writes:

> Faith-rooted organizing also understands that a fair hearing of different perspectives is necessary for truth to emerge. . . . To prioritize the perspective of the poor for the sake of the common good does not imply the devaluation of the gifts of those who are not poor. Instead, it acknowledges the necessity of the dance of solidarity.[8]

We recognize that building diverse teams comes with challenges. One is that people from different perspectives may struggle to communicate with each other, which can increase conflict. A 2022 study found that a vital factor for the success of diverse teams is psychological safety, or "a shared belief that team members will not be rejected or embarrassed for speaking up with their ideas, questions, or concerns."[9] As you build your Transformation Team, we encourage you to consider the appropriate forms of diversity and create the unity and safety needed to pursue God's best future.

We partnered with one congregation enthusiastic about building a Transformation Team that was both intergenerational and multiethnic. The senior pastor and youth leader worked together to form a team that represented diverse perspectives and experiences. However, early challenges emerged when two of the older members of the team quickly dismissed the perspectives of two younger participants. The senior pastor realized the group had not created a safe environment, so she spent significant time with the two older members outside of the regular meetings, focusing on how to respond to a more diverse team. After these two older members were specifically invited to listen to and value all perspectives, they responded with more grace and openness to the younger members, which built trust across the entire team.

Three Essentials to Energize a Committed Transformation Team

As you build a Transformation Team that can help your culture become more vibrant and vital, our research and experience (with both successful and unsuccessful change efforts) point to three essentials in identifying, inviting, and igniting a committed team.

Essential #1: Match Your Team's Authority to Its Responsibility

One of the most common roadblocks a Transformation Team encounters is that their responsibility outweighs their authority. In other words, teams are assigned to carry out tasks they lack the power to initiate or enforce. For instance, countless youth leaders are tasked with helping a church become more intergenerational (Checkpoint #1). While the youth leader may have authority over what happens in the ministry with youth, he or she most often lacks authority over other generations. Or we've known people of color who are hired into lower- or mid-level staff roles with a mandate to increase ethnic diversity, promote multiculturalism, or lead racial justice efforts for the overall congregation (Checkpoint #2) without having the authority to enact widespread change.

When you have chosen or are tasked with leading change, it is best to pause and ask yourself (or discuss with your team) a few questions:

Do I have the authority to execute the change I need to make?
If not, whose support or partnership do I need to secure?
And what might be their questions or concerns?

In the example of LLUC, the pastor guiding the effort held a significant level of positional authority. However, he did not have direct oversight of all areas where changes needed to take place. So, he specifically recruited the leaders of each of those areas to join the Transformation Team. By gathering those people on one team, he coalesced the authority needed to carry out the required shifts.

Approaches to responsibility, authority, and power dynamics vary greatly based on the context, tradition, and racial or ethnic background of a congregation. For example, we recognize churches whose history or governance is more personality-centered or hierarchical may struggle with additional barriers that make it tougher to empower a Transformation Team. In these cases, your Transformation Team will need to devote additional time or intentionality to really understand the interests of those in power. Or, as another example, in many Black and immigrant (especially Asian and Latina/o) churches, power distance—or the disparity of power and authority within any given organization or society—is a significant force. The greater the power distance, the greater the potential authority gap and the more certain you need to be that you have the authority required to guide your church toward God's best future.

If you are in a leadership role in your congregation but don't possess a significant amount of "formal authority," you'll likely need to consider how you can invite those who hold more seniority or authority (perhaps a supervisor, senior pastor, or church board member) to support the initiative. If this is the case, our best advice is to take the time to listen to and empathize with whoever holds the authority you believe you need. Pause and try to step into their shoes. Consider the questions they may be asking, the pressures they may feel, or the goals they want to achieve. If it's difficult for you to do so, look for the right opportunity to request a meeting. Ask open-ended and probing questions about their ideas, preferences, and concerns. Take time to truly listen and step into their world, rather than trying to convince them or argue why your way is best.

In these cases, it's even more important to understand and speak in language that matches what your supervisor values most, which involves empathizing with their greatest motivations and leadership style. If your supervisor is passionate about growing the church, share how your request furthers that goal. If they care deeply about aligning with Scripture or engaging your neighborhood, highlight how your vision fuels progress toward those objectives.

Also recognize that leadership styles and communication preferences matter. We know one senior pastor of a prominent historic Black church in the upper Midwest who is known for inviting robust and direct dialogue from his staff and leadership, which is sometimes intimidating to others. As a leader with influence inside and outside the walls of the church, he often relies on his team to help him determine where he should allocate his time. There are occasions when he and his team do not see eye to eye. In such instances, his preference is for his staff members to do their best to persuade him instead of shrinking back. He once even challenged a staff member, "Haven't I earned the right to have you convince me?" For this leader, a well-reasoned argument is important. Those of us who work closely with similar leaders need to understand their favorite communication styles as we navigate the realities of church culture and seek to lead up.

Finally, if you want to help your supervisor get on board, we encourage you to lead with both wisdom and courage. There are times your supervisor will be privy to information you are unaware of (and that may require them to maintain privacy or confidentiality), which could impact their decision or the timing of a shift. It may be that their no is really another way of saying "not right now." Trust flows in both directions, and you'll earn more trust and long-term support for being a Future-Focused Church by working closely with them in these seasons.

One practical way to understand the level of authority your team needs to move forward is to consider two topics: (1) *complexity*, or how simple, straightforward, or multifaceted the change is, and (2) *conflict*, or how much resistance or frustration the change might bring. Assess the changes you want to make, perhaps related to the 3 Checkpoints or other priorities, in light of these two variables, rating both on a 1–5 scale (with 5 being the most complex or likely to bring high conflict). The higher the score assigned by you or your Transformation Team, the more authority your team might require.

Essential #2: Get the Right People on the Bus

In his research-based book *Good to Great,* Jim Collins asserts that one of the principles of great companies is that they focus on "First who . . . then what."[10] Collins uses the metaphor of a bus to explain that if you as a bus driver want to transport a group of people, you can't push the gas pedal and speed off to your desired destination before others have a chance to board the bus. Instead, the strongest companies are intentional about WHO is on the bus. They want to have the right people in the right seats so that, together, they can figure out where the bus should go.

We believe this principle is crucial for Future-Focused Churches. Once you've considered if your scope of authority matches the scope of your changes, take time to carefully reflect and ask: *WHO do I need on the team to develop the strongest possible future direction?* If your church keeps a directory or database of members, we've found it helpful to review that information and consider who might be a fit—particularly if you're in a small or medium church.

As you're assembling WHO can best help you journey from HERE to THERE, you might be tempted to utilize a team that's established or already has authority to carry out change. In most cases, we'd encourage you not to do so. We find that most already-existing teams (such as a church board or elders) hold enough existing responsibilities that they don't have the time, margin, or brain space to shoulder additional change work. Further, they might not offer enough divergent thinking to help imagine and chart a better and more faithful future.

It's better to establish a special team whose main agenda is shaping and guiding the change work. While you'll need to recruit a diverse and broadly representative team, the tension you'll need to navigate is forming a team that carries the interests and perspectives of the specific people or groups they represent but is also sufficiently well-aligned with the overall church for the desired change to make progress. Simply assembling a broad group without a clear shared focus and ability to place other interests ahead of your own (Phil. 2:4) will stall your progress.

As you know, we *urge* you to involve people from a wide range of ages, genders, ethnic and cultural backgrounds, perspectives, and

> In pursuing the 3 Checkpoints and other priorities, we believe the strongest teams tend to range from five to twelve people, depending on the size of your ministry and the scope of the change. If you have a team smaller than five, you run into the pitfalls of members missing meetings (and thus losing momentum), challenges generating enough ideas, and potential lack of representation from across your church. If you have a team much larger than twelve people, it's difficult to keep the team focused and cohesive, as well as to consistently gather everyone's input.

roles in the church. If a particular group of people will be affected by the change, you're wise to include a representative in the team shaping the decision. Where appropriate, we urge you to consider including younger voices—teenagers and young adults—in the mix.

Sometimes creating a diverse Transformation Team means that you or other leaders will have the opportunity to advocate for communities within your church that may feel poorly represented. One of the churches we've worked with had a desire to become more ethnically and culturally diverse but struggled to create substantial pathways for that commitment to seep into its marrow. As we assessed the church, we concluded that cultural diversity was only visible at the most superficial level—they sometimes sang worship songs, read Scripture, and prayed in other languages. After guiding the leadership through a listening tour to hear from different members, it became clear that their team's lack of diversity was the biggest barrier to meaningful change. They realized they were acting as cultural gatekeepers as much as theological guardians. In one of the debrief sessions, one of the longstanding leaders of the church generously offered, "I think we need to make sure that our team is made up of the diversity we want our church to have in the future. If we can't expand to include that

> If you could use support on your change journey, visit FullerYouthInstitute.org to find coaching, consulting, or speaking from the Fuller Youth Institute.

diversity, I'm happy to give up my seat to someone from another background and would encourage a few of you to do the same."

That's future-focused leadership in action.

Consider the following questions, as well as people who might provide the necessary experience and insight, as you complete the chart below.

Identifying the Right People for Your Transformation Team

QUESTION	INDIVIDUALS OR GROUPS OF PEOPLE
Which people may be the most receptive to the changes we'd like to see? (This might include those already known to be interested because of what they've said or done.)	
Who may be most resistant to the changes we'd like to see?	
Who are influential people in our congregation who might care about the potential change?	
What specific skill sets or areas of insight and expertise will we need on our team? Who might have these insights and experiences?	

Essential #3: Invite and Onboard On Purpose

After God has helped you match the right people on the bus with the scope and authority needed, you can intentionally invite and onboard those people to join your change mission. Too many future-focused leaders stumble because they're clear about what they want to achieve and WHO they want to involve, but they fail to communicate the need and responsibility precisely and power- fully. While many in your parish or ministry are probably already overcommitted or lack disposable time, we urge you to assume that most people crave a sense of purpose and want to contribute to something important and meaningful.

First, that means you shouldn't say someone's no for them. Don't let the fact that people on your invite list are busy or hold important roles outside your church disqualify them or cause you to remove them from the list. Sometimes those same people have been pray- ing for a meaningful way to serve—and your invitation is the right answer to that prayer. In addition, don't underestimate those who may not hold "prestigious" positions. Wisdom, insight, godly char- acter, and strong leadership abilities are often found in places we may easily overlook.

Second, pause long enough to be sure the initial invitation matches the importance of the work at hand. If you're going to work on a vital project, we recommend you not put an announcement in the church bulletin asking for volunteers or send out a single email to a large group asking people to volunteer. While those approaches work for some efforts, they won't do for a significant future-focused change. Instead, you might begin with asking a group for intentional nomi- nations. Try to step into the shoes of each person you plan to invite. Ask yourself, What would make this invitation meaningful and clear to *this person*? For some, that might start with a text. For others, it may be a conversation over coffee, boba, or a meal. For others, it might be a clear and direct email. Find what works for each person, and do your best to speak their language when you make the ask.

One church in our change interviews emphasized the importance of starting with *why* in their invitations and earliest team meet- ings. The pastor understood she was inviting people into a complex process to discern God's best future, so she needed to spend much more time explaining the rationale for the potential change. Taking sufficient time to build the case for *why* deepened the group's com- mitment to overcome the hazards and obstacles that might prevent their progress.

Finally, as God nudges people to say yes to your invitation, be ready with a plan to orient and onboard them. Here are several approaches we've seen work well in other churches. We invite you to choose one or more that are most helpful for your context:

- In high school English class, you might have learned that good journalism addresses the topics of who, what, where, when, why, and how. Use these as framing questions to describe the impact and details of your project.
- Create (or have the group create) a one- to two-page document or five-minute video that outlines your initiative's essential elements.
- Send everyone a short survey (no more than five to seven questions) that invites them to share their ideas, give initial reactions to your ideas, and speak to the biggest questions they're asking. Review the responses in advance and be ready to share your reply at an early meeting.
- In your first meeting with the group, refrain from launching right into the work and planning. Take time to make sure people understand the assignment and give people a chance to share their excitement and questions verbally.

As you recruit your team and begin the early work, we encourage you to meet for approximately seventy-five to ninety minutes every three weeks. While you can certainly adjust those meetings for your context and topic, we find that if you meet more frequently or for longer periods of time, people tend to get overwhelmed by the commitment and don't have enough time to do work in between meetings. If you meet less frequently, it's difficult to maintain momentum, or if someone misses a meeting, they might go two months without engaging in the discussions. Periodically, we'd encourage you to consider scheduling a more intensive "big picture" half day together, or even a full day or overnight retreat.

We also encourage you to create space in and around your meetings for people to build relationships with each other. One of the best ways to do this is through sharing meals, stories, and experiences. The subsequent stronger team bonds will allow you to navigate the ups and downs that come with a culture change process, which can be testing for everyone.

When Should I Disband My Team?

Most Transformation Teams are not designed to exist forever. Your team should likely disband after the change work has been achieved. In some cases, that might be after a few months. Often more complex change work can take a few years. After your group has met for an initial period of time, we'd encourage you to ask every three to six months if the group should continue in its current format. Sometimes you might need to give team members the opportunity to drop off, in turn giving you the opportunity to add fresh voices and new energy. Instead of disbanding altogether, you might also consider meeting less frequently, such as once every few months, or setting a time six months down the road when your group will meet again to evaluate progress and determine your future activities.

Grounding Your Transformation Team in Prayer

One of the best activities you can engage in with your Transformation Team from the start is prayer. Invite members to pray for the work ahead of you. Recruit select members or ministries of your church to join you in asking God for wisdom and clarity for the work ahead. Spend personal time with the Lord, preparing your own heart for what God may want to do through you. In fact, before you read much further, we'd encourage you to pause now and ask for God's guidance as you shape a Transformation Team.

Our prayer is that your church would experience the same unity, intentionality, and team engagement as LLUC. During our change interview with their pastor, we asked what advice he would offer to a team just getting started. He paused before sharing, "Listen a lot. Not just once. Keep listening. Keep going back to the well of listening to young adults, to older members, and to everyone. Listening well to as many diverse people as possible will never hurt your team. It will form the deep relationships and understanding you'll need to move forward."

REFLECTION QUESTIONS

For the future-focused change God is leading you to consider, how much *complexity* (how simple, straightforward, or multifaceted the change) and *conflict* (how much resistance or frustration) are involved? Rate both items on a 1–5 scale (with 5 being the most complex or likely to bring high conflict). What are the implications for the level of authority, size, and duration of your Transformation Team?

Which of the lies leaders believe about building a team are you or your Transformation Team most likely to believe? How might you engage the corresponding truth?

How does your team's authority correspond to its level of responsibility?

Who should you include in your Transformation Team? If your team has already started gathering, who might you consider adding to the team?

How might adding to the diversity of your team (e.g., age, culture and ethnicity, gender) strengthen your work?

What might be one of the most important activities for your team to engage in over the next one to three months?

What role would you like prayer to play in the work of your team, as well as in your own life and leadership, as you're seeking God's future for your church?

People Support What They Help Create

"If our church doesn't get more young people soon, we are going to die."

This was the warning one of the leaders at Port Orchard Seventh-day Adventist Church in Washington State shared with Dustin during his 2017 interview to become the senior pastor. They wanted him to know right away just how badly their church was shrinking and aging. Of the ninety congregants, only a few were between eighteen and thirty-five. In that season, the church's future didn't seem too bright.

After Dustin accepted the pastorate, the leader's warning continued to reverberate in his mind and soul. So, he vowed that every time a young adult joined their worship service, he would personally meet them, get their contact information, and try to connect afterward.

After a year of connecting with every young adult who visited their church, Dustin had a list of over forty names. He and his wife had already been meeting with a handful of young adults, but in 2018, they felt God calling them to expand their group and invite the entire list to a midweek young adult Bible study in their home. While Dustin's leadership was a needed catalyst, he knew this couldn't simply be a ministry *for* young adults; it needed to be a ministry *with* young adults.

As the Bible study grew, Dustin regularly asked participants, "What would you love to see God do through you?" Eventually a collective answer bubbled to the surface: given the preponderance of young health professionals in the group, they wanted to organize a free health clinic to benefit the surrounding community.

The growing crop of young adults presented a health clinic proposal to the church board. While its members were pleased that the young people were taking such initiative, they still saw more problems than potential. *How will we pay for this? Why would we want to invest so much energy in something with unknown impact? Can these young adults really pull this off?*

While it looked like the proposal might get stalled by these questions, a respected board member suggested the board vote to decide whether the young adults could keep working out the details. The vote passed, and God guided the young adults' subsequent planning. Within a few months, they identified a partner organization, secured a public school location, raised over $20,000, and recruited more than 150 volunteers. The day of the free clinic, the church offered 350 free dental, vision, medical, and physical therapy services. They also offered prayer to every patient they served. Given how many church members had been involved and how the neighborhood appreciated that Port Orchard Seventh-day Adventist Church was so tangibly there for them, the church hosted a second clinic the next year too.

During those initial years, the church realized how thrilling it could be to work together intergenerationally. "How can we involve young adults in this?" became a common question brought up in church decision-making. Young people were empowered to serve in church leadership roles, facilitate worship teams and small groups, and develop other churchwide ministries. There was a new aura of respect and appreciation for people from different generations that opened doors for greater impact in the community.

Dustin began talking with the young adults about planting a new church in Tacoma, thirty minutes south of Port Orchard. During the pandemic in 2020, the vision for LifeBridge Church was birthed.

Since many of the young adults who had led the health clinics lived in Tacoma, they became key leaders on the church plant's core team. Over the last four years, LifeBridge has hosted twelve free health clinics, mobilized one thousand volunteers, served two thousand patients, and provided over a million dollars' worth of free dental, vision, and medical care to the community. Thanks to this work and LifeBridge's intentional relationships with their diverse neighbors, the church came to be even more ethnically and racially diverse than its surrounding community and more engaged with missional outreach.

Both at Port Orchard and at LifeBridge, God used these young adult–led experiments to intersect with the future-focused 3 Checkpoints. They were led by young people, they were used by God to develop leadership gifts across the diverse generations of the church, and they impacted the local community. As Dustin summarizes, "We were amazed at the miracles God did when we rallied behind a handful of emerging, passionate young leaders."

Help Your Congregation Move from the Stands to the Playing Field

What would you love to see God do through you?

Dustin's simple but strategic question helped turn both congregations into Future-Focused Churches. Dustin could have imposed his own ideas for local outreach on the twentysomethings, but instead he prayed that God would birth kingdom dreams inside of them, thereby expanding WHO was shaping the church's steps toward the future.

As Dustin's two congregations highlight, people move from passive consumers to passionate champions when they are involved in envisioning and creating a Future-Focused Church. After interviewing over 400 leaders from 130 countries, respected leadership theorists John Kotter and Dan Cohen summarize their single most important message: "People change what they do less because they are given *analysis* that shifts their *thinking* than because they are *shown* a truth that influences their *feelings*."[1]

As Dustin experienced with the launch of his church's young adult Bible study and the free health clinics at both churches, people best see and feel the power of positive cultural changes when *they* are the ones to help imagine and implement them.

Put more simply, *people support what they help create.*

As we've journeyed with churches like Dustin's, we've consistently seen God move people out of the stands and onto the field because of this. So, if you're encountering resistance to your good ideas, or if you're simply struggling to get people engaged in what you think is a worthwhile change, spend less time getting people on board with *what you created.* Instead, spend time engaging people to *create something together.*

Sometimes people help create—and thus come to support—through a heavy lift of time and energy. Like the young adults in Dustin's Bible study, their hard work causes them to truly own current ministry initiatives or help launch new ones.

Other times the investment is smaller—perhaps wise input or periodic coaching. The board members in Dustin's initial church knew their questions and concerns provided the guardrails the young adults needed to effectively care for their neighbors.

Whether through minor, moderate, or major involvement, as you ask people to share their dreams and then rely on their resources, time, skills, and input to make those dreams a reality, you broaden WHO is part of your Future-Focused Church work.

As you envision WHO you should involve in change efforts in your church or ministry, consider four concentric circles of people. The innermost circle represents *You* as a leader. The change effort starts with someone, and that's likely you or one to two others who initially raise the need for change. The second circle represents your *Transformation Team,* and the third circle represents your *Overall Congregation.* The outermost circle corresponds to the *Broader Community* outside of your congregation whom you hope to love and serve.

Notice how, as you continue to involve more people and widen your net to include the overall congregation, God expands your change effort.

FIGURE 4.1

WHO to Involve in Change Efforts

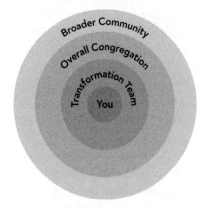

Empowering a Community of Co-Creators

Whatever our role is in a church, our human ability to create stems from our Creator God. As leading contemporary artist Makoto ("Mako") Fujimura teaches, "We find our creative identity in God . . . God is the great Artist, and we are God's artists, called to steward the creation entrusted to our care."[2]

As we partner with the Transformation Team or our community more broadly, we celebrate that all people—across all cultures and time zones—share this in common: we are each made in God's image. Just as all three members of the divine Trinity are in relationship with each other, so we as God's creation are intended to be in community with each other. In recognizing that all three members of the Trinity have distinct gifts and roles, we can celebrate that each of us has been given distinct talents to purposefully shape our world. As Paul celebrates in Ephesians 4:11–12, "So Christ himself gave the apostles, the prophets, the evangelists, the pastors and teachers, to equip his people for works of service, so that the body of Christ may be built up."

Despite Paul's focus on the leadership task of equipping believers, when American individualism is combined with the current Christian celebrity culture, it's tempting to think of leaders in another light, almost like leading actors. Though well-intentioned, we often, as leaders, end up making ourselves the star of the story, focusing on what we do *to* or *for* people instead of what is done *with* and *by* them.

Future-Focused Churches don't let their leader put on an (often impressive) one-person show. Instead, they view their leader as one member of a diverse cast of talented writers, actors, set designers, musicians, and ushers creating masterpieces together with an audience of One. As Danish theologian Søren Kierkegaard reminds us, God is the ultimate audience, and the congregants are the "actors." The role of the minister is as the "prompter" to remind the congregation of their (sometimes fuzzy or forgotten) lines.[3]

Future-Focused Churches who empower people to create and support ministry recognize that a leader's role is not to fit people into *their* show but rather to discern how God is at work *in others* and expand those contributions. Ideally, the entire community is supporting each person in playing the role God wants them to play as part of ongoing discipleship. Pastors certainly have a unique part to play in mobilizing the community through their preaching, mentoring, and leadership, but all of that work is like tributary streams that flow into the larger river of seeing the community's gifts mobilized. As Dustin saw with his young adult medical professionals who wanted to offer a free health clinic, that river can grow and become a powerful force for kingdom change.

While we think it's best when leaders are proactive and seek out a team of co-creators, we also believe God is always at work raising up new leaders who help the tide rise. One example of this is the Robloxian Christians, an online youth-led ministry founded on the Roblox gaming platform in 2011 by an eleven-year-old who wanted a space for friends to pray and talk about faith in Jesus. Robloxian Christians was serving 1,400 members by 2013 and continued to grow significantly in the following years. It describes itself as "A multi-denominational ministry that defies geographical and demographic borders faced by other physical churches."[4] This community was founded well before the COVID-19 pandemic, and since then, we have seen a proliferation of faith communities integrating more online approaches to outreach and discipleship.[5] All that to say, you might have people in your congregation right now who are ready to contribute their gifts and leadership to the streams of creativity and impact emerging from your community; they just haven't yet been given the opportunity.

Catalyzing "People Support What They Help Create"

We think most leaders want to see that river of empowering co-creators rise and crest in their church culture and community but don't yet know how to start. Or leaders perhaps do know how but are focused on other tasks and priorities and struggle to find time to build others' capacities. Our hope is to equip leaders to increase the momentum and flow in all those WHO we journey with by providing tangible action steps for all three elements of this key phrase:

People . . .
support . . .
what they help create.

Catalyst #1: People

The first catalyst is embedded in its first word: *people*. Based on our study of Future-Focused Church leaders, we have identified two key steps to help you steward the *people* on your transformational journey—starting with the Transformation Team and then quickly expanding to the rest of your congregation.

Step #1: Earn and Extend Trust

We agree with Stephen Covey that groups can make progress toward their goals at "the speed of trust."[6] In fact, the theme of trust occurred frequently in our interviews with Future-Focused Church leaders.

In the midst of widespread institutional distrust held by all generations, especially teenagers and young adults, we have our work cut out for us. In a national survey of diverse thirteen- to twenty-five-year-olds by Springtide Research Institute, only 14 percent indicated they trusted organized religion completely, and 39 percent expressed they had been harmed by religion.[7] In other words, young people are almost three times as likely to say they've been harmed by religion as they are to trust religion. While older adults seem to (or maybe do) have greater trust in institutional religion, it is still prudent to consider how any change initiative needs to build trust with all generations.

For all leaders, trust is like a boomerang. The more we extend it to others, the more it comes back to us. When we as leaders don't trust others, they in turn don't trust us.

One of the best ways we can extend trust to others is to involve them as creators and supporters. Robert was a youth pastor at a Black church of six thousand people in Texas. He took over the youth ministry after it had shrunk from three hundred to twenty-five teenagers. The youth were still connected with the church and its worship services but didn't attend any youth ministry gatherings. Wanting to extend and build trust, Robert strategically poured into a group of twelve to fifteen teenagers, who then took on leadership roles within the ministry and poured into others. Soon the youth ministry was back to three hundred members, and it kept growing.

Feeling ownership for the youth ministry, the middle school and high school student leaders embodied Checkpoint #3 by proposing to Robert that they host a new conference to reach the unchurched. With administrative support provided by Robert, the young people launched a three-day conference to reach their peers. The teenagers determined the theme, picked the topics, chose the speakers, and ran the logistics and "merch" store. For a decade, an average of two thousand local teenagers attended this conference, led and shaped by student leaders from the church, and the youth ministry ultimately grew to six hundred teenagers. Because Robert trusted his young people, they trusted him and the church. Propelled by that trust, the church rocketed toward a more vibrant future.

Step #2: Map the Relationships and Influence in Your Church

You constantly cross paths with your people—both digitally and in-person—but have you ever thoughtfully mapped the relationships and channels of influence in your church? Have you figured out how those networks of relationship, trust, and influence shape WHO is helping you become a Future-Focused Church?

If your answer is no, don't worry—you're not alone. Neither had John Keim, the student ministry pastor at a large church in Indiana. The church launched in the 1980s as a thriving and entrepreneurial faith community that magnetically drew young adults. But after thirty years of traction with young people, John and the rest of the executive leadership team realized that somewhere along the way, they had lost momentum. They were still impacting their local community, but as much of their city aged, their church members were aging too.

Unlike previous changes that were largely under John's student ministry purview, God revealed to John that prioritizing Checkpoint #1 through a church culture that emphasized young people required a broader group of supporters WHO could champion change. He could be the advocate and point person, but he needed the backing of the executive leadership team. To his delight, five of the church's six executive leaders were able to join a Growing Young Summit. After being immersed in the summit training and shaping the church's subsequent action steps, the entire executive team enthusiastically endorsed a greater across-the-board emphasis on young adults.

While the creative involvement of the executive team was crucial, John knew it wasn't enough. His next step in expanding WHO was involved in change was to map the channels of ministry influence across the church and identify which leaders were essential for the church to grow young. Spanning from ages twenty-two to sixty-five, those fifteen leaders represented different generations and different church functions—ranging from discipleship and local missions to communications and IT.

The church had repeatedly launched "big and flashy" young adult programs, but none of these led to long-term systemic change. Eventually each of these programs died out. John knew he needed a more organic, head-to-toe culture shift to include and empower young people. For several months, he met with those fifteen leaders to read through *Growing Young*, reflect on its six core commitments, and share stories of how God was making their community more hospitable to young people. As a result of John involving diverse leaders in an extended learning and change process, those leaders became more proactive about intergenerational connections in their own ministry areas.

One of the most vivid shifts toward being a Future-Focused Church happened mostly by accident because of a small crisis one weekend during worship. Somehow the children's ministries rosters had not been delivered to church classrooms. In a pinch, the children's director gave her keys to a group of teenagers so they could deliver the rosters to each room. Ironically, this same handful of teenagers had been onstage in the main worship service an hour earlier before a few thousand church members as part of the student worship team, but in their eyes, *getting the keys to the church* was a bigger deal than that!

As John summarized, "I don't think we would have learned about the power of small acts—like handing the keys to young people—if we had not intentionally mapped out and engaged departments across the church and then responded to the planned and unplanned opportunities God gave us to elevate young people."

Earlier we shared the four concentric circles of WHO is involved in taking your church into God's best future. We hope you've prayerfully identified the right members for your Transformation Team in the second circle. To help you likewise map out the departments or people groups WHO are key for success in the third circle of your congregation, we've created the chart below.

Mapping Your Congregation

QUESTION	INSIGHTS
Building on the insights from your Transformation Team questions, what are the distinct ministry areas or groups of people in your church? (Note: you might choose to list those in the column on the right, or you can draw a "map" of your physical church or ministry building or space and use that diagram to identify the ministry areas.)	

QUESTION	INSIGHTS
Within those ministry areas or groups of people, who is particularly influential, well-connected, or relied on by others for insights or communication?	
How might you provide updates to the people above? How might you seek their input as you enact future-focused change?	

Catalyst #2: Support

As we map WHO is in our churches and lower the walls that separate us, we are ready to more fully engage people's *support* by taking our next two key steps.

Step #1: Practice Keychain Leadership

In the *Growing Young* study of diverse churches that aren't aging or shrinking but are thriving and engaging fifteen- to twenty-nine-year-olds, one of the research-based images that has gained the broadest traction is *keychain leadership*. By "keys," we mean leaders' capabilities, power, and access that carry the potential to empower all generations but especially young people. As we hand over the keys—sometimes literally, like with John Keim's church, and other times metaphorically—so teenagers and young adults can use their gifts to benefit the community, everyone is changed. Young people gain new skills and confidence, and older generations are inspired by young people's innovative energy and creative spirit.

As you become a more Future-Focused Church, the keys you offer those WHO are part of your change journey come in all shapes and sizes. You can hand large and thick keys to others when you ask them to get involved in tackling some of your biggest problems—like an unbalanced annual budget, struggles in representing the ethnic diversity of your surrounding communities, or conflict-laden team or church board meetings.

Or sometimes the keys you offer are smaller and more bite-sized. (We're not advocating for swallowing keys, but we think you get the idea.) Our former senior pastor, Greg, handed a small but meaningful key to my (Kara's) daughter Krista during one of his sermon preparation seasons. Knowing he needed input from younger generations, Pastor Greg invited Krista, then an eighth grader, and a few other teenagers to meet in his office one Tuesday afternoon and discuss the Scripture passage he was preaching five days later.

Since that was seven years ago, I don't remember what the passage was. Neither does Krista. But I do remember her telling me after the meeting that one of her major pieces of advice was that Pastor Greg's prayers should be "shorter." (In case you're wondering, Krista is now twenty-one years old and still appreciates shorter pastoral prayers.)

I also remember the ten-minute drive from church to home after I picked her up. She gushed with enthusiasm that Pastor Greg had listened to *her ideas.* His openness to listening to her perspective, and following up with a few additional questions that Tuesday and afterward, made Krista feel even more at home in our church's worship services. In just a few hours, Greg handed her a fairly small key that yielded big benefits for Krista, our pastor's preaching, and the congregation that following worship service.

Step #2: Agree on the End Goal; Give Freedom on the Journey

As we deepen and widen WHO is helping us become a Future-Focused Church, what's scary about handing over keys is that we lose control. We might think we are handing over keys to a stable four-door sedan, but somehow in the hands of our people—especially our young people—that sedan morphs into a semitruck.

Or a motorcycle.

In the midst of involving people in all 3 Checkpoints of our Future-Focused Church, we need to find the right balance between alignment and exploration. As we share keys, the question becomes, How do we stay aligned enough to avoid chaos while simultaneously granting enough freedom to enable creativity?

One of my (Ray's) leadership growth areas has been threading the needle between being empowering and being directive. I tend to lean toward the former, but I am learning that different team members need, and even want, different types of support. As I've been actively encouraging team members to utilize their imagination, I was pleased when one of them recently shared excitedly, "Most of my [ministry] career has been executing the ideas that others passed off to me, but I appreciate that you are asking for my mind too." Other team members, however, have experienced my efforts at empowerment as me being too hands-off or not giving enough clear direction. A key point of my learning (and balance I'm trying to find!) is how to provide the clarity some team members need (especially in the early stages of a project), be available to respond to confusion as it emerges, and create systems both of support and encouragement along the way.

Catalyst #3: What They Help Create

In the midst of handing over substantive keys, clarifying the desired end goal, and giving all sorts of freedom on how to accomplish that goal, God allows us to experience one of the true joys of leadership: inviting people to *help create God's future for our faith community*. Here, there are three big steps you can take.

Step #1: Ask the Right People the Right Questions

One of our best ways to broaden WHO is helping create and support progress toward being a Future-Focused Church is to ask questions. Since everyone's time is short, we want you to ask the right people the right questions. As you consider what those questions are for you, we recommend using the following as a guide.

FIELD GUIDE:
THE RIGHT QUESTIONS

Never make a statement if you can ask a question instead. This is one of our favorite rules of thumb—in both leading and parenting. In the Gospel accounts, Jesus asks more questions than he answers. More specifically, Jesus only answers three of the 183 questions he is asked, and he asks 307 questions himself.[8] Do the mental work ahead of time, as well as in the moment, to turn statements you would like to make into questions you can ask.

Leverage a powerful default question: What is God inviting us/you/me into? The three of us have benefited greatly from both individual and group spiritual direction, especially those highly transformative moments when we discuss, "What is God inviting us/you/me into?"

Repeat two powerful default phrases: "I'm curious" and "Tell me more." If conversation stalls and you want to go further, ask others to tell you more or prod them into deeper waters by sharing what in their statement or question piques your curiosity.

Create your list of tough Future-Focused Church questions. On your own or with a group, draft a list of tough Future-Focused Church questions you can tackle with various leadership groups when the time is right. Keep that list handy as a go-to discussion tool for important individual or group meetings with wise mentors or stakeholders.

Ask multiple mentors the same tough questions. Create your own unofficial advisory council by asking a handful of leaders you respect to help you solve the same tough ministry challenges. Pay attention to themes and overlapping answers.

Seek input on the 3 Checkpoints of being a Future-Focused Church. How do others feel like God is already moving in the 3 Checkpoints of discipling young people, forming a diverse community, and tangibly loving your neighbors? What dreams do they have for God's best future for your church in those three areas? Perhaps even try asking a version of the question Dustin asked his young adult Bible study: *What would we love to see God do through us?*

> While we encourage you to use questions more than statements, we understand that there are race, gender, and power dynamics that need to be considered. Questions can unlock creativity and imagination, but they can also communicate uncertainty. Be mindful of who is in the conversation and whether asking questions might place you or others in a less powerful, or more tenuous, place in the conversation.

Step #2: Spend Extra Time Getting the Input of Those Who Resist the Vision

While it can be tempting to avoid people who disagree with our Future-Focused Church vision, it's far better to maintain communication with those WHO disagree with us. Instead of keeping our distance, we are better off drawing toward them. My (Ray's) father-in-law, whom I respect greatly, has faithfully pastored at the same Korean American immigrant church for nearly three decades. He finds that the church members who seem most opposed to a new vision or changes are often among those who care the most about the church. While there may be those who want to stir up conflict for unhealthy reasons, the majority of the time people simply want to be understood and want to understand the implications of the new vision or direction. He's helped me see how important it is to move toward dissenters with discernment. I try to create a lot of space for disagreement on the teams I lead and include the helpful divergent thinking of all those who are committed to the mission, vision, team, and those we serve. One of the ways I do this is by being as transparent as I can and letting people know I value their transparency. I remind people that it's better to *say now what you might regret not saying later*, creating space for them to be honest about their reservations or concerns.

As you move forward toward a more Future-Focused Church, work to make regular contact with those who are the most adamantly opposed to change. Whether it's coffee on a weekday morning or a few minutes of conversation after a worship service, find time to hear from, listen to, and enter into dialogue with dissenters, contrarians, and those who are in opposition to new ideas and plans. It can sharpen your own understanding, expose your blind spots, and help you fill in the gaps. While you may not come to full agreement, look for the kernel—or basket of kernels—of truth in their feedback so you can glean from their wisdom and address their concerns. Further, spending extra energy, time, and resources in the short-term can produce long-term benefits.

One of the biggest challenges that can occur when co-creating with others is when they enthusiastically offer ideas that may not fit the church or team's direction. In these cases, reflect on if there is some value in the idea that may not be immediately apparent during a first discussion. There might be a way to incorporate the idea, even if it involves a slight (or significant) redirection. Or perhaps engage a small group in discussion around the idea in order to help the person suggesting it see the pros and cons. In other cases, your role as a leader will involve explaining to someone why their idea will not be incorporated (yes, even if it disappoints them).

▶ If You're Feeling Overwhelmed . . .

We'll say it again: leading change can raise your blood pressure, feel paralyzing, and make you want to throw in the towel. If you're feeling like the work of inviting your church or ministry to support and create with you is overwhelming, you're not alone. Remember, you don't need to finish the whole journey right now; you simply need to take your next faithful step.

Step #3: Report How You've Used Feedback

It turns out that we're usually more committed to learning from others' feedback than they think we are. Our problem isn't that we don't listen or don't alter our course based on others' input. Our problem is that we forget to loop back to share specific ways that others have shaped our course of action. After all, people can't support what they help create if we never tell them that they are, in fact, helping create the future of our church.

Whenever possible, text, email, or call someone whose feedback has impacted you to thank them for how their perspective changed your thinking, communication, and actions. Better yet, take them out for a meal, connect with them, and share, face-to-face, how their input made a difference. An Asian American church planter we know grows his church by doing four consistent things: (1) taking newcomers out to eat, (2) listening intently to them, especially about their frustrations, fears, and hopes for a faith community, (3) finding ways to incorporate their feedback, and (4) pausing to let them know how their sharing impacted him. Almost always, he follows up with a second meal. During that second meal, he shares his reflections on what they initially shared and, where possible, lets them know how he is integrating their feedback into church realities. This gives them a profound sense that their pastor not only listens but applies what he hears from them.

Sometimes we can both show *and* tell others how they are part of helping us move from HERE to THERE. That's what happened when Keith decided to involve his deacon board in an upcoming youth group scavenger hunt. In an effort to build intergenerational connections between teenagers and the church's leadership, Keith asked each deacon to wear a particular hat, scarf, jacket, or pair of shoes and wander around a nearby shopping mall for ninety minutes on a Friday night. Keith's students were divided into teams and given descriptions of those specific apparel items. When students located that item of clothing, they then had to complete a short task (e.g., burst into song, form a human pyramid, create a spontaneous cheer) before that deacon would sign off.

Needless to say, the deacons and teenagers shared a lot of laughter and made vivid memories. Those Friday night connections spilled into subsequent worship services and other church gatherings as those students and deacons made a point to greet each other, sit together, and even catch up on the past week.

Four months later, when the deacons had to make across-the-board budget cuts, guess which was the only major area of the church not to receive any cuts? Yes, you're right; the student ministry was spared.

Do people tend to support what they help create? While your results might not always be so tangible, Keith, Dustin, and a host of other Future-Focused Church leaders would answer with an exuberant yes!

REFLECTION QUESTIONS

For whatever change your church or Transformation Team is focused on in this season, on a scale of 1–5 (with 1 being "very little" and 5 being "a lot"), how much are you involving the overall congregation?

In what ways have you seen it be true in your church or ministry that *people tend to support what they help create?*

How would involving more of your congregation in future-focused change help lessen potential resistance to culture change?

How would involving more diverse people in the change you're envisioning help build trust?

What silos could be broken down if you engaged more of your church in helping create the change?

How could you hand keys to others, especially younger generations, being clear on the end goal while still giving them freedom on the journey?

Zone 11

HERE

Where You Are Now

If any of you lacks wisdom, you should ask God,
who gives generously to all without finding fault,
and it will be given to you.

JAMES 1:5

Mapping the Journey—HERE

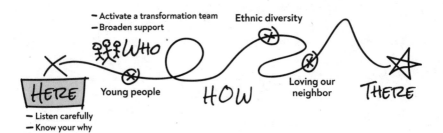

As you and your Transformation Team navigate the four zones of your Future-Focused Church map, it's critical to discern your church's current HERE.

Your guiding question for this zone is:

> Where are we now, and why are we HERE?

We've intentionally placed HERE as the second section of the book because it's crucial to understand key elements of your past and present before you try to move into your future THERE. We've accompanied leaders and faith communities who move quickly toward their picture of the future only to find they wasted time by making poor decisions because they lacked history or context.

As you engage in the work of listening and reflecting on where your church has been and is now, we encourage you to remain open and respond without becoming defensive. Involve a diverse group in the process and consider a wide variety of possibilities as you reflect on why you are where you are.

EMOTIONS ON THE JOURNEY

As you start talking more about change with others, we want you to be aware of, and responsive to, the emotions you're experiencing. Consider the following prompts:

- As I think about moving into the work of listening, I'm excited about . . .
- If I'm honest, I'm apprehensive about . . .
- With everything that's on my plate, when I think about making space to better understand our HERE, I feel . . .
- For the good of my own heart and soul, sometime soon I should talk with someone I trust about . . .

PRAYER

As we attempt the challenging task of understanding all the reasons we are HERE, we take comfort in God's promise in Ephesians 2:8–10 that

> it is by grace you have been saved, through faith—and this is not from yourselves, it is the gift of God—not by works, so that no one can boast. For we are God's handiwork, created in Christ Jesus to do good works, which God prepared in advance for us to do.

So, on your own or with your team, take a few moments to ask God to guide your future-focused change through these recommended prayer prompts:

- That you and the Transformation Team would have courage knowing you are "God's handiwork, created in Christ Jesus to do good works."

- To strengthen you and your Transformation Team by God's grace as you listen carefully and deeply to the right stakeholders in your church or wider community.

- To understand the deeper realities, causes, or implications you might either celebrate or lament that explain why you are HERE.

- For nothing to hinder the "good works" God wants to bring to fruition through your church.

5

Leadership Begins with Listening

Today, Wollongong Church is ecstatic that forty of their hundred or so members are children and teenagers.[1] These forty young people aren't just half-hearted attendees; they're contributors who help lead prayer sessions, offer worship service greetings, sing in the worship team, contribute to the multimedia team, give input in board meetings, and shape important decisions. The church, which is multi-ethnic and largely comprised of immigrants, recently baptized ten young people.

Just five years ago, it was a different story. Then, only five children and teenagers were involved.

So, what changed? What made the difference at Wollongong Church?

Leaders who listened.

As one church leader described, "First, we got on our knees in prayer and asked where God wanted us to go. Second, we listened to young people and asked them to be involved in leadership. We paid attention to their preferences about where they wanted to be involved, what they hoped to do, and the changes they wanted to see. Through relationship and partnership, we helped younger people understand and believe they're part of the overall church and not just a number."

In other words, they listened to God and listened to young people. And we couldn't agree with their approach more.

Scott Cormode, our colleague at Fuller Seminary, is well-known for opening his classes and lectures with the phrase (often written on a whiteboard): "Leadership begins with listening."[2] While leading a Future-Focused Church certainly isn't *only* about listening, we agree it is *most effective* when it starts with listening.

Five years ago, as Wollongong Church led with listening, they realized that while they had a history of being warm and welcoming, that hospitality was more present-focused than future-focused. Close relational connection was mostly enjoyed by the adults who were already part of the congregation. Young people's involvement (and especially their leadership) was an afterthought.

Wanting to prioritize youth discipleship, leaders initiated conversations with young people, intentionally listening to their ideas, questions, and concerns. The leaders then spent time listening to God in prayer and mulling over what they had heard. Next, they prioritized listening to other adults and leaders in the church—including the church board (who held decision-making power). While the adults and decision-makers in the church certainly valued young people, some weren't sure teenagers and twentysomethings could be trusted with real positions of leadership or real influence in important decisions.

Along with the entire Transformation Team, the church leader we interviewed took these concerns in stride and continued to advocate for teenagers. He helped the church board listen to, and better understand, its young people—especially by inviting the board to experience the young people's leadership in action. Over time and through intentionality, the board's mindset changed, and they became more open to the leadership and influence of young people.

Often young people's roles started small and then grew. As one example, an adult leader congratulating a teenager on great work as a church greeter half-jokingly offered, "Maybe next you should preach a sermon." This adult wasn't prepared when the teen replied, "I'd love to do that!"

That adult knew this was a key moment to demonstrate true listening and a wholehearted belief in this teenager, so he went to the pastor and the teenager's parents and advocated for the young man to preach. That adult took the time to mentor and coach the teen, who went on to offer one of the shortest sermons in recent church memory. Still, his preaching opened the door for other young people to offer sermons.

As the adults continued to listen, they realized that some young people (like the teenage preacher) were ready to merge into leadership opportunities right away. Others needed a more gradual on-ramp and smaller leadership opportunities to build their confidence. Either way, what mattered most was that church leaders calibrated not to adult opinions about pace but to young people's passions and readiness. The church leader we interviewed was adamant that encouragement, mentoring, and reciprocal relationships were essential to young people becoming more involved in the church.

Like most future-focused change processes, progress was accompanied by some bumps in the road. Such as one occasion when a few minor elements in a worship service under teenage supervision didn't go well. When the singing was enthusiastic but off-key, and the sermon was passionate but poorly organized, a handful of well-intentioned adults pointed out to the teenagers what they could do better next time. A few teenagers were crushed by what they received as critique. Thankfully, other adult leaders who were relationally closer had cultivated trust such that the teenagers shared with them how they were feeling. Those adults listened and offered the support needed for the teens to bounce back and try again, and even incorporate some of the other adults' suggestions in future worship services.

That's why, today, Wollongong is a Future-Focused Church, making progress in the direction God is leading them. That trajectory and future feel warm and bright . . . for all generations.

Why Listening Can Be Your Superpower

Similar to Wollongong Church, as you accurately discern your HERE, we believe God can make listening your Transformation Team's superpower.

Since listening is both simple and basic to human relationships, we find it often gets neglected in churches' efforts to move into the future. As leaders, we sometimes gravitate toward shifts or skills that are flashier or more public. After all, Spider-Man can shoot webs from his wrists and swing from skyscrapers. Wonder Woman has superhuman strength. Batman and Iron Man are billionaires with easy access to powerful technology. Careful and intentional listening doesn't necessarily stand out as a visible and transformative superpower like that, does it?

What makes us think that *listening* is so important in future-focused change?

First, businesses today have realized the power of listening. Have you taken a flight, used a ride-sharing app, ordered a product online, or streamed a movie—and immediately been asked to rate it or provide other feedback? That's because successful companies realize that listening carefully and understanding you means they're more likely to sell you their future products.

A recent study traced how senior leaders often become insulated and disconnected from what's really happening within their organization. The authors write that leaders "often trap themselves in information bubbles, a result of their overconfidence and outdated ideas about leadership."[3]

Ouch.

"Information bubbles" form when we as leaders tend to surround ourselves with people who agree with us or echo our perspective, causing us to lose touch with other views and hindering our ability to adjust. We've certainly experienced this with pastoral leaders in many churches and ministries, and at times been guilty of it ourselves.

In her book *Leading Change While Loving People*, our friend Yulee Lee outlines how change processes often bring volatility and uncertainty to participants because "we don't treat people as partners, or as co-creators, in the change process. Rather, we take the easier approach, which is to lead change through command, control, and fear tactics."[4] Instead, Lee outlines a relational communication process that highlights the power of listening, discernment, relationships, and trust.

The wisdom of focusing on listening doesn't only emerge in the business world or organizational research. Listening was praised centuries earlier in Scripture, where it is frequently upheld as admirable and wise. Proverbs 18:13 warns, "To answer before listening— that is folly and shame." James 1:19 teaches, "Everyone should be quick to listen, slow to speak and slow to become angry."

This emphasis on listening is even more powerfully demonstrated in the concept of *the incarnation*—the reality that God became human through Jesus Christ. As John 1:14 proclaims, "The Word became flesh and made his dwelling among us. We have seen his glory, the glory of the one and only Son, who came from the Father, full of grace and truth."

Let those words from John sink in for just a minute. The all-powerful God of the universe entered into our world through Jesus and took on human form. Listening well to another person requires a strong sense of presence and empathy. The Christ we serve walked as we walk and has felt what we feel. As other passages in the New Testament emphasize, Jesus can empathize with our weaknesses (Heb. 4:15). Furthermore, Jesus modeled listening to his disciples, those he met in his ministry, and even those with whom he disagreed (see Mark 10:35–44; Luke 24:13–35; John 4:1–26). Yes, we reflect the example of Jesus when we listen carefully to others.

Given the focus on listening found in Scripture and in today's organizational research, we believe your leadership begins with listening. God will use listening to help you understand your church's current HERE and guide your next steps toward one of the 3 Checkpoints or other priorities.

To inspire you to tap into this superpower in your church, let us share three benefits that come from listening and what you can do with what you hear along the way.

Benefit #1: Listening Reveals People's Mental Models

Every day, every one of us carries around mental models. A *mental model* is the way we see and make sense of the world. It's what we think the world *should be*. For example, when we say "church," a picture almost certainly comes to your mind. Is it a small group of people in a home? A large group of people in a worship service? A building? Whatever you picture sheds light on your mental model of a church.

In his book *The Fifth Discipline*, management expert Peter Senge champions the importance of mental models, writing, "Mental models are deeply ingrained assumptions, generalizations, or even pictures or images that influence how we understand the world and how we take action. Very often, we are not consciously aware of our mental models or the effects they have on our behavior."[5]

You and your church's progress in the 3 Checkpoints varies based on your mental model. Some churches might equate prioritizing and empathizing with young people with making sure the preaching relates to the needs of young people. Others could assume that it's not just about preaching *for* young people, it's about preaching *by* young people (no matter how short the message may be!).

For Checkpoint #2—embodying the ethnic diversity of God's kingdom—Revelation 7:9 offers a mental model of the church as representing people from every nation, tribe, and language. This can be very different from the mental model of a historically monocultural congregation. For example, I (Jake) grew up in a congregation that was historically Dutch Reformed and, when I was younger, almost exclusively White. As our geographic community became increasingly diverse, it took time for many longstanding members to see the need for our church to reflect these new realities in our worship, discipleship, and relationships.

Similarly, for Checkpoint #3 of tangibly loving our neighbors, one parish's mental model might lead them to believe they need to give away more money to worthy causes or share their faith more boldly. A nearby ministry might interpret the same Checkpoint as their collective obligation to become more vocal about local justice issues or engage in discussions around climate change.

Whatever the topic, Senge explains that the key to mental models is unearthing them and bringing them to the surface so they can be discussed and considered. This is rarely as simple as asking someone, "What is your existing mental model about _____?" The vast majority of us are unaware of our current mental models.

Sometimes, your careful listening to another person sheds light on their assumptions about what something should be. Often, however, you'll need to dig deeper into people's initial responses by asking follow-up questions like, "Help me understand why you view it this way?" or "Have you ever looked at _____ from this perspective?"

Mental models can lead people and churches to say and do things that seem downright crazy. Once I (Jake) was coaching a church from a historic denomination and joined the board's monthly meetings. In most meetings, as the board encountered difficult topics or challenges, they would turn to me for ideas and suggestions. Sometimes I offered direct advice; often I encouraged them to reflect on how they imagined Jesus would respond to that situation.

Apparently, I spent a little too much time bringing up the J-word. After several months of navigating a particularly difficult scenario, the board once again asked my advice, and I again invited them to consider how Jesus might respond to the situation. One of the elders slammed his fist loudly on the table and blurted out in frustration, "You need to stop bringing Jesus into everything! After all, we know what we're supposed to do as _____!" (Yes, he shouted the name of their denomination to fill in that blank.)

Implicit was his mental model that they didn't need to consider Jesus' response because they needed to put their denominational traditions first. The other elders in the room looked around awkwardly as the gravity of his outburst sunk in. It was a keen reminder of the power of mental models to shape our behavior.

Maybe you avoid that toxic mental model, but there are probably other subtler ways each of us get locked into unhealthy mental models. Perhaps you're overly deferential to your church's past, or you swing to the other equally unhealthy extreme of ignoring your church's history. You may carry a mental model that young people are naive and lazy, or older people are ignorant and stuck in their ways, or people who think differently than you do are wrong. The next time you find yourself listening to others who see life and leadership differently, pause long enough to consider if you have an existing mental model at work.

Benefit #2: Listening Lowers Resistance and Builds Empathy and Trust

When introducing changes in your church, you'll almost certainly encounter resistance from someone or somewhere. We've consistently found that church leaders are able to decrease resistance as they take time to understand their current HERE through intentional listening that builds empathy and trust.

When you listen with empathy, you are able to feel how others feel. More often than not, the person you're listening to can tell whether you understand, resonate, and *get them*. When someone else senses you actually care about their perspective and place in the church, trust is built. This trust is the track on which change can move forward more quickly and with significantly less opposition.

▶ As a reminder, we define *empathy* as the ability to understand where someone else is coming from and put yourself in their shoes.

Truly listening with empathy might first require a change in your perspective. Instead of trying to get people *to understand you*, you need them to feel *understood by you*. Said another way, people don't care how much you know until they know how much you care.

Peter Cha, professor of practical theology at Trinity Evangelical Divinity School, would often tell me (Ray) that "shallow listening" isn't enough in leadership. Instead, leaders need to engage in "deep listening," which better reaches the core of the concern.

As an example, a former colleague of mine profoundly offended a group of racialized minority students when he shifted the direction of an event that had been traditionally shaped by the community's Black members to serve a different agenda. The students asked for a meeting to try to repair the damage that had been done and restore the relationship that had been broken. I shared with my former colleague that it was very important for him to take time not just to listen to what they were saying but to hear the heart behind what they were saying—to understand how and why they felt betrayed. I encouraged him not to take a defensive posture or position but to simply empathize with their pain, whether or not he fully agreed.

Unfortunately, he spent the entire meeting doing "shallow listening" that missed the depth of their pain and longings. Most of his responses felt more to the young people like reactive rebuttals. As one student expressed in their personal reflections, "How could a pastor be so dense and defensive that he completely failed to see or hear what is going on in the room? All we wanted was an apology. All we got was gaslighting."

My colleague was listening to respond, not listening to understand. Deep listening begins with a commitment to comprehend and pay attention to the issue beneath the issue. What could have been a moment of healing turned into years of mistrust between him, his department, and members of that community.

One recent study on the importance of listening in change found that empathetic and nonjudgmental listening helps those who are listened to feel less anxious and more self-aware, and also to have less extreme and one-sided attitudes toward a scenario or argument.[6] Lowering anxiety and helping people move beyond one-sided attitudes is especially important in the current polarization we're experiencing in the US. Social media, politics, and culture overall seem to reflect increasingly entrenched and opposing perspectives rather than demonstrating civility, unity, and mutual respect. While we do not offer a simplistic solution for moving beyond intense polarization in your church, we believe empathetic listening is one tool to help your congregation move toward Jesus' prayer for his followers to demonstrate "complete unity" (John 17:23).

As we practice "deep listening," we can better identify the shifts we need to make to be more hospitable to those we hope to love and serve. One church in the Northeast that describes themselves as "conservative" in their theological beliefs about gender identity learned that their segmentation of youth into male and female groups alienated those who identified as nonbinary. While not changing their theology about gender identity, they decided to eliminate "girls" and "boys" small groups and instead offer small groups that weren't assigned by gender for every grade in high school. As the pastor explained, "We still believe what we believe, but we've

▶ As you consider your approach to LGBTQ+ persons, we encourage you and your community to engage in careful reflection on Scripture and your tradition. While there is a wide variety of theological perspectives, given recent Gallup research indicating almost 21 percent of Generation Z Americans who have reached adulthood—those born between 1997 and 2003—identify as LGBT,[7] it's important to prayerfully discern how to love and serve all young people, including those who identify as queer or as allies of those who are queer.

heard from nonbinary teenagers that they feel far more welcome when we don't make them choose male or female."

Benefit #3: Listening Fuels Your Ideas and Insights for Next Steps

One final very pragmatic reason listening can be your superpower is that it yields dozens of ideas and insights to inform your next steps. Perhaps you've sat in a room by yourself or with your Transformation Team and hit the mental wall of being stuck. Out of ideas. Not sure how to move forward.

We've been there too.

Choosing to listen widely and carefully helps you discern ways forward you might never have thought of. This requires a shift from just seeking input about *my ideas* to a wider embrace of *our ideas*.

From a theological point of view, this taps into our understanding that the Holy Spirit often can, and will, speak through the people of your community. If you're together seeking God's direction for the future, it makes sense that God is likely to provide insight, ideas, and direction to—and through—dozens, or even hundreds, of people. Your church will generally benefit when you tap into God's power and wisdom pulsing through a wide number of Jesus followers and community members.

We once worked with a congregation in which two senior leaders had some sense of what it would look like for them to be a Future-Focused Church, but they felt they had significant gaps in their understanding and ideas. They decided to conduct one-on-one and small group interviews with a cross section of the church. Those interviews yielded fifteen major themes for what the church might do next. We then helped them distribute a survey that asked the entire congregation to vote for their top themes, add any new themes, and offer practical ideas for how the church might move forward on those themes.

When the results were tallied, over 95 percent of the church was aligned and supportive of pursuing four of the themes (with three of those themes mirroring our future-focused 3 Checkpoints). What's more, the congregant responses generated ten to fifteen solid and specific action steps for how the church might get started.

Shortly after the survey, one of the pastors shared the results with the congregation: "From the beginning, we believed God would lead us into the best future for our church by speaking through our congregation. Our leadership has listened to you, and here are the four priorities you've encouraged us to move forward on." Since the pastor didn't frame the future around her ideas or a small group of leaders' ideas but rather *the congregation's ideas*, the leaders faced very little resistance in rolling out the cultural changes.

How to Execute an Effective Listening Strategy

While there are many ways to listen, we recommend aligning your listening strategy with the approach of Appreciative Inquiry. As the name suggests, Appreciative Inquiry is a listening strategy that shifts focus from deficits to strengths. It posits that the questions we ask shape the conversations we have, and those conversations shape our focus and reality. By focusing on the positive, we end up leading toward a brighter future.[8]

We find Appreciative Inquiry aligns well with Paul's admonition in Philippians 4:8: "Finally, brothers and sisters, whatever is true, whatever is noble, whatever is right, whatever is pure, whatever is lovely, whatever is admirable—if anything is excellent or praiseworthy—think about such things."

Sometimes it is misunderstood as *only engaging in listening* but not taking action. We would counter this misunderstanding by pointing out that the listening of Appreciative Inquiry is conducted *for the purpose of launching and driving change.*

Another misconception about Appreciative Inquiry is that it intentionally ignores pain or brokenness that needs to change. But our experience with churches is that when we focus on the bright spots of what's going well, we will inevitably identify and discuss the bare spots of what we lack. Appreciative Inquiry doesn't silence discussion about where we're falling short of God's best for our present or future; it just doesn't start there. We affirm that our churches must push beyond a toxic positivity that pretends everything is going well when things are actually going poorly. Appreciative Inquiry can help accomplish that goal.

As you incorporate Appreciative Inquiry to discern your HERE, let us share several key questions to ask on your listening journey.[9]

Who Should We Listen To?

Who should you listen to? As many people as possible.

The more people you listen to, the higher your chances of success in leading toward the future.

We realize, however, that you don't have unlimited time, so try capitalizing on the key insights you've already gained by reflecting on the questions below with your Transformation Team. These questions build on those you may ask of your team and overall congregation by helping you consider the branches of your congregation to whom you most need to listen.

- Who in the overall congregation will be most affected by the changes we seek?
- Whose permission or support will we need to make the changes?
- Who might be the most resistant to the changes?
- Who might have key insights or essential ideas related to the changes?

Your goal in answering these questions is to surface those in your community who can help you gain a solid understanding of your church's present HERE. Depending on which Checkpoints or other priorities you emphasize, your Transformation Team should listen most closely to those with the greatest experience and expertise on those topics. In the case of Wollongong Church, leaders first listened to the teenagers in the church (as those who would be most affected by their emphasis on Checkpoint #1). The next group they listened to was the church board (as the group whose support they needed to make the changes).

While there are many ways to listen (including a short survey, email, or text message), we most often recommend churches engage in synchronous, live conversations (in-person or through an electronic medium such as Zoom or Google Meet). There is little that replaces the power of human connection over a meal, a cup of coffee, or another venue that allows for direct connection and communication. These meetings can take place one-on-one, or perhaps in small groups of one listener with three or four congregants. If you've taken our advice to develop a five-to-twelve-member Transformation Team, you can divide and conquer to listen to up to one hundred people fairly quickly (if each person on the team has three or four conversations, and each conversation involves three or four people).

Regardless of your Checkpoint or change topic, we strongly recommend listening to people from a variety of age groups (younger, older, and in between), different racial and ethnic groups and genders, plus both dissenters and supporters, staff and key leaders, as well as those from different ministry areas or affinity groups. You'll also want to be intentional about listening to those beyond your congregation and in the broader community you hope to love and serve. Consider those who might be immediate physical neighbors living across the street or near your church building, as well as schoolteachers or administrators, leaders of nonprofit organizations, area business owners, or perhaps local government leaders. The selection of these groups can be informed by the goal of your change effort, and the questions asked can be adapted slightly to apply to members of your broader community.

While your listening process can extend over a variety of time-frames, we'd encourage your Transformation Team to allocate at least two months to dedicated listening. Complex change initiatives might spend more time listening, while simpler change efforts might spend less. No matter the time, we can't stress enough the importance of allocating it. We've heard from many churches in our training initiatives that the time they spent listening was the most fruitful of all tasks and created more buy-in than anything else.

What Questions Should We Ask?

Your questions need to be tailored to the changes you want to make.

That said, we'd encourage you to leverage Appreciative Inquiry by focusing on what is hopeful and life-giving instead of what people dislike or want to change. While some of your questions should certainly invite dreaming about what could be different, emphasize questions designed to elicit the strengths and assets of your parish or ministry. If you're unsure how to shape the questions, include a few brainstorming partners from the groups most likely to be affected. For instance, one church that wanted to better understand the perspective of young people recruited a few teenagers and young adults who were gifted in communication to help draft their questions.

Several questions that might be helpful across a variety of contexts and change scenarios include:

- What do you love most about this church? If there's a particular story or example that comes to mind, please share it.
- Tell us about a moment when you really experienced God or felt God's presence. What was that like, and why was it meaningful?
- What do you hope or dream for the future of our church?
- What is it like to be a ____ (teenager, senior adult, etc.) today? What do you really enjoy about this stage of life, and what is important for others in our church to know about your perspective?

- What ideas do you have for how we might connect with, or serve, our community to make it better?
- What are the assets in our congregation, or what strengths do we have as a church community, that could be leveraged for the good of our neighborhood?
- Who is someone in this church (an adult, mentor, leader, or younger person) who means a lot to you or has made a difference in your life? What is it about this person that stands out to you?
- Think of someone you want to invite to church but may not yet be comfortable inviting to our church. What would our church need to look like or do differently for you to be comfortable inviting them?

What Should We Be Listening For?

As you practice empathetic listening, hopefully you are communicating to the person sitting across the table (or screen) that you are interested in their opinions. In addition, you are also paying attention for confirmation or new insights that connect to potential changes to become a more Future-Focused Church. In the case of the listening at Wollongong Church, they were particularly mindful of how teenagers might want to lead and shape the congregation.

As you listen, we cannot overemphasize the importance of *nonjudgmental listening* and the power of maintaining a *nonanxious presence* as a leader. Especially as you listen to younger people, those in your wider community outside your congregation, and others who may be different from you in one way or another, you're likely to hear things that make you uncomfortable. In our experience, many young people have strong opinions on topics like mental health, the church and its relation to the LGBTQ+ community, climate change, race, and other social justice topics. In general, as you're listening, we recommend you don't jump in with a counterpoint—especially if you hear something with which you disagree. Ask curious questions and attempt to understand why the person you're talking to holds their perspective. In your later reflections with your team, you can discuss what you heard and its implications. To prepare for nonjudgmental listening and develop a nonanxious presence, we've seen some teams roleplay and practice their listening questions (and potential responses) in advance.

In the chart below, on the left is a prompt to consider and on the right is space to enter what you've heard from spending time with diverse people. We'd encourage you to use this chart or create your own version that fits your specific purposes.

Listening Insights

Mental Models: What are people's expectations related to this topic or proposed change?	
Building Empathy: What are the feelings people have toward this topic? What specific hopes, dreams, fears, or pains have been shared?	
Ideas and Insights: What specific ideas emerge that inform our next steps?	

What Should We Do with What We Hear?

As each person on your team listens, a best practice is to note key insights or themes during, or shortly after, the conversation. Ask someone on your Transformation Team to curate and compile those written or typed notes. Then perhaps invite one person to take the lead, or work together with others from your Transformation Team, to identify themes based on key categories (perhaps the three categories of Mental Models, Empathy, and Ideas and Insights from the chart above). Together, discuss the significance of those themes and how particular stories and ideas might inform your next steps.

Echoing the mantra that "people support what they help create," it's often powerful to create a written or video summary of what you've heard and share that with stakeholders in your church or the overall congregation. This documents that you're in a two-way conversation and want the process to be shaped by the faith community as a whole and not just your Transformation Team. As much as possible, highlight how insights from listening have made a difference in your plans.

What Other Forms of Listening Are Available?

Up to now, we've focused on human interaction through one-on-one and small group conversations. This is intentional, because we find that building relationships and trust is often the glue that holds change processes together. While we implore you not to skip over the important relational process of listening, there are many other processes to help you listen effectively.[10] Consider how some of the following might supplement your relational listening process.

Church surveys. You can use many free or low-cost services to craft a high-quality survey, or you can employ a research or ministry organization to help you. We recommend you use clear questions, keep the survey as short as possible, and test it with a few people before sending it out more broadly. You can also use social media creatively by sharing short questions through your relevant channels and garnering responses publicly and in real time.

US Census data. The US government collects data on the demographics and trends of your community. You can visit Census.gov and gather free, recent information particular to your neighborhood or community.

> FYI offers a Growing Young Assessment, which is an academically validated survey tool that provides vital insights about a church's effectiveness with young people. Diverse churches nationwide have benefited from how it harnesses the collective insights of the entire congregation to provide a true picture of reality. Visit FullerYouthInstitute.org to learn more.

We once worked with a church who told us their city had few young adults and was predominantly White. When we pulled together their demographics, the data revealed that a very high percentage of the community consisted of young adults as well as a diverse collection of races and ethnicities. It's just that the everyday habits of the congregational leaders rarely took them to spaces where they would intersect with younger generations or greater ethnic diversity.

Observation. We're often in such a hurry to move from one event to the next that we fail to pause long enough to notice what's happening around us. As another method of listening, we'd encourage your Transformation Team to arrive early to a church service or ministry gathering (following all appropriate safety guidelines for your context) and locate yourself where you can observe people, conversations, and interactions. If your future-focused goals are to engage more in your surrounding community, you might pay attention to interactions and dynamics at a public park near your church, a sporting event or shopping mall, or other appropriate public settings. What needs, feelings, or ideas are sparked by this form of listening?

When Leadership Doesn't Begin with Listening

In the spirit of Checkpoint #1, one church decided to emphasize young people right away. Before they attended any of our training, the senior pastor declared during a Sunday morning worship service, "From now on, we will be a church laser-focused on engaging and incorporating young people." It didn't take long before this pastor began to hear whispers of frustration and resistance, which then grew into emails of complaint and requests for meetings to discuss concerns about this new trajectory.

Nearly all of the complaints were from those in older generations who voiced, "You don't understand the identity of our church. We don't leave other generations behind to focus on young people." Underneath their handwritten letters and emails were fears about the church becoming a community that didn't value senior adults, which was something they had seen happen at nearby parishes.

Once the pastor began the training and attended our in-person summits highlighting that *leadership begins with listening,* he was immediately hooked. He realized he had moved too quickly to make changes without listening. He gathered with his Transformation Team, and together they concluded that while some damage had been done, God could rescue and redeem their change process.

The pastor and the team constructed a careful process to listen to the congregation, especially their senior adults. As they asked about the church's history, identity, and greatest strengths, they recognized that many of these senior adults—or even their parents—had been part of planting this church decades ago. They shared that the present church was founded when another congregation in a neighboring city realized their young adults were moving to this new community for college. There was no church from their faith tradition near the college, so as that church from the neighboring city reflected on their values, they decided to plant a new church within close proximity to the campus.

Upon hearing the church's origin story, the pastor confirmed with the senior adults, "You're telling me that the identity of our church is that we were planted by a group of people who paid attention to the spiritual needs of younger people, were willing to give and contribute sacrificially to respond to those needs, and then came together across all generations to provide solutions—even when those solutions required risk-taking and new ideas?" The senior adults nodded their heads, unsure why the pastor needed confirmation on what was so obvious to them.

Through intentional listening, the pastor had appropriately grasped the power of the church's HERE and began to share in worship services, "From now on, we are going to be the church we have always been and live out of our core history and identity. We will be a risk-taking community who pays attention to the needs of those around us, especially younger people, and work together to meet those needs."

Much to the pastor's delight, he received a new batch of letters and emails from senior adults, this time expressing full support. Younger people and families loved the direction as well. The Transformation

Team pursued many of the same changes they were considering previously—with almost no resistance.

Similar to the leaders in Wollongong Church, this pastor and the Transformation Team chose to intentionally listen (even if this pastor mistakenly didn't listen at first). God used that listening to reveal mental models, people's hopes and fears, and ideas for the future. The listening changed the church's perspective and direction and fueled next steps that were better aligned with God's best future for the community.

When you begin your leadership with listening, you'll discover tangible benefits for your future-focused change process almost immediately. These insights will position you well for the next chapter's vital task of clarifying your *why*.

REFLECTION QUESTIONS

For whatever change your church or Transformation Team is focused on in this season, on a scale of 1–5 (with 1 being "very little" and 5 being "a lot"), how much listening have you recently done related to that change?

What are the mental models (pictures or expectations of the way something *should be*) people hold related to the change or topic you're focused on?

Utilizing the resources in this chapter, what would a process look like for your team to listen well and build empathy and trust? Who will facilitate the listening, what questions will you ask, and to whom will you listen?

In addition to listening through one-on-one and small group conversations, how might you utilize other forms of listening (such as surveys, census data, research, and observation)?

How can your Transformation Team report back what you've learned from listening, highlighting how that feedback is impacting and improving your plans for the future?

Once you complete your listening, what key themes, stories, or ideas did you hear? What should you do next, in light of these?

Know Your *Why*

New York City's Marble Collegiate Church is one of the oldest Christian churches in the United States, tracing its founding to 1628. With a celebrated history of transformative ministry in New York and throughout the US and the world, the church has learned how to respond and adapt over nearly four hundred years.

Recently, however, serious questions surfaced about the present and future vibrancy of Marble Church. Having nurtured many generations of children, teenagers, and young adults over four centuries, the congregation had aged significantly during the last few decades. While there was an abundance of older generations in church membership and attendance, there were only a handful of children and teenagers regularly present for their Sunday morning worship services.

The church's leadership wisely recruited two veteran leaders to leverage their rich history and understand the church's current HERE, while simultaneously guiding the church into the future. One of leadership's top priorities was to raise the profile and value of children, youth, and families. The congregation was supportive in principle but still resisted actually incorporating younger people in Sunday morning services and particular areas of the overall church.

As the pastors and other leaders listened carefully to better understand that friction, they began to unearth the strong mental models governing much of the church.

As Marble's leadership envisioned change, they realized that the congregation's mental model for the weekend worship service was that it was primarily for adults, with excellent music and world-class preaching, and should otherwise be respectful, orderly, and excellent. Certainly, there were other places for young people to engage in the life of the church, but it was an unspoken expectation that those should be ministry areas that were less visible and not disruptive to the adults.

To move beyond that existing mental model, the leaders needed to better address and explain *why* this current understanding was so prevalent.

There's a chance you've heard of Marble Collegiate Church, as it has been one of the more prominent and influential churches of the past century—largely tied to its previous pastor Dr. Norman Vincent Peale. Dr. Peale assumed leadership at Marble in 1932 and served as senior minister for fifty-two years. During this time, church attendance grew significantly, as did the church's radio broadcast and TV ministry. Peale also wrote the book *The Power of Positive Thinking*, which has sold over five million copies and influenced many Christian leaders.

Given Peale's prominence and the church's influential broadcast ministries, it became paramount that the Sunday services were on time, excellent, well-ordered, and, above all, *quiet*. When you're responsible for an international broadcast that influences tens of thousands of global viewers, producers don't want any crying babies, interrupting children, or rambunctious teenagers. Based on these values, the church understandably developed a particular culture and strategy for weekend worship. Success and effectiveness for accomplishing their mission were built on a worship service designed almost exclusively for adults.

The hidden cost of this approach? Their younger people learned they were to be seen but not heard.

Fast-forward to today. In order for the pastors and church leaders to move forward, they couldn't merely introduce new ideas or programs. They had to address the deeper *why* of what motivated the church, where it found its identity, and what it meant to be successful. Yesterday's successes had become threats to tomorrow's sustainability.

Marble's leadership moved forward by helping the church construct a new *why* for the future. This new *why* didn't happen overnight, and it didn't leave their past behind. The pastors and leaders made the case, through preaching and programming decisions, that younger people can and must play a vibrant role in the life of the overall church. They emphasized that while excellence and order honor God, so do seeing lives transformed and people (especially younger people) knowing and following Jesus Christ. They introduced the wider congregation to the power and value of an intergenerational community, and they helped adults and senior adults understand what today's teenagers and twentysomethings are seeking in a faith community.

Yes, even a congregation with a rich past can have a brighter future.

While Marble's cultural changes are far from finished, as of this writing they're headed in a hopeful direction and have thoughtful strategies and plans in place. What propels them toward the future and fully embracing all 3 Checkpoints is that the leadership and congregation have taken the time to *know their why*.

Not every church has the prominence, history, and national influence of Marble Collegiate Church. But even if your church is less than a year old, your current mission, programming, culture, and steps toward the future are driven by a *why* that beats at the church's core.

You Are HERE . . . but *Why*?

Imagine you visit the doctor because you've battled a serious headache for the past couple of days. Any doctor worth their salt needs to conduct a thorough examination before offering a diagnosis. This examination will take several factors into account, including your past health, any medicines you're taking, and, if needed, perhaps some scans or other tests. Malpractice might occur if your doctor took one look at you, didn't ask questions, and recommended you take an over-the-counter pain reliever—only for you to later find out you had a serious medical condition warranting more aggressive treatment. Knowing the medical *why* makes all the difference in what's prescribed.

The same is true for your church. Understanding your church's ministry history, values, and other root causes of its current culture can shed light on how you got HERE and how you'll get THERE next.

I (Jake) once served as a youth pastor in a local congregation, and at first I wondered why it took so much time to build trust with the majority of the staff, parents, and teenagers. Listening to some wise church members who understood the church's culture and history revealed that I was the church's seventh youth pastor in the past ten years. From the day I started, several people were anticipating the day I would leave the position. It was only after I entered my second year in the role that key stakeholders began to trust my leadership and potential for longevity.

Why were some parents and leaders apprehensive about my leadership? They had been conditioned by past experiences that youth leaders only stay for a short amount of time and don't invest long-term. For me to really make progress on next steps, I needed to understand that history and subsequent expectations.

Too Many Church Leaders Don't Start with Why

In his bestselling book *Start with Why*, business author Simon Sinek observes that our world doesn't start with asking *why*. He argues that many leaders and organizations are clear about *what* they do, and some can outline *how* they do *what* they do. However, when it comes to *why*, Sinek writes,

> Very few people or companies can clearly articulate WHY they do WHAT they do. When I say WHY, I don't mean to make money— that's a result. By WHY I mean what is your purpose, cause or belief? WHY does your company exist? WHY do you get out of bed in the morning? And WHY should anyone care?[1]

When it comes to church leaders and congregations, we fall into the same trap. Many of us are busy with our *what* and our *how*. But a smaller percentage of us are crystal clear about our *why*. And even fewer of our congregations and Transformation Teams operate daily out of a crystal clear *why*.

Don't get us wrong: at a very general level, most churches are steeped in a general familiarity about our *why*. Faith communities broadly have a sense that we're operating out of faithfulness to God, or to make disciples of Jesus. However, too often those statements become just that: statements. They operate in the background and can become stale or overly general, lacking specific application and a tangible motivation for our day-to-day work.

Whether your desired cultural changes are related to young people (Checkpoint #1), increasing ethnic diversity (Checkpoint #2), tangibly loving your neighbors (Checkpoint #3), or other priorities, at some point people will ask, "*Why* are we doing this?" or perhaps, "*Why* haven't we done this before?" We recommend you be ready with a clear and compelling answer.

Identifying Adaptive Issues

Knowing your why informs the type of change you're dealing with and the corresponding interventions you'll need to deploy. In his seminal work distinguishing forms of change, Ronald Heifetz describes *technical problems* as those for which we "do, in fact, have the necessary know-how and procedures."[2] When facing a technical problem, you can easily locate the solution, or perhaps an authority figure or expert can solve it with or for you. Furthermore, once the problem is solved, things will go back to status quo.

An *adaptive challenge* is more complex. Heifetz characterizes adaptive challenges as

> not amenable to authoritative expertise or standard operating procedures. They cannot be solved by someone who provides answers from on high . . . they require experiments, new discoveries, and adjustments from numerous places in the organization or community. Without learning new ways—changing attitudes, values, and

behaviors—people cannot make the adaptive leap necessary to thrive in the new environment.[3]

To further contrast the difference between the two, Heifetz and coauthor Marty Linsky use an analogy of taking your malfunctioning car to a mechanic.[4] Most of the time, this is a technical problem because the expert (a mechanic) solves the problem and (hopefully!) the car goes back to normal. However, if the same problem is repeatedly caused by the driving habits of a particular family member, a technical solution will not solve the core challenge. Every time the family member's driving causes the problem to recur, taking the car to the mechanic will become both expensive and time-consuming. The adaptive challenge, in this case, is influencing the family member to change their driving beliefs and behaviors.

Applying this to the church, as you ask, *Why* are we HERE?, some answers are more *technical* while others are more *adaptive*. Perhaps you haven't had any new guests at your worship services or gatherings in years, and you realize it's because your church doesn't have an appealing website, or you need better physical signage on the road. Those are technical responses.

Or let's imagine you attract lots of new visitors, but none of them stick around longer than a first service or ministry activity. If you take the time to ask a few of them why, and they share that your church is the least welcoming, most unfriendly church they've ever visited, your challenge is probably adaptive. It would require changing congregants' attitudes, values, and behaviors—which may not come easily or quickly.

Knowing Your Why Requires Wisdom in Christian Leadership

Richard Osmer, a practical theologian from Princeton Theological Seminary, outlines the importance of Christian leaders having an answer to the question, *Why* is this going on? In his book *Practical Theology*, Osmer shares how early in his first postseminary pastorate in a small town in the mountains of eastern Tennessee, the church placed a swing set in a picnic area so children could play outdoors after worship while the parents had fellowship time.[5]

Shortly after the swing set was installed, Osmer arrived at the church to find it gone. It was now cemented into a new location behind the church. After some investigation, it was discovered that the longtime church treasurer had hired a small group to move it in the middle of the night. This caused no small amount of frustration, so a church meeting was held and a vote cast, and that day the swing set was returned to its original location, set again in concrete.

Osmer tells of visiting the church treasurer (which he was not excited to do), who promptly quit her position and told him she was quitting the church as well. It was at that moment he realized his seminary education had not prepared him with the skills and knowledge to make sense of this prickly situation.

Through some careful detective work, Osmer discovered that the church treasurer was married to a man who had been part of the church until his death years before. To honor her husband, the church treasurer gave money to build the covered picnic area where the swing set was initially placed. Since so much time had passed, no one remembered how or why the picnic area had been constructed. And so, no one had asked the church treasurer, whose family made that picnic area possible, how she would feel about the inclusion of a swing set.

Hence the treasurer's middle-of-the-night, clandestine relocation of the swing set. (We imagine you could tell your own swing set story too!)

The following weeks and months took Osmer through an in-depth, on-the-job process of exploring *why*. He dug into the importance of honoring family members in small church communities, the role of family systems theory in understanding complex relationships, and how the field of psychology could shed light on this church treasurer's possible feelings. Throughout his processing and discussions, Osmer had to sharpen his detective skills to understand what was happening and *why*, and to offer a pastoral response.

Consider Your *Why* through Three Timeframes

As God sharpens your sense of HERE and *knowing your why*, that process can be aided greatly through your careful listening work. If you haven't already done so, thoughtfully and systematically reflect on what you and your Transformation Team heard during your listening, noting specific observations, questions, and threads about *why* that wove through your conversations.

As you seek to make sense of what you hear, be extra mindful of the three timeframes involved in any change: your church's past, present, and future. In fact, we recommend your Transformation Team reflect through a threefold process of looking back (past), looking around (present), and looking ahead (future).

Timeframe #1: Looking Back at the Past

When you look back, you reflect on your church's history. Consider the example of Marble Collegiate Church again. Its successful development of a massive broadcast ministry informed its culture, values, and current realities. As a result, for a season, younger people were not actively welcomed into the worship services since they might distract the listening audience.

To help you look back, consider trying a few of these exercises.

Investigate Your Church's Founding Narrative

Is there a story that encapsulates how or why your church (or ministry, tradition, or denomination) was initially founded? Discuss that founding narrative with your Transformation Team and its implications for why your church does what it does today. As one example, we've experienced Pentecostal and charismatic denominations and churches that trace their founding narrative to the early twentieth-century Azusa Street Revival and its significant, fresh move of the Holy Spirit. We've also experienced Methodist churches that trace their founding narrative to John Wesley and his eighteenth-century approach to ministry that was known both for its organization and for being with people in everyday life (outside of formal church gatherings). Those founding narratives about faith movements and denominations inform the current identity of affiliated churches.

As another example, the Chinese Community Church of Washington DC (CCCDC) was founded in 1935 as a faith community that helped Asian Americans preserve their cultural and faith heritage. In the heart of DC proper, it has provided a growing Chinese American population with religious services, social services, and a community to call home. The hallway of the church displays a photo board that tells the history of the church—including stories of God's faithfulness.

As the Chinese American population has largely moved to the suburbs of the DC area, the church's English Congregation pastor, Joshua, a Korean American, actively wrestles with the church's core identity. I (Ray) have had fruitful discussions with him to consider how he could steward the history and heritage of his church as a historic Asian American church. One of the key conversations we've had is around preserving the name of the church as a way to honor its historic founding. Such questions about name change are common in ethnic minority churches that are experiencing demographic changes from a variety of forces, including gentrification.

As the immigrant Chinese population in the area has diminished, the church's leadership has considered emphasizing the geographic location of the church by changing the name from Chinese Community Church to Chinatown Community Church. When Joshua surveyed the landscape, he realized that they were not only the sole Chinese church in DC proper but also one of the few Asian American churches in their area. As of this writing, he is still processing what the identity of the church is becoming, but he is resolved to honor its roots. Joshua has been intentional in including the church's history as part of their membership orientation, maintaining a good relationship with the non–English speaking congregants, and ministering to the remaining Chinese population living at a nearby housing project. In addition, they run a Chinatown Service Center that supports immigration efforts through the church and is seeking to serve the broader Chinatown neighborhood even as its Chinese population rapidly diminishes.

Construct a Congregational Timeline

A second exercise that might help you uncover elements from the past is to build a congregational timeline. On a large piece of paper or electronic document, draw a long line. A dot on the far left side

FIGURE 6.1

Congregational Timeline

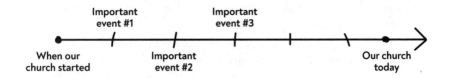

represents when your church started. The far right side represents today. Depending on how long your church has been in existence, identify five to fifteen (or more) significant turning points in the life of your church. As a Transformation Team, ask, "What events have been most important in shaping the life and ministry of our community?" Briefly write or depict each point in its place along the timeline. Reflect as a team on what those events reveal about *why* your church does what it does today.

Explore Key Questions about Your Past

A third exercise to contemplate the past involves constructing good questions for your team to reflect on together, such as those listed below. You might also incorporate some of these questions as your team listens to community members.

- When were one or two times our church was "at our best" or fulfilled our mission with excellence? What might we learn from those moments or experiences?
- Has our church faced a challenge similar to what we're facing now at some point in the past? What did we do at that time that either helped or hindered our progress?
- In what ways have our church's culture or leadership helped or hindered our effectiveness as a church in the past?

Timeframe #2: Looking Around in the Present

Looking around means considering the various cultural factors *today* that are influencing *why* your church does what it does. We are going to offer several helpful exercises to thoughtfully assess your current reality, but feel free to brainstorm other methods as a team. If you have community members with specific expertise, perspectives, or wise insights, consider inviting them to team meetings to share.

Name Your Church's Current Reality

First, there is power in simply naming your church's current reality. As a team and using a piece of paper, electronic document, or perhaps a whiteboard, jot down your team's responses to the following questions:

- What are the current demographics of our congregation? When we consider the percentages of people who fit into particular categories of age, gender, race and ethnicity, socioeconomic status, geographic location, and other demographics, what does our current reality look like? How does that embody or reflect who we want to be? How closely do we reflect the geographic community in which our parish is located?
- If Jesus were to walk through our neighborhood and visit a worship service or ministry at our church, what might he say to our team?
- How would we describe the current culture of our church? What are our church's greatest values? What are the activities we repeat without even needing to think about them? How does this reflect the culture or values we want to be central?

Leaders may want to work ahead to prepare for this conversation by gathering (or assigning team members to gather) demographic information ahead of time. As you meet and discuss, notice similarities among team members' answers; if the answers differ, discuss why they vary.

During an extended discussion at an all-church fall retreat, one predominantly Chinese church with which I (Kara) am connected realized that while its members valued tangibly showing love to each other, various generations expressed that value differently. Older Chinese adults who wanted to show they cared regularly asked teenagers and twentysomethings direct questions like, "Have you eaten?" and "Are you dating anyone?"

For sixtysomethings, those two questions demonstrated care about the young people with whom they were speaking. But to the young people, who felt more distant from this older generation's manner of expressing care, that pair of direct questions felt intrusive. As one college student expressed, "There's no way I'm going to invite my friends to church if adults are going to ask them such personal questions."

When older generations explained *why* they asked those questions, young people became more empathetic and gently suggested alternative questions that were more hospitable and welcoming, like, "How can I be praying for you?" or "Is there any way I can help you this week?"

Conduct a SWOT Analysis

One of the most powerful tools we have found for quickly making sense of our current reality with our own teams is a *SWOT exercise*. SWOT stands for Strengths, Weaknesses, Opportunities, and Threats. Strengths and weaknesses are factors internal to your organization that you can control (or at least influence), whereas opportunities and threats are external and usually beyond your control or influence. For example, a weakness could be that your church is not spending or budgeting money very efficiently. (It's internal, and your church has some control over your budget.) A threat would be if the national economy plunged into a recession and your congregants had less money to give. (This is external because you presumably can't control the national economy; if we're mistaken and you can, please let us know because we'd definitely like to chat!)

To engage in a SWOT, invite your team to brainstorm and write down (using a whiteboard or electronic document) what seem like the most important strengths, weaknesses, opportunities, and threats given the future-focused changes you're contemplating. Keep brainstorming until you have at least five to seven responses under each category.

But don't stop there. Under each category, invite your Transformation Team to vote for the one or two responses that seem most important. In the end, you should have one or two top strengths, weaknesses, opportunities, and threats. Once you have your final list, discuss the implications for the changes you face.

Uncover Mixed Messages

As another option for "looking around," consider where your church is experiencing *mixed messages*. Mixed messages occur when you or someone in a leadership position communicates something that can be confusing or interpreted in a way that doesn't result in clarity. As a team, ask, "What mixed messages might be at work in our church, and what might we do to find greater clarity?"

Some examples of mixed messages are telling the congregation you want to emphasize intergenerational relationships and connections but failing to provide any practical space or programming to make those a reality. Or wanting to expose your congregation members to people who live, love, or vote differently than they do while simultaneously being a faith community that avoids tension.

Timeframe #3: Looking Ahead to the Future

As we move forward to the next zone—THERE—we want to offer a couple of introductory exercises for how you might consider your *why* as you look ahead to the future.

Name Problems and Opportunities

One inspiring way to identify your *why* for the future is to consider two sides of the same coin—with one side being the local and global problems currently existing that make it necessary for your church to carry out your mission, and the other being the future difference that would be made if you successfully fulfilled your mission.

In a Transformation Team meeting, start by asking, "If our church ceased to exist today, what progress would not be made over the next few years? What are the challenges or problems that would exist, or perhaps even get worse, because our church is no longer involved?" Try to be as vivid and descriptive as you can.

The other side of the coin focuses more on the positive by inviting your Transformation Team to reflect, "If our church was fully accomplishing our mission and doing everything we hoped for over the next few years, what positive differences might we make? What local or global work might get better or stronger because our church is involved?" Similar to the first exercise, this can fuel your team's collective passion and help you dig into *why* God is calling you toward a particular future.

Identify Barriers and Challenges

Another future-focused exercise is to consider the cultural barriers or challenges that prevent your church from deeply living out your *why*. Shape your team discussions with questions such as these:

- As we move forward in this work, are there any elephants in the room? These might be big issues that exist and are hard to ignore, but we nonetheless avoid talking about or addressing them. How can we begin engaging these elephants?
- Is our church suffering from vision fatigue? Have we been so focused on the future, or have we changed our vision of the future so frequently, that people are exhausted and need rest before we introduce even more change?
- Are we appropriately focused on the root causes of a problem or opportunity, or are we stuck focusing on symptoms? As we look ahead, is there anything behind or beneath the presenting issues we need to more strongly consider?

We once worked with a church in Iowa that wanted to emphasize Checkpoint #1 and better disciple its teenagers. The church staff asked, "What would be the best way to spiritually form the young people in our church?" Their conclusion? The best approach would be spiritually mature adults who walked with those young people.

That aha moment was quickly followed by an internal wake-up call that they didn't have enough spiritually mature adults in the church. So, they decided to double down on adult discipleship, which would yield more mature Christian adults who could then invest in teenagers and twentysomethings. They invested more resources in the faith formation of adults and urged those more mature adults to prioritize impacting the next generation.

Name Your *Why* by Constructing and Testing Hypotheses

The point of exploring *why* you are HERE isn't just an abstract theoretical or theological exercise. The goal is that this deeper reflection on topics like adaptive change and considering the past, present, and future informs your team's practical next steps to become a Future-Focused Church. Unpacking your *why* should unearth key insights related to young people, ethnic diversity, and tangibly loving your neighbors as well as other cultural changes you seek.

Like the doctor who needs to do a careful examination to diagnose why someone may have a headache, your role as a Transformation Team is to diagnose your church's core problems or opportunities and propose solutions or paths forward that respond appropriately. Ron Heifetz argues powerfully, "The single most important skill and most undervalued capacity for exercising adaptive leadership is diagnosis."[6]

Much like you may have done when you were in a high school science class, you may find it productive to construct and test hypotheses to diagnose *why* you are where you are. A hypothesis is a proposed explanation for something that can usually be tested. It's another tool in your toolbox to explain *why* something is occurring.

The process for testing hypotheses is relatively straightforward. Once you've encountered something you'd like to change or a problem you're trying to solve, ask each team member to finish this statement: "_____ is happening because _____." Take time to evaluate and discuss, and see if you can come to agreement on the root cause. This is your diagnosis.

As one example, we've conducted deep listening with various communities who serve youth leaders through the TENx10 Collaboration. In those conversations, we've discovered that while there is a significant amount of training resources designed for White and suburban contexts, there are fewer training resources designed primarily for racialized minorities and urban communities. As our leadership team explored these complex realities, someone proposed, "The lack of resources designed primarily for communities of color and urban leaders is largely because many of those training organizations lack funding and access to needed resources to build their capacity." While there are complex realities at work in this situation, that was one hypothesis our team could discuss and explore to find potential ways forward.

Then, move from diagnosis to proposed action through an if-then statement. You can do this by inviting each team member to fill in what's missing in the following sentence: "If we _____, then _____." The idea is to identify a potentially fruitful strategy or approach, then name what the intended result might be.

We're encouraged by the ministry of Charlie Dates, who currently serves as lead pastor for Salem Baptist Church and Progressive Baptist Church (a historic Black church in Chicago that was on its last leg). Prior to Charlie's pastorate at Progressive, the median age of congregation members was over sixty-five, and the leadership knew they needed to hire a senior pastor who was much younger than the majority of their congregation was used to (or, frankly, comfortable with). As the hiring committee members deliberated, they tested a hypothesis by musing, "*If* we don't hire this young pastor, *then* our church may not be vibrant . . . or even around in ten years." Convicted by this hypothesis, the congregation took a chance with someone who they wondered might be too young. However, their decision paid off. Over the next five years, the church grew vibrant in energy and more than fivefold in number.

Other examples of if-then statements in churches include:

If we keep funding our youth ministry position at half-time, *then* we will continue to see high turnover in the role and discouragement among our kids.

If our youth discipleship activities are disconnected from relational ministry and interaction with the wider congregation,
then we may fail to effectively form the faith of an entire
generation.

If we keep elevating or hiring leaders who don't reflect the diversity of our surrounding neighborhood, *then* we'll have a
harder time truly welcoming our neighbors.

If we don't preach or engage on social and political matters
(even when they may be uncomfortable or controversial),
then our congregants will be informed and formed by alternative sources.

If we don't explicitly declare our commitment to communal
righteousness and social justice, *then* people who are skeptical and cynical about the church may never walk through
our doors.

Note that at this point in your change efforts, you don't need a
final answer, so don't worry if your team members hold different
perspectives, advocate for different hypotheses, or feel stuck. The
key is getting your team to consider the deeper, and even sometimes
multiple, *whys* by diagnosing and testing potential ways forward.

Follow Jesus' Lead

At any point in defining your HERE, it's prudent to pause and ask if
you're modeling Jesus and following his lead. This is especially true
when you're asking questions about *why* you are where you are, and
how that *why* might inform your next steps.

In the Scriptures, Jesus regularly addresses *why* questions. In
Matthew 5, during the Sermon on the Mount, he offers a series of
provocative statements with this beginning: "You have heard it said,
but I say to you . . ."

Covering a wide range of topics, Jesus showcases his followers'
current mental models and then reinterprets and offers a counterintuitive approach. Most often, he does so by looking deeper, or

considering *why* the command was originally given. In this and other circumstances, Jesus often doesn't give a straightforward answer but challenges people's assumptions, history, or core beliefs.

As you seek to lead changes to become a Future-Focused Church, we think you'll do well to follow Jesus' example and ask *Why?* Marble Collegiate Church needed to consider their culture, identity, and what it meant to be successful. Your church might need to wrestle with different questions, but you almost certainly will need to pin down *your why.* As you engage in this work, we urge you to persevere until you get to the bottom of *why* things are the way they are and to be willing to challenge the status quo to help your church become more faithful and effective. When you get that far, you're in good company—with Jesus!

REFLECTION QUESTIONS

On a scale of 1–5 (with 1 being "not at all" and 5 being "very well"), how well do you feel your church or ministry knows its *why* (in terms of the past, present, or future)? Share with your Transformation Team the reasoning behind your answer.

What might be one of "yesterday's successes" in your church, parish, or ministry that could be a major liability to your future vitality?

Based on the description of an *adaptive challenge*, what are one or two adaptive challenges your church currently faces?

What is your church's *founding narrative*, or an important story from your history that shapes your congregation? How does that story shape your *why*?

How do the current demographics and culture of your congregation shape who you are today? How closely do they reflect who you want to be? How about your neighborhood or city?

Considering a change you'd like to make, what is your response to the statement: "____ is happening because ____"? After sharing and discussing your responses to that, how would you fill in these blanks: "If we ____, then ____"? How similarly or differently do your team members frame responses to those same prompts?

THERE

Where God Is Leading

"For I know the plans I have for you," declares the LORD,
"plans to prosper you and not to harm you,
plans to give you hope and a future."

JEREMIAH 29:11

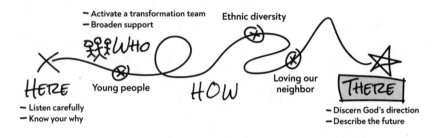

FIGURE Z3.1

Mapping the Journey—THERE

As you and your Transformation Team navigate the four zones of your Future-Focused Church map, the two chapters in this section will address how to discern God's best for your future THERE.

Your guiding question for this zone is:

> **Where is God leading us?**

We encourage you to discern your THERE by involving a wide variety of people identified during your WHO efforts, along with a deepened sensitivity to where you have been and where you are now that you've gained from your HERE work. Also keep in mind that THERE does not invite you to determine the future of your church in a vacuum but to carefully discern where *God* desires you to go.

To reiterate what we said in chapter 1, we understand that change isn't as simple as moving from one static HERE to one static future THERE. Christian leadership in today's world involves preparing for, and being able to pivot into, multiple potential futures—as outlined in the diagram below.

FIGURE Z3.2

Mapping the Journey—Multiple There

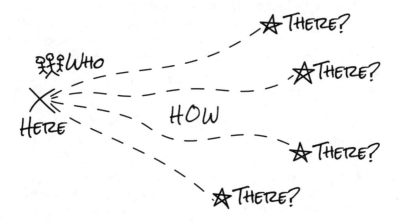

EMOTIONS ON THE JOURNEY

In the midst of the excitement about dreaming together about God's best future for your faith community, take a few moments to attend to your own emotional journey through the following prompts:

- As I think about dreaming about the future of our church, I feel . . .
- Based on my past experience with this team or other teams in trying to discern where God is leading, I feel encouraged that . . .
- And yet at the same time, I'm anxious about . . .
- For the good of my own heart and soul, soon I should talk with someone I trust about . . .

PRAYER

We take great hope knowing that God is the initiator and guide of all change in our churches, parishes, and ministries. So, we invite you (on your own or with your team) to pause and reflect on the words of Galatians 6:9 to "not become weary in doing good, for at the proper time we will reap a harvest if we do not give up" through the following prayer prompts:

- To not be overwhelmed by the amount of change and lack of clarity about the future of your church but instead be filled with hope.
- To wisely include a wide variety of perspectives as you do the good work of seeking God's most important themes and values for your future.
- For your discernment and description of the future to be an appropriate balance of fidelity to your past and boldness to engage new frontiers.
- To reap a great harvest of disciples who make disciples as you pursue God's best future for your church.

Discerning God's Leading
When the Future Is Unclear

New Movement Church was struggling to discern their future. They had articulated a clear mission (or *why*) of "making disciples of Jesus" and were committed to the 3 Checkpoints of being a Future-Focused Church. Still, finding clarity and a unified strategy to move their people to God's best THERE proved elusive. Their community and the wider world were changing so quickly, they were navigating the COVID-19 pandemic, and so much seemed up in the air.

Knowing this uncertainty was untenable long-term, New Movement joined Fuller Youth Institute's Growing Young Cohort to gain strategic momentum and shift their church to be more hospitable to younger people. As coached by the cohort process, their Transformation Team gathered for a series of meetings, prayerfully asking God to guide their journey. They didn't want to lead the church into *their* best future but into *God's* best future.

In preparation for one team meeting to discern their THERE, each member was instructed to take time to reflect on Bible passages that spoke both to them personally and to the congregation more broadly. When the team gathered, more than one team member had been drawn to Jesus' parable of the prodigal son told in Luke 15:11–32. As they read that passage aloud and discussed its meaning and implications, the Transformation Team sensed that the Holy Spirit was up to something. They were especially captivated by the image of God as a loving father who offers forgiveness and celebrates when a child returns. There was a deep resonance and confidence that *this* was the direction they had been seeking.

New Movement's Transformation Team excitedly discussed what this parable might mean for their congregation if they adopted a similar posture—particularly toward younger people. What if they were fundamentally a community of love and forgiveness? What if they weren't marked primarily as being legalistic and, if they were honest, a bit stuffy (which the pastor admitted was a characterization with some degree of truth)? How could they model God's empathy and warmth in their willingness to *not just walk but run* toward those who had drifted from God or the church?

Eventually they settled on a core vision that embodied the future-focused 3 Checkpoints and guided their change process: *We want to be a church that throws a party and celebrates when anyone who walked away from God comes back to God.*

Their Transformation Team next drafted two paragraphs that imagined a hopeful future for their church five years from now, along with the activities and relationships that would be pervasive if they took this vision seriously. The subsequent half-page document was hopeful, empowering, and motivating to the entire congregation. While it didn't call out every new program to launch or every shift to make, it offered a clear THERE to discern if they were moving closer to, or further away from, their shared goal.

Over the past several years, while much in our world and New Movement Church's wider community has remained uncertain, living out the parable of the prodigal son has functioned as the church's North Star. It has given them a shared direction, a set of values, and enough clarity to follow God's leading THERE, even when so many aspects of the future remain hazy.

Why It's So Hard These Days to Plan for the Future

We've reviewed dozens of top-selling church leadership, outreach, and youth ministry books from the past few decades, as well as been part of many popular church training conferences. Broadly, we've noticed an underlying assumption that the list of effective ministry practices is relatively static and predictable—such that any leader could plan with confidence toward a relatively stable future.

In this previous stabler world, many churches that grew were those with a compelling senior pastor or charismatic leadership team who could cast vision and skillfully move their church THERE. Oftentimes these well-known leaders also wrote books and head-lined conferences to share how they aligned staff and the overall congregation around an appealing strategy that yielded results. The good news? They could teach you to do it too.

But that predictability is an artifact of the past.

These days, we hear very few pastors (from any region, faith tradition, or size parish) describing such stability. Today, planning for the future is more difficult.

Predictability has been replaced with constant pivoting.

As one leader shared, "Early in my pastoral leadership, it felt like what I needed to do was cast a clear vision for the future during one of my sermons, and then people would be supportive, give financially, and lean in to help us move that direction. But things are so much more complicated today. Part of that was due to the changes and shifts from COVID, but it also feels deeper than that. It feels like every week I'm needing to learn new skills, respond to new challenges, and discern a new future. It can be exhausting."

Simultaneously, shifts in our wider society have led to adjustments in human development and behavior, especially among young people. Developmental psychologists have recently coined terms such as *extended adolescence* and *emerging adulthood* to describe how the process and timeline of becoming an adult has changed. Consider for a moment that in 1970, the median age of getting married was twenty-one for women and twenty-three for men, compared to twenty-eight for women and thirty for men today.[1] In 1970, the average age for women having a first child was 21.4, increasing to age twenty-five in the year 2000,[2] and age thirty by 2019.[3] During this longer season before marriage and parenthood, young people are left to navigate complex realities and decisions about what job(s) to take, what college to (maybe) attend, if and who to date or marry, where to live, and much more.

While increased options may seem appealing, they can be debilitating. We've heard from today's teenagers and twentysomethings that they struggle not only with FOMO (Fear Of Missing Out) but also FOBO (Fear Of Better Options).

If you're from an older generation (and especially if you grew up with middle-class realities and options), you might resonate with *the world as it was*. Life certainly wasn't easy, but it was more linear. There was more of a recognized, or default, path to follow. If you're from a younger generation (especially Millennial or Gen Z or Gen Alpha), or if you didn't grow up with financial privilege,

FIGURE 7.1

World as It Was

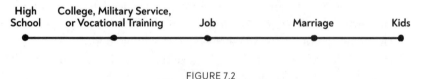

FIGURE 7.2

World as It Is Now

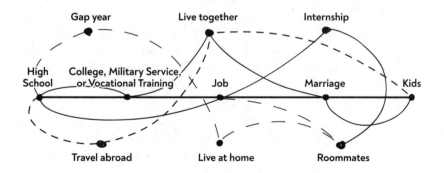

> We recognize that any image or metaphor falls short in providing the full nuance and representation of varied and diverse people and experiences. While this "world as it was" diagram largely reflects the White, middle-class experience of many in the US population over the past few generations, it doesn't encompass all realities or journeys. While your journey is unique and may or may not fit this diagram, we want to emphasize the main point: the journeys of today's young people into adulthood are increasingly complex.

you more likely resonate with *the world as it is now*. Life is complex, full of twists and turns. We're not labeling either reality as "good" or "bad"—we're simply stating they are the worlds in which we live and in which our churches and ministries function.

The problem? So many of our church systems, structures, and processes were designed for *the world as it was*. This doesn't mean our churches are "bad" but rather that we need to move toward more adaptive thinking and develop the ability to learn and adjust as we journey toward a less certain THERE.

Indeed, much of the writing and research in the business world over the last few decades has shifted away from long-term strategic planning to short-term planning coupled with rapid testing and iteration, as well as design thinking.[4] The takeaway here is that your church can't simply choose one future ten to twenty—or even five—years from now and plod along toward that stable THERE. You have to prepare for multiple potential THEREs, as we outlined in chapter 1.

As New Movement Church demonstrates, being a Future-Focused Church means developing a picture for tomorrow that is both clear enough to guide and flexible enough to adapt. That way, as you take faithful steps toward THERE, you can also prayerfully adjust and revise along the way.

Know What Will Never Change

While it may seem counterintuitive in a book about change, we urge you to first become laser focused on what will never change.

FIGURE 7.3

Mapping the Journey—Multiple Potential Futures

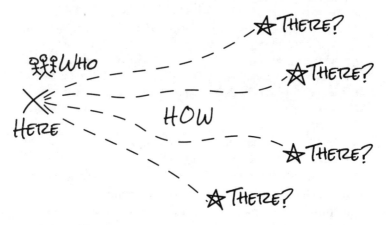

Based on their survey of highly effective, long-standing, for-profit companies, Jim Collins and Jerry Porras conclude that "truly great companies understand the difference between what should never change and what should be open for change, between what is genuinely sacred and what is not."[5]

One commitment that should never change is a *core purpose*, which is "the organization's reason for being . . . it doesn't just describe the organization's output or target customers; it captures the soul of the organization."[6] Given this definition, your church's core purpose should be closely related to your mission. But while your core purpose addresses *why* your church exists, your mission addresses *what your church does*. For example, the mission of your church may be to make disciples of Jesus. Your core purpose should

> ▶ We are using the phrases "core purpose" and "core values." You might instead use terms like "vision," "mission," or "strategy." The labels aren't as important as making sure your church is aligned around a cohesive framework that paints a clear picture for God's THERE for your church and community.

address the question, Why does our church need to make disciples? It could be a sentence like: *Following Jesus brings true hope, peace, and joy for all people and our world.*

Another influence is *core values*, which are "the essential and enduring tenets of an organization. A small set of timeless guiding principles, core values require no external justification; they have intrinsic value and importance to those inside the organization."[7] For example, a church that has built its ministry on Acts 2:42–47 might elevate values that emerge clearly from that passage, such as fellowship or hospitality, generosity, prayer, teaching, and worship.

We believe a church's core purpose and core values don't operate in a vacuum or emerge based on the whims of a new leader or team. While you should certainly be creative and consider your church's unique context, your core purpose likely stems from essential scriptural principles related to making disciples, embodying the kingdom of God, or experiencing the abundant life of following Jesus.

We coached one church that went to great lengths to discover their particular core values. They hosted congregation members in town hall meetings, conducted listening sessions in adult classes and small groups, and gathered their elders for prayer and reflection. In the end, they landed on the values of discipleship, worship, mission and evangelism, prayer, and teaching. When that final set was presented at a churchwide meeting, a congregant raised her hand and pointed out that those five paralleled the core tenets and activities of the early church in Acts 2:42–47. While church leaders were glad they had done the hard work of listening to their community, it was a lesson that their values weren't so much something "new" to invent but rather a timeless scriptural reality for them to identify.

▶ Other scriptural examples you might lean on to draw your core values include Jesus' command to love God and love your neighbor in Matthew 22:36–40 or the fruit of the Spirit in Galatians 5:22–23: love, joy, peace, patience, kindness, goodness, faithfulness, gentleness, and self-control.

Rather than feeling limited, they felt greater freedom to innovate and explore how to embody those timeless principles in today's reality.

Leaning In to Congregational Imagination

You were likely skilled in the craft of imagination from a very young age. I (Jake) am regularly blown away by the ingenuity of my two young sons' imaginations, often associated with a Star Wars, Harry Potter, or Ninjago story they've read or seen.

We believe our churches would do well to recover more of a childlike imagination. Quoting the prophet Joel, Peter proclaims in Acts 2:17, "'In the last days,' God says, 'I will pour out my Spirit on all people. Your sons and daughters will prophesy, your young men will see visions, your old men will dream dreams.'" Our faith history and scriptural foundations invite us to be people of imagination.

Craig Dykstra, former vice president of religion at Lilly Endowment Inc., describes how over time, artists and lawyers develop an intelligence, or a way of knowing, that helps them see in ways others can't.[8] In "Imagination and the Pastoral Life," he suggests that congregations and pastoral leaders can develop a similar sense of imagination—most often connected to a

> deep, sustained and thoroughgoing engagement with the scriptures and with a sound theological tradition that brings the word of God into an ongoing history of endlessly contemporary thought and practice . . . [as well as] a reliable understanding of what makes human beings tick, of who people are and how they operate.[9]

In other words, pastoral and congregational imagination don't simply happen overnight but are the result of faithful and intentional work honed over time.

Thankfully, while discerning THERE for your church is important and invites your church's best contributions, it doesn't entirely depend on you and your people. Dykstra adds, "The pastoral imagination is not something to be achieved or attained. It comes as a gift. At the very heart of pastoral ministry lies the good news of a power that is not our own, a labor that ultimately is not our work, a grace that is not of our own doing."[10]

In *The Prophetic Imagination*, theologian Walter Brueggemann argues that imagination is a core prophetic task, writing that the Old Testament prophets

> were concerned with most elemental changes in human society and . . . understood a great deal about how change is effected. . . . The task of prophetic ministry is to nurture, nourish, and evoke a consciousness and perception alternative to the consciousness and perception of the dominant culture around us.[11]

Biblical prophets invited others to imagine a THERE that was yet to be realized, sometimes through reinterpreting what *was*, by challenging what *is*, or by dreaming what *might be* through a new or fresh perspective.

As we engage in the work of imagining our THERE, it's vital we participate in the process with an open mind and open heart, ready for the Holy Spirit to convict us about areas where we need to stretch or grow. Notice, for example, Peter's sermon during the growth of the early church in Acts 2 that concludes, "Repent and be baptized, every one of you, in the name of Jesus Christ for the forgiveness of your sins. And you will receive the gift of the Holy Spirit. The promise is for you and your children and for all who are far off—for all whom the Lord our God will call" (vv. 38–39). As we're prayerfully developing our own future-focused imagination, it's important to observe that Peter *doesn't* say, "You've been doing everything exactly right. Keep doing what you've been doing." Realizing a new future often requires adjusting our direction—sometimes through a 180-degree turn.

Wheaton College professor Esau McCaulley advises that when we turn to Scripture for guidance on the future, "The question isn't always which account of Christianity uses the Bible. The question is which does justice to as much of the biblical witness as possible."[12] In other words, we shouldn't simply form a picture of exactly what we want our future to look like and then scour Scripture for a passage or two that justifies that direction. We need to take the whole counsel of God into consideration, read through the lens of Scripture as a grand narrative, and discern how the ethics and commitments of God's kingdom apply to our community.

Fully realizing the 3 Checkpoints may require small or large shifts, perhaps starting with some level of conviction or repentance for habits and attitudes we've developed over a long time. For example, when it comes to a church that reflects the ethnic diversity of the kingdom of God (Checkpoint #2), I (Jake) mentioned that I grew up in a historically Dutch Reformed congregation that was almost exclusively White. From my vantage point as a kid in West Michigan, I assumed (incorrectly) that most people's experiences in the area were similar to mine.

Later in seminary, I came across Yale professor Willie James Jennings's writing in *The Christian Imagination*. He describes his experience of being a Black Christian in Grand Rapids, Michigan, growing up around the same predominantly White and Dutch Reformed tradition. Jennings insightfully unpacks significant ways leaders from that tradition misunderstood his own rich Christian experience in the Black church, including devaluing and doing harm to his journey into Christian scholarship and leadership. He shares one poignant example of when a few members from a local congregation who were engaging in neighborhood missionary work visited him and his mother at their home when he was twelve. The church members offered what seemed to be rehearsed speeches and were clearly intent on sharing their perspective—without first seeking to learn or understand, in which case they would have realized Jennings's mother was a pillar of the local Missionary Baptist Church.[13] Reading about how Jennings's experience was so different from my own, despite interacting with the same theological tradition in the same geographic area, challenged (and still challenges) me to develop greater self-awareness and sensitivity as I serve in the church and our diverse world.

As you pursue the following exercises to imagine your church's future, stay open to how the Spirit may guide and convict you.

Six Exercises for Imagining Your Church's Future

As you seek to fully discern God's THERE for your church, we invite you to gather your Transformation Team, look for opportunities to involve your wider congregation, and engage in some of the following exercises. While you consider your faith community's THERE, we urge you to consider the 3 Checkpoints of emphasizing and empathizing with young people (Checkpoint #1), modeling the ethnic diversity of God's kingdom (Checkpoint #2), and tangibly loving your neighbors (Checkpoint #3), in addition to other divinely inspired Checkpoints in your more vibrant future.

Please note you do not need to engage in all of the exercises below (unless you want to!). Each is meant to cater to and leverage different strengths, areas of focus, and styles of imagination. We invite you to begin by trying the two that best fit your team and context. Any of these could be completed in one or more team meetings lasting between forty-five and ninety minutes. These exercises can also be utilized in any ministry-visioning or goal-setting meeting and don't need to be reserved for long-term change work.

As one final note, we'll add that a prerequisite for engaging in productive exercises around imagination involves *hope*. As we've said, we believe the best days of the church are ahead. If you're serving in a context that feels especially polarized, divided, or full of

> ▶ **How Far into the Future Should We Imagine?**
>
> As we said, it's difficult to consider what the future might look like even three to five years from now . . . let alone in ten or twenty years. In our experience, there's no perfect time horizon to use as you plan for the future. The advantage to a longer time horizon is it allows your team to really dream as if anything is possible. However, we find many churches benefit most from a shorter three- to five-year window, as it's far enough out that significant change can happen yet near enough that it feels tangible. We invite your team to discuss the time horizon that feels most appropriate to your context and the focus of your change.

conflict, that hope for the future of the church might feel especially dim or distant. Just as Jesus' disciples experienced intense fear and hopelessness when their world was turned upside down after Jesus' resurrection, we invite you to lean in to the promise that Jesus will make all things new (Rev. 21:5) and that a light shines in the darkness, which the darkness has not and will not overcome (John 1:5). Even if you're not sure at this moment that the best days of your church are ahead, we invite you to suspend disbelief and imagine the great future God may have in store for your church.

Exercise #1: Imagining Your Future through Scripture

New Movement Church imagined their new future through Scripture. To engage in this exercise, you need your Transformation Team and a Bible for each person. In advance of the meeting, invite each team member to consider one or two passages of Scripture that are meaningful to them and could inform God's THERE for your community. Examples of passages that often emerge are Acts 2:42–47, Matthew 28:16–20, John 17:20–26, and Revelation 7:8–17 or 21:1–4, but there are *many* more passages that might speak to your congregation specifically.

During the team meeting, begin with prayer and invite God to guide your discussion and reflection. Next, ask each person to read aloud the passage(s) they selected once or twice. Encourage the team to practice active listening. After all team members have read their passages, discuss what stands out to you. Are there particular themes, images, words, or pictures that are particularly helpful or appealing?

Then ask, *How might one or more of these passages inform where God is leading our church?* Attempt to come to some form of consensus, or at the very least a list of the most prominent themes.

Exercise #2: Imagining Your Future by Revisiting Your Past

In advance of your meeting, invite team members to consider stories or moments in your church's past that are particularly important to define who your church is now. In the language of Collins and

Porras, these might be stories that have shaped your church's *core purpose* or *core values*. If your team has done some of the recommended listening work in previous chapters, you're already a step ahead. Consider if there are important stories or moments from your history that have emerged once or, better yet, multiple times during your listening. If you haven't taken the time to hold listening conversations with individuals or small groups, you might consider doing so in advance of this team meeting.

As your team meets to discuss inspiration from your church's past, your goal is not to overly romanticize the "good ole days." Instead, your objective is to identify foundational elements of your church's past and identity and consider how those might inspire your church's progress toward the 3 Checkpoints and other future-focused priorities. Invite members of your team to share memories, stories, or examples from your founding as well as other highlights and turning points in your church's past. Then take time to discuss, *What elements from our church's past and history might be most important as we consider the future God is leading us into?*

Exercise #3: Imagining Your Future through Future Hopes and Dreams

Earlier, we referenced the prophetic words from Acts 2:17 and Joel 2:28 about God's Spirit being poured out and God's people of all ages seeing visions and dreaming dreams. Your church may do well to consider this invitation as you imagine your future.

Again, we recommend you gather your Transformation Team. If your team doesn't include younger and older members, we suggest inviting them to join this meeting (and maybe your team from now on). In advance, let attendees know they will participate in a meeting geared to envision hopes and dreams for the future.

At the start of the meeting, share the following: *Imagine you've been asleep for several years. Suddenly, you wake up to discover it's five years from now and all that you've hoped or longed for is happening in our church [or ministry].*

Give participants five to ten minutes on their own to visualize what they see. Then invite each person to share snapshots of those hopes and dreams. As each team member shares, take notes—perhaps on a whiteboard or in an electronic document. After everyone has shared, reflect on the common themes that emerge or the moments that spark the most excitement or resonance. Based on that reflection, invite the team to collaboratively craft a response to the statement: *Five years from now, we want our church to . . .* See how much consensus and clarity emerge from that discussion.

In a past training event, we invited a group of diverse younger people to share their hopes and dreams for their own churches. Here's a snapshot of what they envisioned:

- That it would be more Jesus-y . . . or in other words, like Christ.
- It would be known as a place of belonging. Where we receive one another because we recognize we are all made in the image and likeness of God.
- That it would boldly speak against racism, sexism, division, and greed. That we would make space to talk about those challenges with each other. And we wouldn't let these conversations separate us.
- Where adults would stop trying to entertain us and boring us with long sermons. Instead, we long for the church to be a place in which we learn about God, a place where we are invited to reflect more often, and a family that would help us grow spiritually.

As another variation on this exercise, you might reflect on one young person in your church, perhaps one under age ten. As a group, brainstorm the dreams you have for that young person when they are in their twenties. What do you hope they will do, who do you hope they will be, and how do you hope the church will have shaped their life for the better? Your goal is not to try to predict or control that young person's life but to hope and dream the best for them. After completing your sharing, take time to reflect together on what your church would need to do, or how it might need to change, to help young people have this experience.

A youth pastor at one church in our training, whom I (Kara) coached, completed this story exercise for a male and a female student in the high school ministry. His dreams for their future highlighted the adults who invested in them, the way the two teenagers felt at home in the church, and how their church empowered them to purposefully use their gifts. Every time he saw those two students, he would think about the visionary story he had drafted for their futures.

Somewhat sheepishly, he finally shared the stories with those two teenagers. These students were so inspired by the youth pastor's pictures of their future that he decided to write future stories for a few more students. Sharing those went so well that he encouraged his adult volunteers to draft future stories for the teenagers in their small groups. Most leaders ended up reading those stories to the students, which prompted the teens, in turn, to craft future stories for each small group leader.

As the lead pastor heard about the waves of stories washing their way through the high school ministry, he quickly got on board and suggested more of the church draft these stories for each other. Thanks to his support, those future stories eventually became a key step in the church creating unique discipleship plans for hundreds of young people and adults.

All because the youth pastor imagined a different future story for two teenagers.

Exercise #4: Imagining Your Future by Reflecting on Needs in Your Community

Another way to imagine God's THERE is to focus outside your church's walls. As a team, consider the greatest needs in your community, and how your church might respond. You might find inspiration from the admonition in Jeremiah 29:7 to "Seek the peace and prosperity of the city to which I have carried you into exile. Pray to the LORD for it, because if it prospers, you too will prosper." In the spirit of Checkpoint #3, dream about what it might look like to seek the good of your city together.

You can also get creative and active by taking your meeting outside the church building. Consider a prayer walk during which your team explores the area around your church, paying attention to what you observe. Ask for God's presence and blessing on the people, buildings, and outdoor spaces you encounter. After the prayer walk, reconvene as a team and discuss all you noticed and felt. Together, brainstorm what your church would be like in the future if you prioritized meeting the primary needs in your community.

For another variation on this exercise, you might suggest that Transformation Team members meet with various community leaders or organizations. First, brainstorm who you might meet with, including teachers or school administrators, local government officials, social service leaders, law enforcement officials, or business owners. Invite each member of your team to meet with one or two community leaders, asking questions related to the needs of the community or the organization they lead that help you glean from their wisdom. Brainstorm how your parish could better help, or advocate for, those in need. Then reunite as a team to discuss your insights and their ramifications for the future of your church.

One historic Asian American church in Chicago was seeing a significant departure of young people from their communities once those young people left for college. After the murder of George Floyd, the Asian American Christian Collaborative (that I, Ray, help lead) hosted a march from Chinatown to Bronzeville, Illinois. We marched from a historic hundred-plus-year-old Chinese church to a historic hundred-plus-year-old Black church. Nearly two thousand Christians showed up, with the vast majority being Asian American Christians. During the march, one of the leaders from the historic Asian American church leaned over to me and said, "I wish the young people who left would've stayed to see this. This is the type of thing they wanted us to do." This march provided a new imagination for many Christian leaders on what the church's efforts toward racial reconciliation might look like, led by fellowship between Asian American and Black Christians.

Similarly, what imagination might your church discover by getting outside of your building and into your community?

Exercise #5: Imagining Your Future through the Inspiration of Others

We're big advocates for Jesus' prayer in John 17:20–23 that the church might be *one* and brought to *complete unity*. If we and our churches can be living answers to Jesus' prayer today, we can move toward future-focused opportunities for collaboration, sharing, and learning. If one church or ministry has insights or ministry activities that are effective, those can be shared to inspire other churches, either locally or nationally.

As your team considers your church's THERE, we encourage you to pay attention to what you can glean from other churches. Visit their worship services or gatherings, noting what you can learn from or what works well. Perhaps take time to search online or attend a church training conference to be equipped with new skills. We certainly don't want to encourage a mindless reproduction of other faith communities, but with the right posture and perspective, you may be able to discover key insights that help you build future momentum internally.

When one well-known and highly respected church decided to prioritize Checkpoint #1 by designating one weekend per month as "intergenerational worship" time and canceling all weekend youth services, dozens of youth leaders and pastors at other churches used their example to accelerate their own church's momentum toward Checkpoint #1. Some ended up likewise designating one weekend per month for intergenerational worship, while others launched intergenerational justice activities, vocational mentoring programs, and other contextual experiments. Whatever intergenerational steps they took, that journey was faster and easier because of the credibility gained from the example of the admired church.

Exercise #6: Imagining Your Future through Communal Discernment

As one last exercise to help you imagine God's THERE for your church, we invite you to widen the group of participants beyond just your Transformation Team by engaging in communal discernment. While there are multiple ways you can practice this that may be consistent with your church's culture or theological tradition, we've observed two options work particularly well.

The first is to extend an open invitation to your entire congregation to gather for a prayer meeting, or series of prayer meetings, to seek God's direction for your church moving forward. Open the prayer gathering with some words of welcome and framing, and perhaps share a few key verses of Scripture consistent with the theme of seeking God's guidance. Then participate in a guided and prompted or perhaps more open and free-flowing time of prayer (whatever fits your tradition) for clarity about the future of your church. Consider inviting your people to share ideas or insights that emerge either at the end of, or between, prayer meetings.

The second option is to host church town hall meetings. These can often be effective immediately after a church service as long as people receive advanced scheduling notice. We facilitated a meeting like this for one congregation who was told in advance they were going to have a meeting to discuss the future of the church. At the start of the meeting, we framed that we wanted to invite people to share hopes and dreams for their church that were good, positive, excellent, and praiseworthy (Phil. 4:8). We were clear this was not a session to complain or share what wasn't going well. We then opened up two microphones. For nearly forty-five minutes, congregation members of all ages shared their hopes and dreams. The key themes of these "open mic" comments became the foundation upon which the church built their future direction.

What to Do after You Imagine the Future

After you've completed the exercises, you should have a long list of potential ideas, directions, and activities for the future of your church. Next, we'll guide you in how to translate that list into something more focused, cohesive, and tangible that can propel you toward your THERE. But for now, we want to highlight that, when it comes to finding the future for a church, we cannot simply leave the past behind. Our past and future are inextricably linked. Often the best way to find God's tomorrow is through a deep connection to our yesterday.

This truth is well demonstrated in Peter's sermon in Acts 2. Jesus has just ascended into heaven, the Holy Spirit has come at Pentecost, and Peter stands to address the diverse group that has gathered as Jesus' disciples speak to them in a variety of languages. The passage says that the people are *amazed and perplexed* before Peter addresses them (v. 12).

As Peter offers a sermon that will lay the foundation for an early Christian church of thousands of people, he envisions the future by appealing to the past. Peter doesn't simply leave the past behind and paint a compelling vision of what the future will entail. Instead, as we describe earlier in this chapter, Peter quotes the prophet Joel (vv. 17–21). He recounts what Jesus has done (vv. 22–24). He invokes King David (vv. 25–28). Then he declares that Jesus is Lord and Messiah and invites people to repent and be baptized in Jesus' name (vv. 29–41).

Similarly, we believe you will find God's best future for your church not only by looking forward but also by looking back. By building your confidence in Jesus as Lord and Messiah and the One you (and all of us!) are to trust and follow for the future. By considering where you have been in the past, and how that journey has shaped your values, purpose, identity, and mission for the future.

While your THERE may be unclear, we hope you share our confidence that you follow a God who has promised to walk with you.

REFLECTION QUESTIONS

On a scale of 1–5 (with 1 being "not at all clear" and 5 being "very clear"), how clear does your church's future feel for five to ten years from now? Discuss your ratings and your rationale for that rating.

Does your church seem like it was designed more for "the world as it was" or "the world as it is now"? Why did you choose that response, and what are the implications for the future of your church?

What are some of the elements or aspects of your church that should never, or will never, change?

Based on one or two of the imagination exercises your team chose, what are some of the key takeaways or insights that should shape where God is leading your church, parish, or ministry?

How could you invite more people into the process of imagining God's THERE for your community?

Crafting, Quantifying, and Communicating a Vivid Description of the Future

For nearly two thousand years, vivid descriptions of the future from Scripture have captivated the imagination and provided direction for Christ followers. While we are far from scholars on the book of Revelation, we believe its words, as well as those of Jesus in the book of Matthew, invite us into stories of hope. Consider the following snapshots from Scripture, which you may know well:

Revelation 7:9–10: After this I looked, and there before me was a great multitude that no one could count, from every nation, tribe, people and language, standing before the throne and before the Lamb. They were wearing white robes and were holding palm branches in their hands. And they cried out in a loud voice:

> "Salvation belongs to our God,
> who sits on the throne,
> and to the Lamb."

Revelation 21:1–4: Then I saw "a new heaven and a new earth," for the first heaven and the first earth had passed away, and there was no longer any sea. I saw the Holy City, the new Jerusalem, coming down out of heaven from God, prepared as a bride beautifully dressed for her husband. And I heard a loud voice from the throne saying, "Look! God's dwelling place is now among the people, and he will dwell with them. They will be his people, and God himself will be with them and be their God. 'He will wipe every tear from their eyes. There will be no more death' or mourning or crying or pain, for the old order of things has passed away."

Matthew 25:31–40: When the Son of Man comes in his glory, and all the angels with him, he will sit on his glorious throne. All the nations will be gathered before him, and he will separate the people one from another as a shepherd separates the sheep from the goats. He will put the sheep on his right and the goats on his left.

Then the King will say to those on his right, "Come, you who are blessed by my Father; take your inheritance, the kingdom prepared for you since the creation of the world. For I was hungry and you gave me something to eat, I was thirsty and you gave me something to drink, I was a stranger and you invited me in, I needed clothes and you clothed me, I was sick and you looked after me, I was in prison and you came to visit me."

Then the righteous will answer him, "Lord, when did we see you hungry and feed you, or thirsty and give you something to drink? When did we see you a stranger and invite you in, or needing clothes and clothe you? When did we see you sick or in prison and go to visit you?"

The King will reply, "Truly I tell you, whatever you did for one of the least of these brothers and sisters of mine, you did for me."

You get the idea. The authors of Scripture, and Jesus in particular, knew how to inspire and capture people's imaginations by offering stories of what God was like or snapshots of what might happen in the future. These stories convincingly highlight the diversity of God's people, the power of God's presence, the end of pain and suffering, and divine righteousness and justice.

If you are the leader of a church or Christian ministry, you are part of a rich lineage that offers hope, shares stories that captivate, and uses words and pictures to clarify your congregation's future THERE.

In your efforts to move your congregation toward God's best THERE, we encourage you to do the same. If you want to be a

Future-Focused Church, it's critically important to craft, quantify, and communicate a vivid description for the future.[1]

Moving from Imagination to Activation

In the previous chapter, we provided six exercises to help you imagine God's future for your faith community. While these exercises offer inspiration and nascent direction, the work isn't complete until you've translated your initial imagination into something tangible and actionable. Too many Transformation Teams land on something *they're* excited about, and then they fail to do the work of communicating it to the overall congregation so *everyone* can be equally enthusiastic. The clearer, more widely owned, and more captivating your church's picture of the future, the more likely you are to activate people and accelerate toward THERE.

We've found churches make progress in crafting a vivid statement by integrating the wisdom of Scott Cormode, who describes vision as a shared story of future hope.[2] We're compelled by this description of vision because it captures that it is ideally *shared*, meaning those who need to be part of the vision see themselves in it. It's also often powerful in a *story* format. As human beings, we find ourselves in stories and use them to make sense of our lives. Finally, it is a story of *future hope* that is centered on the unparalleled good news offered by Jesus Christ.

A compelling picture of a *shared story of future hope* is exemplified in Dr. Martin Luther King Jr.'s description of the Beloved Community—a diverse community made up of generous peacemakers committed to justice, equal opportunity, empathy, and love.[3] The notion of a Beloved Community—a community where everyone is cared for that is void of hunger, homelessness, and hate—is compelling. King paints a vivid picture of a better future:

> As I stood with them and saw White and Negro, nuns and priests, ministers and rabbis, labor organizers, lawyers, doctors, housemaids and shopworkers brimming with vitality and enjoying a rare comradeship, I knew I was seeing a microcosm of the mankind of the future in this moment of luminous and genuine brotherhood.[4]

Similarly, in another speech honoring W. E. B. Du Bois, King gives his audience this invitation:

> Let us be dissatisfied until rat-infested, vermin-filled slums will be a thing of a dark past and every family will have a decent sanitary house in which to live. Let us be dissatisfied until the empty stomachs of Mississippi are filled and the idle industries of Appalachia are revitalized. . . . Let us be dissatisfied until our brothers of the Third World of Asia, Africa and Latin America will no longer be the victims of imperialist exploitation, but will be lifted from the long night of poverty, illiteracy and disease.[5]

In both examples, King imagines a future in which we view every person as a precious image bearer of God, even if we disagree with them or were taught to think of them as "less than." King envisions a society where compassion outpaces condemnation, where love is shown to those who lament, where tenderness is expressed to those in turmoil, where self-sacrifice overshadows selfishness, and where safety is provided to those who suffer. In this Beloved Community, difference doesn't lead to disdain, disagreement doesn't lead to dehumanization, and darkness doesn't win. King's notion of a Beloved Community paints a picture of the community the church has failed to be but still could be, through faithful and sacrificial obedience. His future picture is vivid enough for people to assess themselves and activate toward God's THERE.

While we may not use the poetic prose of Martin Luther King Jr., we can still make our hopes for the future tangible and more widely owned. We can share a vision for our church communities and congregations. And we can start with three key activities: crafting, quantifying, and communicating.

Crafting: A Vivid Description of the Future

As you begin crafting a vivid description for the future, we'd encourage you to designate a specific time horizon that fits your goals and context. As we've said, that could be three, five, or ten years, or perhaps even twenty years from now. We'd also urge you to limit the length of your final story to no more than a full page—ideally closer to half.

Part of what distinguishes the vivid description you're writing from the core purpose, mission, or vision statement of your church, which are likely one to three sentences long, is length. In addition, this vivid description for your church's future can involve much more creative liberty than your church's mission and vision statement, as you want to make the cultural changes you're seeking tangible and unique to your church's location, context, and theological tradition. Since your core purpose and core values reflect what will not change in your church, it's a good idea to make sure they're clear before you do the work of creating a vivid description. If this hasn't already happened in your work up to this point, spend time as a team reflecting on and, if needed, clearly and prominently communicating

> We're inspired by the vivid descriptions of churches we've interacted with over the years. One of those includes The Dwelling, a North Carolina church plant led by Pastor Emily Norris that began with a vision to serve those who are experiencing homelessness:
>
> > In a world that constantly tells people who are homeless that they don't belong, The Dwelling will be a church that tells them that the world has it all wrong. That there is holiness in their identity as someone experiencing homelessness, that they share a kinship with God who reminds us that we are all wanderers in search of belonging that can be found at the table—where outsiders are no more.
> >
> > The Dwelling will be the space to reflect the radical countercultural nature of the cross—where shame is glory and identity in Christ replaces the damaging narrative that the world so easily affixes to people in the margins. The Dwelling will be a catalyst of education and advocacy, empowering leaders in the margins to use their story and their voices to shift the narrative around people experiencing homelessness. The Dwelling will be a place rooted in sacrament, where daily bread meets real mouths and water calls us all back to the limitless cleansing of grace. The Dwelling will proclaim loudly that resurrection is real.[6]

your church's core purpose—the *why*. Similarly, spend time reflecting on the most important core values that reflect the essential elements or guiding principles of your church or ministry. The clearer you can be on your core purpose and core values, the easier it will be to consider what it will look like to embody those values in your vivid description.

While there are many ways you can craft a vivid description for the future, we recommend the following five-step process.

1. During a Transformation Team meeting, discuss the results of your imagination work from the previous chapter, noting key elements or insights that stand out or fill your team with the most excitement. As much as possible, focus on the 3 Future-Focused Church Checkpoints of prioritizing and empathizing with young people, modeling the ethnic diversity of God's just kingdom, and tangibly loving your neighbors, as well as others that seem particularly relevant for your future. As you picture this preferred future and imagine the changes you seek actually taking place, what would be the key features of your congregation or ministry? What attitudes and actions would you emphasize?

2. After the meeting, invite each person on the Transformation Team to draft their vivid description for the future in no more than one page. Your Transformation Team members can do this writing on their own, or they can enlist the help of friends, family, colleagues, small group members, or other congregants.

3. Gather your Transformation Team again, allowing everyone to share their vivid descriptions. Then identify the key insights and ideas that most resonate with the group. Either during or after the meeting, synthesize these multiple descriptions into one new, vivid description. You might want to designate one person from your team as the initial author of that document or recruit someone else in your church who is a strong writer to curate the multiple versions into

one unified and cohesive version. Try to keep the document
as short as you can (if possible, less than one page).

4. Share the revised document with as many people as feasible,
inviting their feedback. Perhaps each person on the Transformation Team gathers feedback from a few individuals,
a couple of small groups, or other ministries. Specifically
invite others to share what resonates and what doesn't. Take
careful notes on the feedback you receive. Note that if your
vivid description doesn't get people excited, you don't yet
have what you need.

5. In a final Transformation Team meeting, incorporate the
feedback from Step #4 and revise your vivid description.
Your goal is to develop a short, clear, inspiring write-up
that captures God's THERE and can be shared broadly with
the congregation. (You might think of it as a lighthouse or
North Star that can guide your change efforts.)

We worked with one congregation that excelled in collaboratively
drafting a vivid description of THERE. They knew they needed to
make changes to engage more teenagers and young adults in their
congregation, as well as to better reflect the ethnic diversity of God's
kingdom in their community. They first formed a Transformation
Team that met regularly to reflect on the church's challenges and
opportunities, as well as to pray and seek God's guidance. This led
to a season of intentional listening, during which each team member
met individually or in small groups with congregants and members
of the wider community. They asked open-ended questions to invite input about how the church could be more effective and elicit
people's hopes and dreams for the future.

Based on what the Transformation Team heard, they crafted a
vivid description for what their church might look like five years
from now if they were effective in making the hoped-for changes.
Their vivid description flowed clearly from the church's mission and
wove in core values that reflected their particular passions for fervent
prayer, intergenerational discipleship, unwavering hospitality, and
sacrificial service. They took their refined draft on a "vision tour"

to share, listen, and gain feedback from several individuals, small groups, and ministry areas.

They did, in fact, receive quite a bit of input, but it wasn't what they had hoped. Some groups couldn't find themselves in the description or thought it was missing important elements. Despite this critical feedback, the Transformation Team wasn't discouraged. Instead, they mobilized to incorporate the opinions they had heard.

Since their draft wasn't exciting for others, they knew it had to be revised. They eventually landed on a compelling description that was meaningful not just to the Transformation Team but also to the vast majority of the congregation. An unintended benefit was that when they rolled out the final vivid description and began making more specific plans for next steps, several members of the congregation described it as "*our* vision." In the spirit of "people support what they help create," since congregants had a chance to shape the vivid description, they were invested in its success and wanted to contribute to make it a reality. Although the Transformation Team initially had to move more slowly in order to solicit broad feedback and revise their statement based on that input, in the long run they moved much faster than anticipated because of the widespread ownership.

Quantifying: Objectives That Make Your Future Tangible

Once you've crafted a vivid description for the future that captures your church's THERE, you need to land it tangibly by creating goals, metrics, or other achievable markers called Objectives. In *Measure What Matters*, John Doerr explains that an *Objective* is "simply what is to be achieved, no more and no less. By definition, Objectives are significant, concrete, action oriented, and (ideally) inspirational. When properly designed and deployed, they're a vaccine against fuzzy thinking and ineffective execution."[7]

As a team, ask, To truly realize the vivid description we feel God is leading us toward, what major shifts or changes would need to happen in the next one to three years? Take the time to brainstorm several possible ideas, then continue to discuss until you can refine

> In setting longer-term Objectives, some leaders find the additional concept of *Big, Hairy, Audacious Goals* (or *BHAGs*, pronounced BEE-hags; note that some churches prefer Big, "Holy," Audacious Goals but use the same acronym) helpful.[8] As Collins and Porras explain,
>
> > A true BHAG is clear and compelling, serves as a unifying focal point of effort, and acts as a catalyst for team spirit. It has a clear finish line, so the organization can know when it has achieved the goal; people like to shoot for finish lines. A BHAG engages people—it reaches out and grabs them. It is tangible, energizing, highly focused. People get it right away; it takes little or no explanation.[9]

those ideas into a more organized and thoughtful (and short!) list of a few specific Objectives.

Most Transformation Teams find it helpful to parse their Objectives into action steps that are more specific and short-term (e.g., what they hope God will do during the next few months or the next year). In alignment with Doerr's recommendations, our top framework for doing so is to pair Objectives with Key Results (jointly referred to as OKRs).

Key Results provide the steps along the way that help you achieve your Objective. Doerr adds that effective Key Results "are specific, time-bound, and aggressive yet realistic. Most of all, they are measurable and verifiable. You either meet a Key Result's requirements or you don't—there is no gray area, no room for doubt."[10] Using

> We recognize that your church or ministry might already have a framework or language for setting goals that works well. We know some business leaders are most familiar with *Key Performance Indicators* (KPIs) and others simply prefer *Goals and Next Steps*. Feel free to stick with that language and replace our mentions of Objectives and Key Results (OKRs) with that terminology throughout the rest of the book.

the analogy of a road trip, your Objective is the end destination to which you are driving, and your Key Results are the stops you will make along the way.

OKRs can be implemented in a variety of industries and categories of goals. For example, Doerr provides an example of someone whose Objective is to run a 10k in under fifty minutes by June.[11] Assuming it's at least a few months before June, the Key Results to achieve that Objective are to run at least three times per week for at least thirty minutes, increase the distance of the run by one mile each week, and improve mile speed by five seconds each week. The assumption is that if the Key Results are achieved along the way, the Objective will be achieved.

These concepts can often be effectively applied to your Future-Focused Church plan. Your future THERE might include a strong focus on tangibly impacting our world for Christ. Perhaps you've written up a compelling vivid description about what it will look like to accomplish that Checkpoint that includes your wider community seeing your church as an invested and integral partner tangibly working toward the good of your neighborhood. Perhaps you've established that an Objective for making that a reality one year from now is to form a new, strong partnership with a local public school, with twenty-five people from your church tutoring or otherwise volunteering. Key Results to move toward that Objective over the next year might involve a representative from the church scheduling an initial meeting with the school principal or superintendent, identifying a point leader from the church who will maintain the school relationship and guide the overall effort, and recruiting twenty-five congregants who are willing to volunteer.

Or perhaps your future THERE might include a strong focus on empathizing with young people. If your vivid description focuses on greater relational connection between generations, your Objective might be that, three years from now, half of the small groups in your church would be comprised of people from different age groups. A Key Result to help that dream become a reality one year from now would be to establish two small groups that are intentionally experimenting with this approach. Or another Key Result one year from now might be that you've hosted an evening seminar for training different generations to understand each other as a precursor to being in community together—and that thirty people would have attended that event.

The goal is not to make your OKRs complicated or complex but to ensure they are clear, consistent, and well-communicated.

As you seek to make your future more tangible, you also need clear metrics for success so you can determine how close to or far from THERE you are now. In the past, churches have often defaulted to the "ABCs" of metrics: Attendance, Buildings (total size and square footage), and Cash. Those can be useful, and your community is welcome to track them. Most of us probably do already. But is someone's capacity to sit through a church service or gathering really the ultimate measure of Future-Focused Church impact? No, of course not. Neither is the square footage of your meeting space or the dollars you receive and spend.

As your church seeks to discern your future THERE, we urge you to incorporate additional metrics based on the three Future-Focused Church Checkpoints (or other priorities you may identify). Below are several questions and ideas to help catalyze better metrics for your church.

When it comes to young people . . .

- What percent of young people feel known by an adult in your church?
- What percent of adults can name three young people in the church (who are not part of their extended family)?
- How many of your young people are being trained for leadership?
- What percent of your budget is allocated to young people?
- How many young people are sharing their faith or discipling others?

When it comes to ethnic and racial diversity . . .

- How does your overall church congregation resemble, or not resemble, the diverse Beloved Community Dr. King described?

- How does your church resemble or outpace the diversity of your surrounding geographic community? How about your pastoral and congregational leadership groups?
- What percent of your church has close friends who are from a different ethnicity or racial group?
- In what percent of worship services are ethnic and cultural diversity highlighted and celebrated through music, rituals, testimonies, and the sermon?
- How often is racial justice discussed and taught?
- Does your community model the multiethnic and multicultural kingdom of God to the watching world?

When it comes to tangibly loving your neighbors . . .

- How much of your church's resources are allocated directly to help those in need?
- How many partnerships with community organizations does your church maintain?
- What percent of your adults and young people are serving in your church and surrounding community?
- How much do you think your neighborhood or town would notice if your church disappeared?

One hint about timeframe: we find most churches overestimate what they can accomplish in one year and underestimate what can be done in three or five years. Keep that in mind as you're working with others to plot your own set of goals.

Communicating: Leveraging Your Venues, Channels, and Meetings

Your carefully crafted vivid description for the future, as well as the goals or metrics that make it tangible, will not drive the changes you seek unless they are appropriately communicated to and embraced by the necessary stakeholders and then your wider congregation.

Change expert John Kotter highlights that one of the main errors change leaders make is "undercommunicating the vision by a factor of ten."[12] Based on his team's research, Kotter outlines that the total amount of communication that goes to an employee over three months is 2.3 million words or numbers. The typical communication about a change initiative in that organization normally amounts to about 13,400 words or numbers. This means that a change in an organization, perhaps even a significant change, represents 0.58 percent of all communication employees receive.[13] No wonder employees often can't keep up with the changes happening around them.

In our experience, we've found a similar dynamic in churches. A Future-Focused Church might desire to better partner with their geographic community, involve more people in diverse small groups, or recruit additional volunteers for the youth or young adult ministry. To move forward, leaders might advertise in weekly (paper and

▶ Keep in mind that cultural differences can also impact the number of words used and how words are used. For example, in *low context cultures*, words alone provide most of the meaning that is conveyed. In *high context cultures*, nonverbal cues often do a lot of the communicating—whether through body language, tone, or the overall context. People who have grown accustomed to a high or low context culture might find it challenging to get their point across in an environment that is less accommodating of their natural style. When communicating across differences like these, try to refrain from assessing one style as "good" and the other as "bad." Ascribing value to a cultural communication style will often diminish the ways others (especially those with less power) tend to communicate. Second, do your best to name the dynamics at play. If you lead with curiosity and genuine appreciation for differences, you can usually find new methods that work for everyone. Third, don't assume that all involved need to communicate the same way. You want unity, not uniformity. Fourth, when there are misunderstandings, seek both clarity and harmony. In high context cultures, harmony is often more important than clarity. In low context cultures, clarity is more important than harmony. You generally need both in order to create a healthy environment that's open to God's best future.

electronic) bulletins, give a short announcement during a worship service, or post on the church's social media channels. One month later, leaders often wonder why the change they introduced failed to take root or have the desired effect.

That's what happened with one church we coached that was disappointed with the scant new people who responded to an appeal for more youth ministry volunteers. When we met with them to debrief their communication process, they were able to name the exact channels they had deployed. However, when we asked them to enumerate other opportunities simultaneously shared through the same venues, they named *eight other ministry areas* also seeking some sort of congregational response (including mission trip fundraising, an upcoming funeral, and a congregational town hall meeting to discuss property repairs). Their important appeal for volunteers in youth ministry was buried in an avalanche of other messages and needs.

As you seek to make changes toward your THERE, don't make the mistake of offering one announcement, giving one visionary sermon, or scheduling one meeting and then assuming you've said all you need to say. People are often distracted when you're trying to communicate and so busy afterward that they quickly forget.

With your Transformation Team, consider the following questions to guide your communication strategy:

- What might be your church's current commitments or priorities that potentially compete with the changes you hope to see? In what ways might they compete, and how might that inform how you communicate? Are there ways your church or ministry might need to say no or "not right now" to some good things to say yes to one or two of the most essential things? (While you may not have the authority to make these decisions, perhaps you can advocate with those who do.)
- Who are a few individuals or groups of people in your church who may be most receptive to the changes you seek? Who may be most resistant, and why? How might you best communicate the needed information to both groups?

- Is there anyone whose permission you need, or involvement you seek, who you should communicate to first or ahead of time? Who are those people or groups, and how will you communicate to them?
- What is the *elevator pitch* for the future changes you seek? In other words, if you had twenty or thirty seconds to explain it, what would you say? If the answer varies based on the needs and interests of different groups of people, how and why would it vary?

Specifically, consider how widely and broadly you need to communicate the potential changes and which channels are best. Below are several venues or channels you might consider. And, of course, if you have a marketing or communications professional in your church, consider inviting them to be part of your team!

- *Worship services*: How might you utilize sermons, testimonies, videos, and announcements? Depending on the length of your change, could you secure a short window once per month to provide an update?
- *Newsletters or bulletins*: How might you periodically include the vivid description you've written, or perhaps a brief update on the progress God is bringing?
- *Digital communications*: How can you use your church's regular email updates, features on your website, video clips, text blasts, or social media channels to spread the word more broadly?
- *Church town hall meetings*: When might you host a special meeting after a worship service to share an extended update?
- *Other one-on-one and small group meetings*: How might you meet with people individually for specific communication and updates? Or how might you go on a tour of multiple small groups, adult classes, or ministry teams?
- *Additional opportunities*: After your team has considered the ideas above, discuss if there are other potential

communication venues, channels, or meetings that come to mind.

While you have a wide variety of communication options at your disposal, change scholar Yulee Lee's research has led her to contend that "change agents can catalyze the need for, connect people toward, and sustain momentum for change best when they use relational communication strategies to influence key stakeholders in the direction of a change mission."[14] In other words, while you may be drawn to broader communication efforts, don't neglect opportunities for more relational communication and influence.

To initiate and maintain momentum toward THERE, we'd encourage you to take your vivid description of the future on a *vision tour*. In your vision tour, you can utilize all relevant communication channels, as frequently as you can and for as long as you can, to communicate your vivid description and OKRs.

You can also conduct a tour at various intervals in your process of discerning God's THERE. In the example we shared earlier of a congregation that participated in our training, communicating their vivid description to small groups and stakeholders throughout the congregation *before it was in a final form* ended up generating widespread excitement, buy-in, and relational support to see that vision brought to tangible reality.

If you find yourself stuck or discouraged as you're creating your picture of THERE, we'd encourage you to lean in to vivid descriptions of the future you can find throughout the Bible. The good news for those seasons when we feel overwhelmed and underskilled is that most of leadership is not about us determining the future of the church on our own but instead leaning in to and applying God's wisdom and direction. Scriptural passages that you and other leaders in your church gravitate toward might contain just the inspiration you need.

REFLECTION QUESTIONS

On a scale of 1–5 (with 1 being "not at all" and 5 being "very well"), how well has your church crafted, quantified, and communicated a vivid description of the future to your wider congregation in the past few years? Discuss your ratings as a Transformation Team.

What is one of your favorite vivid descriptions of the future in the Bible, and why does it stand out?

Once you've been able to follow this chapter's five steps toward crafting a *vivid description of the future*, what are the key elements of your short, clear, inspiring write-up?

What are one or two Objectives that make your vivid description tangible for the future? What are a few short-term Key Results that would help you move toward those more expansive goals?

What are a few specific success metrics (beyond ABC) you can track for your new initiative?

What are the best channels to help communicate your vivid description for the future? What will you do, and by when, to communicate through those channels?

ZONE IV

HOW

Navigating the Journey Together

In their hearts humans plan their course,
but the LORD establishes their steps.

PROVERBS 16:9

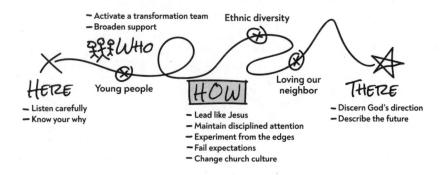

FIGURE Z4.1

Mapping the Journey—HOW

As you and your Transformation Team navigate the four zones of your Future-Focused Church map, the chapters in this section offer tangible advice for HOW you can strategize and execute your journey from HERE to THERE.

Your guiding question for this zone is:

> **What is our next faithful step, and how might we move into a more faithful future?**

We have intentionally placed HOW as the fourth and final section of the book. Too often we find that church leaders jump to HOW without being clear about their HERE or THERE. When leaders like you take time to clarify your HERE and THERE, God often begins to illuminate HOW to navigate the journey ahead. If you have not yet engaged the earlier sections of the book, we strongly encourage reviewing those before jumping directly into this HOW section.

Notice that in the guiding question, we invite you to consider HOW you'll take your *next faithful step*. God often doesn't reveal your entire map for the trek immediately. Instead, God frequently invites you to be faithful to your calling and take one step at a time—even when you don't know what's coming ten—or even two—steps later. As you keep your HERE and THERE in clear view and engage the advice we'll unpack in the next five chapters, we're optimistic these steps will propel you on a journey into God's best future for your church!

EMOTIONS ON THE JOURNEY

As you move into the often-longer-than-expected process of seeking HOW to best make change, we implore you to carve out the time and energy required to care for your own heart and soul. Consider the following prompts.

- At this point in our change journey, I feel . . .
- As I think about the way Jesus led, I'm inspired by . . .
- Based on my past experience in trying new things that didn't go so well, I feel concerned that . . .
- For the good of my own heart and soul, soon I should talk with someone I trust about . . .

PRAYER

Determining HOW to move toward God's best future is not always as clear as we would like. For this reason, we invite you and your Transformation Team to meditate on Proverbs 3:5–6 and "Trust in the LORD with all your heart and lean not on your own understanding; in all your ways submit to him, and he will make your paths straight" through the following prayer prompts:

- To utilize insights from change research and the example of other churches, while modeling the way of Jesus in all you do.
- To enable you to lean not on your own understanding but rather on God's understanding about HOW to best move forward.

- To help you, your team members, and other key leaders trust God more fully.

- To have wisdom for when to pursue change at the core of your church, and how and when to start more on the edges.

Lead Change like Jesus

We believe Jesus is the most effective change leader who ever lived. Period.

Full stop.

The same power that raised Jesus from the dead two thousand years ago continues to change people (including us), families (including ours), communities, cities, and so much more. That same power is available to help you know HOW to move your church toward the 3 Checkpoints and God's best future. And that same power can help you resolve many of the tensions you face as you begin charting HOW to move forward.

Often leaders entering the nitty-gritty process of leading change feel forced to choose between relational outreach and discipleship and keeping the "machine" of their church programs going. In the midst of attending to HOW to move forward toward the 3 Checkpoints, they spend so much energy prioritizing changes needed in systems and structures that changes in *lives* get left behind.

Maybe most troubling of all, at any time, any leader and any Transformation Team can feel—and actually be—stuck.

We want to help you know HOW to gracefully and effectively navigate through these tensions. That's why this entire HOW section is designed to share proven change principles and practices that fuel your community toward the future. To begin, we want to start with what is most fundamental in your forward progress: *intentionally following the example of Jesus.*

When we study the Gospels, we see Jesus following many of the steps in the future-focused map. Jesus activated a Transformation Team (his disciples), involved people in the process of co-creation, listened, asked why, sought God's leading for the future, shared stories, and offered snapshots of a vivid description of the future. Twenty centuries later, we have the privilege and responsibility of following his example.

Want proof of the power of Jesus' example in leading change? There are numerous episodes from the Gospels we could feature, but for now, let's focus on one: John 20:19–23. This passage follows Jesus' crucifixion and burial, just after his disciples have found the empty tomb. While Jesus has appeared to and spoken with Mary Magdalene, he has not yet appeared to all the disciples. On an evening shortly after, the disciples are huddled in a room with the doors locked, fearful of how Jewish leaders might retaliate against them.

From the disciples' perspective . . .

their leader and teacher has been put to death,

their dreams have been reduced to doubts,

their confidence and certainty have been replaced with insecurity and instability, and

they're unsure of how to move forward or even what that future will look like.

If you've felt a sense of hopelessness, chaos, confusion, or fear as you think about the future, you're in good company. So did those closest to Jesus.

It's at this moment Jesus enters the room and declares, "Peace be with you!" (John 20:19). Jesus enters into their humanness and offers hope. He empathizes with their fear and uncertainty and extends his presence and confidence.

After seeing Jesus' hands and side, the disciples are filled with joy. Again, Jesus declares, "Peace be with you!" (v. 21). He then breathes on them, invites them to receive the Holy Spirit, and promises, "As the Father has sent me, I am sending you" (v. 21).

Jesus transforms their fear into hope. And then he commissions them to lead into the future in the same way he had.

Which begs the question: How was Jesus sent?

In his Gospel account of Jesus' life and death, John declares, "In the beginning was the Word, and the Word was with God, and the Word was God. He was with God in the beginning" (1:1–2). In verse 14, John continues, "The Word became flesh and made his dwelling among us. We have seen his glory, the glory of the one and only Son, who came from the Father, full of grace and truth."

We appreciate how Eugene Peterson frames the first part of this verse: "The word became flesh and blood and moved into the neighborhood" (v. 14 Message).

So, how was Jesus sent?

The all-powerful God of heaven was incarnated in human form in the person of Jesus.

Jesus—who dwelled among people like us.

Jesus—who walked as we've walked.

Jesus—who has felt how we've felt.

As Hebrews 4:15 states, "For we do not have a high priest who is unable to empathize with our weaknesses, but we have one who has been tempted in every way, just as we are—yet he did not sin."

Jesus was sent from a place of ultimate glory, peace, comfort, and abundance to a complex, weary, broken world to reveal what God is like. During his time on earth, Jesus invited his disciples and others to follow him, take on his way of life, and invite more of God's kingdom to come to earth as it is in heaven (Matt. 6:10).

In John 20:21, Jesus sends his disciples (and by extension, us) to walk the same path. To incarnate ourselves in the lives of others. To walk with them, dwell with them, and demonstrate what God is like.

While we love thinking about future-focused change and learning from other wise scholars and business leaders, we're not ultimately called to be the most effective ministry CEOs or change leaders.

We're called to be incarnational with others. We're called to follow, model, and be faithful to Jesus—the head of the church.

We Need to Go Back to Our Roots

As we seek to imitate Jesus and help others do likewise, we find the words of theologian Jurgen Moltmann both poignant and powerful:

> When its traditions are imperiled by insecurity, the church is thrown back to its roots. It will take its bearings even more emphatically than before from Jesus, his history, his presence and his future. As "the church of Jesus Christ," it is fundamentally dependent on him alone.[1]

If you find your church in flux, unsure, or insecure, or you want to be future-focused but aren't exactly sure HOW, we invite you to lean in to Moltmann's advice. Instead of being preoccupied with all that is changing or unclear, return to the roots of the church. As you prioritize the 3 Checkpoints, focus more than ever on Jesus and the example Jesus sets.

Your job as a Christ-following leader is not to have all the answers or know the certain way forward but to take on the spirit and approach of Paul in 1 Corinthians 11:1: "Follow my example, as I follow the example of Christ." As Christ-following leaders, we are first and foremost called to repeat the model of, and point people to, Jesus.

Practically, in this present season of change and insecurity for both your church and churches overall, what does it mean to take our bearings from Jesus and lead through the power of the Holy Spirit? Whether your efforts to become a Future-Focused Church are focused most on young people, ethnic diversity, tangibly loving

▶ A powerful exercise we've engaged in personally (and recommend for you and your team) is to read through one or more of the Gospels and ask, *How did Jesus lead change?* We think you'll find it a powerful and fruitful exercise.

your neighbors, or other priorities, allow those efforts to be modeled after change examples gleaned from Jesus.

Example #1: Jesus Invited People to Follow Him—Not an Institution

In Mark 1:16–20, Jesus is walking along the Sea of Galilee and encounters Simon and Andrew casting a net into the lake. Jesus' invitation to them is clear in verse 17: "Come, follow me . . . and I will send you out to fish for people." They drop their nets and follow him.

Notice what Jesus *didn't say.*

He didn't say, "Help me change people's minds on just this one issue."

He didn't say, "Come and help me build a new institution."

He didn't say, "Come be the new volunteers in my program."

Jesus' primary invitation to his disciples was to follow *him.* To spend time with *him,* take on *his way of life,* and try to do what *he was doing.*

We contend that leading change in the church is ultimately about inviting people to trust and follow Jesus.

Is it important that we raise money to keep our activities going? Certainly.

Should we track our attendance and know if we're growing or declining? Probably.

Is it wise to use our facilities and resources well? Yes.

Should we do our best to lean in to research and proven leadership principles to guide our churches as effectively as we can? We sure think so.

But all of those important organizational practices should be an extension of our effort to trust and follow Jesus and help those in our community do the same. As we follow Jesus and help others do likewise, we believe personal, communal, and systemic transformation will result. If we take this seriously, everything we do in the church, including our efforts to lead toward the future, is fundamentally a matter of discipleship.

Unfortunately, not all is well when it comes to the state of discipleship in our churches.

In the early 2000s, the National Study of Youth and Religion sent shock waves through the youth ministry and church leadership community when sociologist of religion Christian Smith concluded that the faith of US young people today was best described as *moralistic therapeutic deism*, which is the belief that:

1. A God exists who created and orders the world and watches over human life on earth.
2. God wants people to be good, nice, and fair to each other, as taught in the Bible and by most world religions.
3. The central goal of life is to be happy and to feel good about oneself.
4. God does not need to be particularly involved in one's life except when God is needed to resolve a problem.
5. Good people go to heaven when they die.[2]

Our friend and Princeton Seminary's Kenda Creasy Dean, who was part of the team guiding the national study, unpacks the meaning and implications of *moralistic therapeutic deism* this way: "American young people are, theoretically, fine with religious faith—but it does not concern them very much, and it is not durable enough to survive long after they graduate from high school. One more thing: we're responsible."[3] What does Dean mean when she states *we're responsible*? She adds:

> The problem does not seem to be that churches are teaching young people badly, but that we are doing an exceedingly good job of teaching youth what we really believe: namely, that Christianity is not a big deal, that God requires little, and the church is a helpful social institution filled with nice people. . . . What if the blasé religiosity of most American teenagers is not the result of poor communication but the result of excellent communication of a watered-down gospel so devoid of God's self-giving love in Jesus Christ, so immune to the sending love of the Holy Spirit that it might not be Christianity at all?[4]

Please keep in mind the research Dean is reflecting on was conducted in the early 2000s (over twenty years ago). This means the teenagers in the study are now likely in their late thirties or older, and many are now passing along the faith they inherited to their own children.

As many churches struggle to demonstrate meaningful change, and the trajectory of the Christian faith in the US is broadly on the decline, we wonder if Dallas Willard, author of *The Divine Conspiracy*, was right when he declared, "Nondiscipleship is the elephant in the church."[5]

In addition to reflecting on these provocative writings by Kenda Dean and Dallas Willard, another practical takeaway is to measure your efforts to lead change against the example set by Jesus. Jesus invited people to follow him, and now invites us as church and ministry leaders to continue inviting people to trust and follow Jesus.

To help you process this example and to spur you onward, consider the following.

Faithful Next Step Questions for You and Your Team

▶ Are your efforts to lead change in your church or ministry clearly and fundamentally about inviting people to know, trust, and follow the person of Jesus? How so, or how not?

▶ In what ways might you be focusing too much on asking people to engage in just one issue, follow an institution or tradition, or spread your preferences as a team rather than following Jesus?

▶ Based on your answers above, are there any shifts you need to make?

Example #2: Jesus Cared for People over Programs

In Mark 6, we glimpse Jesus doing something he did all the time: spending time *with people*. He's with people teaching in the synagogue (vv. 1–6), he sends his disciples out to learn and grow in their ministry (vv. 7–13), he pulls the disciples together to reflect (vv. 30–31), he feeds five thousand people (vv. 32–44), and he touches those who are sick to heal them (vv. 53–56).

That's just one chapter in one Gospel.

Have you ever considered that it would have been much more efficient if Jesus was simply born as Caesar, a government official, or someone who stepped into significant human and organizational power? Imagine how much faster Jesus could have implemented new laws and requirements, inaugurated revolutionary training initiatives, or created mandatory systems that could immediately reach hundreds of thousands of people.

But that's not what Jesus did.

Jesus understood that change in any system boils down to changes in the humans involved. It's about knowing, understanding, and affecting change in the lives of individuals and attending to the feelings that emerge along the way.

Jesus himself was aware of, and expressed, a variety of emotions. Among them, we know that Jesus wept (John 11:35), displayed anger in clearing the temple courts (2:13–25), and had compassion on people (Matt. 20:34).

Jesus was also in touch with others' emotions. In Mark 6:30–32, after Jesus has sent out his disciples to heal people and drive out demons, he gathers them to reflect on their experience. Too many people are coming to them, and Jesus (presumably being in touch with the disciples' exhaustion) offers in verse 31, "Come with me by yourselves to a quiet place and get some rest."

Jesus was not obsessed with progress at all costs. He wasn't so distant from his disciples that he lost touch with their mental and emotional health. While we are supportive of leaders and churches that proactively make progress, create effective structures, and build solid programs, we again hold up the example of

Jesus' leadership. The people mattered more than the programs or OKRs.

As leaders and US residents are experiencing unprecedented levels of busyness and suffering the effects of increased burnout, anxiety, and other mental health challenges, we as change leaders must be intentional about caring for both ourselves and those we lead.

Faithful Next Step Questions for You and Your Team

▶ How attuned are you to the health (mental, emotional, and spiritual) of yourself and those you lead? On a scale of 1–5 (with 1 being "very unhealthy" and 5 being "very healthy"), how would you rate yourself and those in your congregation?

▶ Where might you be placing a focus on progress or programs ahead of love and care for people?

▶ What would it look like for you to follow Jesus' example and put people first in your change efforts?

Example #3: Jesus Prayed for Unity—but Was Willing to Cause Conflict

What might your church consider to be some of the most important truths, convictions, or building blocks of the Christian faith?

Imagine if someone challenged one or more of those beliefs as misguided or completely off base. You'd likely be offended or dismissive, or at least think the person was rude and should probably mind their own business.

What if we told you Jesus was the chief challenger of the first-century faith community? You don't need to spend much time in any of the New Testament Gospels before you come across Jesus questioning, correcting, and redirecting the thinking of people—particularly the Jewish authorities and religious leaders.

In Matthew 5–7, often referred to as the Sermon on the Mount, Jesus' mountainside teachings offer support of, but also subversion of, the popular religious ideas of the day.

When we say "support," Jesus was instructing a Jewish world whose faith and beliefs were drawn from their scriptures at the time—which is our Old Testament. Jesus warns in Matthew 5:17, "Do not think that I have come to abolish the Law or the Prophets; I have not come to abolish them but to fulfill them." In his promise to fulfill the (Old Testament) writings that would have been revered by most of his hearers, Jesus reinforced their belief in God, their desire to love God and love neighbor, their vision for prophecies being fulfilled, and much more.

However, when Jesus dealt with other important topics, such as who is blessed by God, what it means to be salt and light, murder, adultery, divorce, giving to those in need, prayer, fasting, money, worry, judgment, and more, Jesus subverted and challenged common first-century Jewish beliefs and assumptions. While he often affirmed the overall topic at hand, one of his most popular phrases in the Gospels is, "You have heard it was said . . . but I say to you."

> You have heard that it was said . . . "You shall not murder." . . . But I tell you that anyone who is angry with a brother or sister will be subject to judgment. (vv. 21–22)

> You have heard that it was said, "Eye for eye, and tooth for tooth." But I tell you . . . if anyone slaps you on the right cheek, turn to them the other cheek also. (vv. 38–39)

> You have heard that it was said, "Love your neighbor and hate your enemy." But I tell you, love your enemies and pray for those who persecute you. (vv. 43–44)

Jesus wasn't content with his people mindlessly assenting to traditional forms of living out faith. Nor was Jesus satisfied with half-hearted compliance. Jesus wanted his followers to engage fully and knowingly in new actions, even if doing so required significant readjustment of their core assumptions.

Often, as we pursue the 3 Checkpoints, we avoid causing too much disagreement. Or we know a major shift is needed, but we focus on something minor because it feels more achievable. Or we don't pause long enough to consider how we might be missing God's best for our congregation.

In contrast, Jesus wasn't content to splash around in the shallow end, avoiding conflict and ignoring tensions in the name of pseudo-community. He was willing to plunge into the deep end, directly confronting even prominent leaders as needed, reserving his most forceful challenges for religious officials, decision-makers, those in power, and others who thought they spoke for God. Jesus was far more merciful and forgiving toward those who lacked power, were thought to be sinners or far from God, or lived on the edges of society.

Part of Jesus' effectiveness in challenging people was the imagery he employed. He used stories, parables, and everyday examples that people could grasp and apply to their lives. For example, his parables often highlighted agriculture, food, animals like sheep and goats, or familial or other types of relationships. Consider the enduring relevance of the parables of the prodigal son and the good Samaritan (Luke 15:11–32; 10:30–37). Jesus also addressed relevant and hot-button issues such as money, marriage, corruption, and power. In the parable of the rich man and Lazarus (16:19–31), Jesus describes a rich man who receives judgment, while Lazarus (a beggar) receives comfort. Jesus' characters are relatable, which made his stories meaningful and of great consequence to those who heard.

Faithful Next Step Questions for You and Your Team

▶ What widely held or popular assumptions in your church, particularly about Christian community or the Christian faith, might need to be challenged? If Jesus was part of your Transformation Team, what would he be most supportive of in your church, and what might he want to subvert?

> ▶ Are there people in your church or ministry, especially
> those who may be on the margins or lack power, whom
> Jesus might encourage you to listen to or involve more
> fully in this process?

Example #4: Jesus Didn't Just Preach Change; He Modeled It

Jesus certainly spent a lot of time preaching and teaching. He seemed ready to tell anyone who would listen about what God was like and how people could know God and experience more of God's kingdom.

But Jesus didn't just spout words about change. He lived change.

Perhaps one of the most recognizable symbols in the world, depicted through art, jewelry, tattoos, and much more, is the cross. It symbolizes the ultimate sacrifice Jesus made, of which we get a snapshot in Luke 23.

You already know the story well. Pilate succumbs to the crowd's demands, and Jesus is crucified between two criminals. Jesus does not resist his death, despite the crowd's cruel mocking in verse 35, "He saved others; let him save himself if he is God's Messiah, the Chosen One."

Instead, on the cross, Jesus says, "Father, forgive them, for they do not know what they are doing" (v. 34).

Jesus, to the end, models the way of life he has come into the world to demonstrate.

That God is a God of sacrificial love.

That being the Messiah is not about dictatorial power or dominating over others. No; the essence of Christian life and leadership is service toward others.

While we'd love to write an entire chapter (or book!) on the importance and meaning of Jesus' life, death, and resurrection, we'll leave that to the thousands of other commentaries, books, and sermons that already do this well. Here, we'll stick to the implications for your role as a pastor or Christian leader needing help in knowing HOW to change. Clearly, as Jesus invited people into a fundamentally different kingdom and way of life, he didn't just talk about it; he modeled it through his everyday actions.

As you lead toward the 3 Checkpoints, people are probably paying less attention to what you say and more to what you do. Depending on your proposed future-focused changes, odds are good you will not be asked to give your life. But congregants will notice whether or not you really believe and act on what you're inviting others into. They will mirror your commitment and the degree to which you actually live out the changes you seek. Especially if they're young people, they'll have a sixth sense for whether you're authentic about what you claim or desire.

> **Faithful Next Step Questions for You and Your Team**
>
> ▶ How, if at all, might your actions (or the actions of your Transformation Team) discredit the changes you're asking others to consider?
>
> ▶ Beyond what you are currently doing, what else could you do so your actions might more tangibly demonstrate the changes you want to see?

Never Stop Learning How to Lead Change Like Jesus

As we said earlier, we believe Jesus is the most effective change leader who ever lived. But we don't want this to be a quick list you check off to confirm you're keeping a few examples from Jesus in mind during your change process. Instead, we invite you into a deep and transformative commitment to follow Jesus and let his attitudes and actions permeate every area of your change process.

We also bid you to take seriously that leading change in the church is fundamentally about inviting people to trust and follow Jesus.

When you are faced with a challenge in HOW to become a Future-Focused Church, are stuck, or are unsure how to move forward, your best action may be to pause to reflect on how Jesus led change and what he might do in your context.

Whether you find yourself feeling confident and clear on your next steps toward the 3 Checkpoints or are feeling exhausted, unsure, and insecure right now, we leave you with the words Jesus spoke to his disciples in John 20:21: "Peace be with you! As the Father has sent me, I am sending you."

REFLECTION QUESTIONS

On a scale of 1–5 (with 1 being "not at all like Jesus" and 5 being "very much like Jesus"), how well would you say your Transformation Team's change efforts reflect the example and posture of Jesus? Discuss your ratings and rationale as a team.

How might you be inviting people to engage in an issue or build an institution rather than following Jesus? How can you more directly connect the changes you seek to following Jesus?

In what ways might you be focusing on programs over people? What next steps can you take to ensure that people come first?

What core beliefs or convictions are present in your church that Jesus might question, challenge, or subvert?

How can your team go beyond preaching or talking about the changes you seek and instead model those changes?

As you consider the example of Jesus leading change throughout the Gospels, what other ideas, insights, or key lessons stand out that might influence your change efforts?

10

Maintain Disciplined Attention

From "fine" to "on fire."

That's how Marcus described his church's dramatic improvement in their ministry with teenagers and young adults five years ago.

Having served as senior pastor at this small, multiethnic, Midwest congregation for twenty-five years, Marcus had gained both credibility and deep trust. Given Marcus's and the church's vision for kingdom diversity, the church had shifted from being 95 percent White to beautifully reflecting the thirty ethnicities and cultures in their region. Because of Marcus's longevity and the inherent friendliness of the congregation, the church culture was welcoming and warm.

At least for those over thirty.

Teenagers and twentysomethings didn't feel quite so valued and accepted.

As Marcus recounted during our interview, "Our youth ministry matched our denominational expectations, and we received few complaints . . . but there wasn't much enthusiasm either."

Until five years ago. That's when the church decided to give young people the attention needed. The church mustered enough funding to hire an associate pastor whose responsibilities included overseeing the youth ministry.

That new focus on engaging young people unlocked possibilities for HOW the church would move into the future. Whereas before teenagers and young adults hadn't been viewed as potential leaders, now the church board asked the entire congregation to officially and overtly prioritize young people *in every area*.

Worship leaders began integrating teenagers and young adults in all elements of weekend services. Eager for more personal connection with the next generation, Marcus and his wife frequently invited young people to their home for dinner.

When COVID-19 hit in 2020, many older members who feared exposure opted for online worship and withdrew from their church leadership roles, creating voids young people then filled. Given teenagers' and young adults' technological savvy, Marcus was pleased when they ended up "calling the shots" for online worship services, planning both what happened on camera as well as behind the scenes. In the meantime, the congregation's meals and ministry gatherings with young people continued either online or in Marcus's backyard. Young adults started coordinating the church's media department and its neighborhood outreach ministries, and even joined the church's board.

Marcus had wanted to see this sort of momentum with young people for many years but hadn't been able to ignite it given his own full load as the senior pastor. An additional leader who could devote ongoing time and energy to young people was the spark needed to make decades of future-focused progress in just a few years.

As Marcus summarized, "It's like running a relay race. The leader who comes to finish the run is full of energy, so when the baton is passed, that leader takes it to the finish line."

The Need to Maintain Disciplined Attention

You might be thinking to yourself, *I'd love to pass the baton to another leader. But our church isn't in a position to hire a new pastor to give more focus to young people.*

The good news is your church doesn't have to be.

Nor do you have to wait for another global crisis to open new leadership doors for teenagers and twentysomethings.

You can use the resources you have now to expedite progress toward your THERE . . . if you figure out HOW to *maintain disciplined attention.*[1] When you maintain disciplined attention, you ensure your future-focused Checkpoints stay toward the top of your church's always-growing to-do list. You prevent your Transformation Team—and your broader congregation—from getting discouraged by how long change takes. You prioritize your future-focused Objectives and Key Results (OKRs) to protect you and your team from being distracted by ongoing daily duties. You meet regularly to discuss HOW you are progressing to THERE, and what minor, moderate, or major adjustments need to be made in the next week, month, or year.

As you navigate HOW to move from HERE to THERE, maintaining disciplined attention helps you overcome some of the common obstacles that interrupt churches' progress, such as:

- A transition in leadership, especially by the senior pastor or key Transformation Team members.
- Day-to-day busyness of the Transformation Team.
- Difficulties in coordinating schedules.
- Unexpected obstacles.
- Unplanned crises or opportunities.
- Just plain fatigue and weariness.

For Marcus's church, that attention was maintained through a new leader who focused every week on youth outreach and discipleship. But that's not normally how it works in congregations. Typically, it's a handful of *existing* pastoral and congregational leaders who don't just talk about the future but *continue maintaining disciplined attention* on that future until it becomes a reality.

One of the reasons I (Ray) helped start the Asian American Christian Collaborative (AACC) was because there was a gap nationally in Asian American Christians' efforts to connect our Christian faith with public Christian witness—and to connect orthodoxy with orthopraxy. This broad need meant there was no shortage of ideas to pursue, creating an armful (we needed more than a handful) of tasks we needed to complete. Our disciplined and consistent efforts in drafting statements, producing resources, publishing articles, hosting a podcast, organizing panels, and galvanizing nationwide marches (including the March for Black Lives and Dignity, which was featured on ABC's *Soul of a Nation*, along with simultaneous marches in the Asian American community in fourteen cities after the shootings targeting Asian American women in Atlanta) over time brought us into consequential conversations with local, state, and even federal agencies.

Today, we thank God that as a result of all of that focused work (which, given how exhausting it was, had us ready to stop at several points), I and other AACC leaders have been invited to four meetings at the White House in this last year, often as the only Asian American Christians in the room. From the start, we knew that the work of organizing for change was only as good as our ability to follow through, and our follow-through was only as good as our disciplined attention to planning, communicating, convening, and executing the right tasks with the right people.

From our experience with churches and ministries, this ability to maintain disciplined attention is what distinguishes Transformation Teams who complete the change from those who get stalled along the way.

Your biggest threat to becoming a Future-Focused Church isn't some dramatic fatal flaw; *it's lack of follow-through.*

FIGURE 10.1

Mapping the Journey—Disciplined Attention

Maintaining disciplined attention

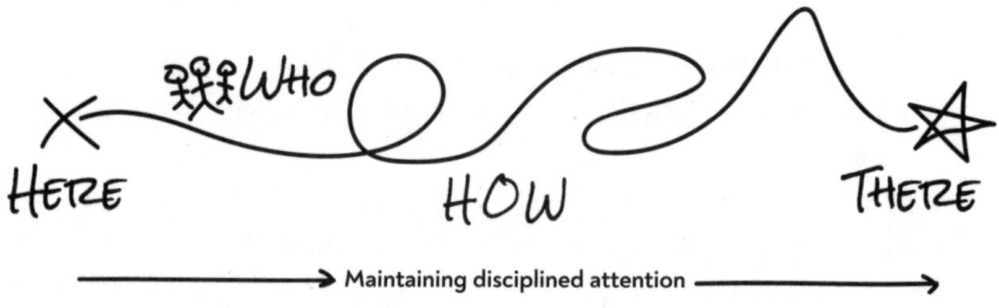

Anyone can read a book on being a Future-Focused Church. The real test is the ongoing attention channeled toward making changes after the last page is finished.

As an example, early in the pandemic, the youth ministry in a large and innovative church in the upper Midwest moved their weekly youth group meetings to Zoom. The Zoom youth group followed their typical in-person meeting pattern of a few games, some worship, a short teaching, and a few minutes of discussion in smaller groups.

Unfortunately, most teenagers quickly tired of living their lives on Zoom (especially given most schools had also moved online). Youth group attendance plummeted from an average of two hundred attendees in-person to well below one hundred participating on Zoom.

So, the youth leader decided to prioritize listening to young people. He and the volunteer team invested hours in one-on-one and small group Zoom and outdoor discussions with teenagers, asking what they wanted and needed most. The answer was clear: they wanted deeper relational connection.

The youth ministry pivoted away from the typical large youth group programming and moved toward an entirely small group model. The youth leader poured his energy and time into equipping and training adult volunteers to lead these discussion groups and build meaningful relationships with young people. Given the smaller format, some of the groups were able to meet outdoors and in-person instead of on Zoom. Within a few months, total attendance for these groups skyrocketed to over four hundred teenagers!

As the church headed into fall 2020, the youth leader continued to prioritize small groups. Together with small group leaders, he celebrated that their ministry had pivoted from a large group program to small group discipleship.

Unfortunately, this new approach didn't last.

As the pandemic emergency faded, the church's overall leadership pushed for a return to fully in-person worship. All ministry activities and ministry leaders were required to resume their large group programs.

The youth ministry begrudgingly complied—and saw attendance drop off precipitously to well below one hundred teenagers on average.

The story of this church highlights the classic axiom we mentioned before: *culture eats strategy for breakfast*. While the youth leader was responsive and strategic in his approach to youth ministry, the shifts didn't last because they couldn't maintain disciplined attention long enough to change the wider church culture.

The importance of maintaining disciplined attention in achieving goals is emphasized by psychologist Angela Duckworth, author of *Grit: The Power of Passion and Perseverance*. In her research on what makes people and organizations effective, she unpacks that it is

> critically important—and not at all easy—to keep going after failure. . . . The highly successful had a kind of ferocious determination that played out in two ways. First, these exemplars were unusually resilient and hardworking. Second, they knew in a very, very deep way what it was they wanted. They not only had determination, they had *direction*.[2]

That's why, as we unpack HOW your faith community journeys from HERE to THERE, we believe your ability to maintain

▶ If You're Feeling Overwhelmed . . .

As you attempt to integrate your previous WHO, HERE, and THERE work with next steps for HOW to make your change a reality, it's normal to be overwhelmed by everything that's on your plate. Know you're in good company with many other leaders in Scripture, throughout church history, and in leadership right now who were entrusted with responsibilities that felt too heavy to carry. Still, they trusted God would give them what they needed for that day or season. Remember you don't need to finish the whole journey right now; you simply need to take your next faithful step. You might also want to review chapter 13, where we offer a suggested timeline and process to help you effectively journey one step at a time.

disciplined attention is like a *gas pedal*. If it is used correctly, you can accelerate your progress. If it is ignored or unapplied, you're in danger of stalling out. And if you push it too much and go too fast, you're at risk of crashing.

Maintaining Disciplined Attention on Emotions

The gas pedal of disciplined attention has two components, the first of which is our emotions. By *emotions*, we mean both our affective response to situations as well as our overall emotional health. As you're becoming a Future-Focused Church, please don't lose sight of the power of emotions in HOW momentum is either accelerated or sabotaged.

Motivating the Elephant

As described initially by Jonathan Haidt in *The Happiness Hypothesis* and later amplified by brothers Chip and Dan Heath in *Switch*, each of us has two parts that drive us: our emotional side, which can be envisioned as an Elephant, and our rational side, which is the Rider. Perched atop the Elephant, the Rider holds the reins and seems in charge. That's sometimes true, but the Rider's control is tenuous because of its small size relative to the Elephant. If the six-ton Elephant and the Rider disagree about which direction to head, the Rider is going to lose.[3]

With all 3 Checkpoints, your parish might intellectually believe they should prioritize young people, diversity, and loving your neighbors. Some of them can even cite Scripture verses that support those emphases. But as you've perhaps found in your own life and ministry, knowing what *should* change isn't enough. You need to be emotionally motivated to *want* to make the change, or at least have the emotional energy to drive forward when your rational belief in the change sputters out.

Based on their data from studying change in 130 companies globally, Kotter and Cohen summarize,

> The core of the matter is always about changing the behavior of people, and behavior change happens in highly successful situations

mostly by speaking to people's feelings. This is true even in organizations that are very focused on analysis and quantitative measurement. . . . In highly successful change efforts, people find ways to help others see the problems or solutions in ways that influence emotions, not just thought.[4]

In other words, as you plan HOW to be a Future-Focused Church, you and your Transformation Team need the emotional Elephant to get motivated.

And stay motivated.

Attending to Elephant-Sized Emotions

As we're trying to keep the Elephant motivated, other counterproductive feelings often threaten to stall our pace. When emotions arise that can trip up the progress of the Elephant, you and your team can counter by first acknowledging those emotions and then maintaining disciplined attention on more life-giving emotions.

> The chart you completed in chapter 5 in the "What Should We Be Listening For?" section can help you identify which emotions are elephant-sized in your own context.

You can counter congregants' *denial* by reminding your church of the *pain* of the current problem through both stories and data.

You're able to respond to others' *sadness* over what is changing with an ongoing vision of *hope* for what the change will mean for your church and all you love and serve.

You can answer *anger* with *empathy* for all those who are being affected by the change and naming tangible potential wins for those with the most to lose.

You can offset any *blame* about who's at fault for the current reality through *collective repentance and lament* over the entire community's role in what has transpired.

Given how tough it is to make changes, sometimes it's we leaders who end up feeling these elephant-sized emotions. That's both normal and OK, and we encourage you to turn to trusted friends and colleagues to help you process your feelings and experience God's grace, hope, and truth in response.

In any change process with diverse stakeholders, you will almost certainly step on land mines that set off all types of explosive emotions. Bringing together diverse people with diverse experiences and diverse levels of power means someone will likely be offended by someone for something that was unintentional. These are the make-it-or-break-it moments of the future-focused change process.

We once worked with a predominantly White Lutheran church located in a neighborhood that was historically White but over the past few decades had become very ethnically diverse. The initial emotions that crept up, particularly in many of the older members who had grown up in the neighborhood, were feelings of loss and fear. Loss, because the neighborhood was becoming less familiar than their experience of growing up and raising their own families. Fear, because they worried about what would happen to the heritage and identity of the congregation (which many of them had helped found) as their neighborhood changed around them.

When a new pastor came in, she empathized with the fear and loss of these church members. She affirmed their current efforts to financially support initiatives in their neighborhood but encouraged them to go beyond only giving money to building relationships with and listening to their new neighbors. In keeping with their denominational identity, this pastor channeled the story and example of Martin Luther, the sixteenth-century Reformer and namesake of the Lutheran tradition, who was willing to challenge existing realities. By retelling elements of Luther's story that embodied courage, boldness, and a willingness to try new approaches (even when they were hard), the pastor inspired the congregation by reminding them a core part of their identity as a church was one of courage and boldness.

Over time, this church began to replace their fear and loss with a sense of possibility and excitement, eager to be part of God's new work in the neighborhood. They developed reciprocal relationships with their neighbors, sought to learn and understand, and ended up opening a community center to support their neighborhood. Now, several years later, the church has become much more integrated with the population of the neighborhood, the leadership and membership are multiethnic, and the future seems bright.

Attending to Your Own Emotions

Given that God has created all humans, including leaders, as emotional beings, any process exploring HOW we can move our church toward the future involves not only the Elephant of our congregation's feelings but also our own Elephant-like feelings as leaders.

As well addressed by Pete Scazzero's toolkit of "emotionally healthy" resources, our emotional health and our leadership cannot be separated. They are one and the same.

In hindsight, reflecting on his pastoral ministry, Scazzero confesses,

> I discovered that my life is a lot like an iceberg—I was aware of only a fraction of it and largely unaware of the hidden mass beneath the surface. . . . It wasn't until I understood that these beneath-the-surface components of my life had not been transformed by Jesus that I discovered the inseparable link between emotional health and spiritual maturity—that it is not possible to be spiritually mature while remaining emotionally immature.[5]

Similar to how we previously talked about the importance of developing a *nonanxious presence*, a balanced and calming presence is essential as you seek to maintain disciplined attention. This doesn't mean you pretend to have everything together or insulate yourself from the complex feelings that can emerge as you lead change. Instead, becoming more in touch with your own emotions allows you to develop a steady presence so you can receive questions, concerns, or frustrations from others without getting overly frustrated or shutting down discussion. Others will likely notice your nonanxious presence and hopefully mirror that posture in their own discussions.

Across racial backgrounds, many churches are actively addressing mental health issues in leaders and congregants alike. Even in many ethnic communities where mental health is a difficult topic to broach, pastors and faith community leaders are realizing that mental health is vital to spiritual health—especially after the COVID-19 pandemic. Recognizing that leadership places significant demands on their mental and emotional well-being, more priests and pastors are incorporating therapy into their personal rhythms and talking about it in public messages.

This is impacting not only their own well-being but also that of their staff and congregations. Seeking to normalize therapy from the pulpit, an East Coast Black congregation dedicated an entire preaching series to addressing mental health. A Midwest Latina/o parish hosted mental health seminars and invited culturally competent licensed therapists to facilitate workshops for leaders and parishioners. A West Coast Asian American pastor found therapy so helpful that he went to graduate school for psychological training and then led his church through a fundraising process to underwrite five sessions of therapy for any member who wanted it. Churches with leaders who publicly prioritize their own mental health resonate with young people who feel at home in communities that engage with the pressures they feel daily.

Maintaining Disciplined Attention on Logistics

We will make more progress in HOW we move from HERE to THERE when we are mindful not just of emotions but also logistics. It's not enough to have the pulse for emotions in and around us; we also need a good plan.

In Exodus 18, a frequently referenced Old Testament passage about leadership, Moses is struggling with the overwhelming load of serving as judge for all of the Israelites. Moses' father-in-law, Jethro, offers needed advice to his son-in-law: "What you are doing is not good. You and these people who come to you will only wear yourselves out. The work is too heavy for you; you cannot handle it alone" (vv. 17–18).

Recently, the Holy Spirit revealed to me (Kara) a fresh leadership insight about Jethro's astute recommendation to empower others. Prior to Jethro offering this counsel, he had spent time with his daughter and grandsons (Moses' wife and sons), Zipporah, Gershom, and Eliezer. I imagine that during that mini–family reunion,

Zipporah shared about Moses' workload and the never-ending needs encountered by a leader like him.

Almost certainly, as Zipporah shared with her dad about their hectic family schedule, one or more of her emotions would have emerged. Bitterness at the demands her husband faced. Envy that others sometimes gained more of Moses' time than her or their sons. Pride that her husband was such a valuable leader. Anxiety that Moses' schedule would never change, and they'd never stop sprinting on this leadership treadmill.

Jethro responded not with platitudes but with a plan. He urged Moses to create a new organizational system in which Moses did what only he could do and other qualified leaders handled the rest, seeking Moses' counsel for only the prickliest cases.

While being overwhelmed is a problem as old as the Old Testament itself, so is the solution: the implementation of a new logistic system. To fully take advantage of the gas pedal of maintaining disciplined attention, your Transformation Team needs a logistic plan to ensure that your future-focused goals don't get sideswiped by other worthy causes in your church's lane.

Designate a Driver, and It Might Not Be a Pastor

Your Transformation Team's change process needs someone who will be its champion and protector. Someone who will make sure that in the midst of all that crowds your to-do list, your future-focused priorities and 3 Checkpoints remain toward the top in big, bold letters. Someone who helps the Transformation Team stay committed and cohesive.

That may be you.

Or it might be someone else.

> While we see definite advantages to identifying one clear driver for this work, we recognize you may need to adjust this for your context. Some churches, for example, may lean toward establishing one person as the main visionary and a second person as the main implementer.

You want a leader who can maintain disciplined attention because they embody the following four characteristics:

1. *They have (or can make) time but also realize the time commitment will fluctuate.* They ideally devote at least two to four hours per week (or more, depending on your congregation's size and complexity) to the future-focused change process, knowing there will be some seasons when the group needs to pause, or they need to invest more time.
2. *They are proactive but don't plan out all the details.* They continually look ahead to your parish's THERE, anticipating potential speed bumps and strategizing how to overcome them, without laying out every detail so people can still participate in a co-creation process.
3. *They are firm but gracious.* They hold team members (including you) accountable for assigned action steps but do so with grace.
4. *They are methodical but can adjust to ambiguity.* They can translate Objectives into granular Key Results while tolerating the inevitable ambiguity as you move toward God's best future.

For your Transformation Team to successfully maintain disciplined attention, there are three additional characteristics that need to be present in either the driver or other team members:

1. *They have relational capital.* They are respected and liked by others in your community.
2. *They are collaborative.* They listen well to others, including (maybe especially) those who disagree with them.
3. *They hold diverse perspectives.* While they are mindful of the feelings of those who are already part of your community, they can simultaneously keep their eyes on the horizon and empathize with those at the margins of, or excluded from, your current community.

In some churches, the best intersection of these qualities is a member of the pastoral or staff team—perhaps whoever oversees youth, young adult, Next Gen ministry, or the education department. Or perhaps your setting is more like other congregations we trained who make more progress when the team leader isn't a pastor but a respected member of the church who knows HOW to galvanize progress toward God's best future.

Given how vital it is that you know HOW to maintain disciplined attention, we will again sprinkle questions for you to process here and at other strategic points throughout the rest of this chapter.

Faithful Next Step Question for You and Your Team

▶ As you read over the qualities of a leader gifted in helping a team maintain disciplined attention, which of your church members or leaders came to mind?

Track Goals

We've previously shared a process of setting OKRs to help you and your community stay future-focused. Maintaining disciplined progress toward these specific goals is where the battle is ultimately won or lost.

If it hasn't been done already, take your vivid description and work as a team to identify four or five OKRs that would help accomplish each goal. Then use the table below (or another version you craft) to plot how to execute those OKRs over the next six months.

Faithful Next Step Questions for You and Your Team

▶ As you plot smaller steps to help accomplish your future goals, what do you find encouraging?

▶ What might trip up your progress?

Tracking Progress Toward OKRs

OBJECTIVE TO ACCOMPLISH?	KEY RESULTS NEEDED TO ACCOMPLISH THIS GOAL?	DEADLINE? AND WHO IS RESPONSIBLE?

Leverage Meetings

The three of us love meetings that are well-designed and bring out the best in other sharp leaders.

Which means that we don't love many meetings.

We're kidding . . .

Sort of.

As we have spent time with Future-Focused Churches and seen the good, bad, and ugly of meetings geared to maintain disciplined attention, we recommend the following tips.

> In chapter 12, we'll equip you to better navigate the tension, or downright conflict, that emerges during the change process.

FIELD GUIDE:
GOOD MEETINGS

Clarify the goal, the purpose, or the desired win. Whatever you call it, clarify ahead of time what you hope is accomplished. Your goal or purpose has to do with why the meeting is happening in the first place, what is expected of those who are attending, and what the meeting intends to achieve. For your meetings, we'd encourage you to try to identify the purpose in one or two sentences.

Make that desired goal or outcome public. Highlight that purpose or desired outcome in email communication ahead of time and on the meeting agenda.

Embrace tension. Author and management consultant Patrick Lencioni wisely highlights that many meetings lack a healthy amount of tension. If the tension is too strong, the meeting might devolve into a shouting match or hurt feelings. If the tension is too weak, you'll avoid the issues that matter most. Finding the right amount of tension, and setting that up early in the meeting, will increase people's level of interest and engagement in the matter at hand.

Designate specific roles and responsibilities. When it comes to defining the roles that people play in creating new direction, we agree with Brené Brown: "Clarity is kind."[6] It's likely one person (potentially you or the driver) needs to be responsible for guiding the team's progress and meeting agendas. Occasionally, it might make sense to have cochairs or coleaders. We've found one of the most common challenges is that teams struggle to meet consistently, so we'd encourage you to assign one person to be responsible for keeping the team meeting regularly. Other roles include note-taking, following up with others outside of meetings to make sure work is completed, and overseeing communication to key stakeholders who are not part of the meeting but need to be informed.

Clarify authority with RACI (Responsible, Approving, Consulted, Informed). When multiple congregants or stakeholders are involved, it's enormously helpful to define a specific RACI role for each: Are they Responsible for the project? Do they Approve the direction? Are they Consulted? Or are they Informed?[7] Your goal as a leader is to have your own A, or Approval, list be as small as possible and involve as many voices as C, or Consulted, as feasible.

Provide key questions ahead of time. While many people, especially busy people, may not want to work ahead of the meeting, there are many who do, especially introverts who benefit from the additional time to process in advance. Further, even if people may not want to "work" in advance, many will appreciate the opportunity to be able to think ahead.

Start with a relational connection. Invite folks to answer a specific share question, even if you only have two minutes to do so by Zoom group chat or you have to limit answers to just a few sentences. The goal is to help break the ice and set a tone for the meeting that invites people to contribute and participate. You might consider questions that focus on a highlight from people's day or why they're excited to be part of the project.

Treat the clock as your friend. Map out ahead of time how much time you want to spend on each item, and make those time estimates part of your public agenda to set expectations for the rest of the attendees. Use a timer to keep everyone's introductions on track. (Let's be honest: we pastors often go long.)

End with specific action steps. Spend your last five minutes together designating action steps, with specific people and deadlines assigned. Email (or otherwise clearly communicate) those action steps, and perhaps also notes from the meeting, to the group in the next few days.

While it is generally wise to stay on track with a planned agenda, it's important to note that cultural differences shape our relationship with time. While some come from more time-oriented cultures, where events tend to start and end at specific times and often lean toward granular planning, others come from more event-oriented cultures, where start and stop times are more fluid and strict agendas can disorient the relationship and community.

To honor those from more time-oriented cultures, do your best to prepare for the meeting, start and stop at the scheduled times, and progress through the agenda. To be mindful of those who are more event-oriented, prioritize relationships, embrace flexibility, and create margin for events and discussion to include a lot of relational time (which often means getting to some agenda items later) and extend past the time allotted.

> **Faithful Next Step Question for You and Your Team**

▶ What one or two changes can you make in your meetings that would improve HOW your Transformation Team maintains disciplined attention?

Meet Every 2–4 Weeks

Your Transformation Team should meet regularly, ideally every two to four weeks, to review progress toward your OKRs and identify current or potential risks and gaps. Meeting more frequently than that can become burdensome; less frequently and you lose momentum. As we've said, many congregational and parish teams have found meeting every three weeks is the Goldilocks "just right" scheduling rhythm.[8]

> **Faithful Next Step Question for You and Your Team**

▶ Given the rhythms of your church as well as the schedule demands of the team helping you know HOW to get THERE, how frequently do you think the team should meet?

Assess Your Available Resources

While the capacity and time of people are likely your most precious resources, it's also important to maintain disciplined attention on:

Finances—Do you have the financial support required to implement the changes that will get your church THERE?

Commitment—Do you have the enthusiastic and public endorsement of senior leaders, as well as the support of those who will most tangibly be impacted by the change?[9]

Community organizations and partnerships—Especially if you are focusing on Checkpoint #3, what community leaders and key stakeholders, or like-minded nonprofits and other churches, could partner to help make your change reality?

Faithful Next Step Question for You and Your Team

- As you pay attention to the people involved, your financial support, the commitment of others, and community organizations and partnerships, where are you a bit light on resources? Where do you feel well covered?

Focus on What's Most Important, and What May or May Not Be Urgent

Churches that effectively know HOW to make progress maintain disciplined attention on what's important, not just what's urgent.

The chart below helps you plot action steps toward your OKRs that are important, regardless of whether or not they are urgent. Note that what is urgent may be driven by stakeholders' strong opinions

FIGURE 10.2

Urgency and Importance of OKRs

	Urgent	Non-Urgent
Important	QUADRANT 1 **Crises**	QUADRANT 2 **Goals and Planning**
Not Important	QUADRANT 3 **Interruptions**	QUADRANT 4 **Distractions**

but may or may not actually be important. Just because it's urgent (at least in some people's eyes) doesn't mean it's significant for your future.

Churches that maintain disciplined attention on the 3 Future-Focused Church Checkpoints and other key priorities seek to hover in Quadrants 1 and 2. They keep their distance from Quadrant 3 and avoid Quadrant 4 at all costs.

In the diagram on the previous page, plot action steps you're taking to accomplish your OKRs. Be as ruthless as possible about whether the steps you are taking are truly important or might actually be unimportant and thus should be de-emphasized.

Faithful Next Step Questions for You and Your Team

▶ Which tasks are the most important for your future progress? Which are unimportant?

▶ How can you offload those unimportant tasks so you maintain disciplined attention on what's most significant for your success?

As leaders moving our church toward the future, what we focus on is likely to flourish. What we ignore may struggle.

Even the best plan to help you know HOW to grow your 3 Checkpoints will sputter and stall without an intentional effort to maintain disciplined attention. Just as Marcus's church at the opening of this chapter devoted resources to keep working their plan, they simultaneously made progress on the next step in their future-focused map: they launched new endeavors that engaged diverse young people.

In the case of Marcus's church, a global pandemic was the catalyst for these new initiatives. The good news for you is that it doesn't take a crisis of such magnitude to open the door for your faith community to launch new ventures. You can open new doors of future-focused change at any time—including now.

REFLECTION QUESTIONS

For whatever change your church or team is focused on in this season, on a scale of 1–5 (with 1 being "not doing well at all" and 5 being "doing really well"), how well are you maintaining disciplined attention?

As you envision HOW your church will make changes, how motivated is your Elephant, or your emotions?

What emotions do you need to attend to in your church or in yourself?

Who might be the best champion, or driver, of the change you're envisioning?

What resources do you already have access to that will help you get THERE? What resources might you lack, and how might you either gain them or compensate for them?

11

Experiment from the Edges

What do you do when your church members, or other key leaders, resist making shifts for the future?

That was the question Keegan, the youth pastor at First Church of the Nazarene, wrestled with when the rest of the church wasn't willing to quickly embrace intergenerational relationships and worship.

Keegan's answer?

He banded together with the church's community engagement pastor to integrate young people in the areas the two pastors could best influence, including the church's beloved summer mission trip to Guatemala. Starting with this trip did not feel as central to the life of the overall church and likely wouldn't bring about immediate widespread change. But Keegan and the other pastor knew that generating energy at the edges of the church was better than no momentum at all.

The two pastors intentionally recruited a diverse blend of sixty participants—nineteen teenagers and forty-one adults over thirty. At the first monthly planning meeting, all the teenagers sat together. The adults sat on the opposite side of the room. Everybody seemed fine with that separation.

At that first meeting and every subsequent planning meeting, Keegan shared with the group, "Adults, we know you might think our trip will be more efficient without teenagers. Teenagers, you might think the trip will be more fun without adults. But we are going to serve together."

While preparing for their second meeting, Keegan realized progress would best be made toward the church's ideal intergenerational future if teenagers took the lead. He strongly encouraged the young people to sit in groups of two or three with other adults around the tables. He even printed "get to know you" questions that helped break the ice. But the intergenerational climate was still pretty chilly.

In the third meeting, after Keegan's by now familiar, "We are going to serve together" speech, Bill, an adult not connected with the youth ministry in any way and skeptical of working with teenagers, raised his hand and asked, "Keegan, how much time will I have to spend with teenagers before you stop bugging me about it?"

Keep in mind, he asked this *in front of nineteen teenagers!*

Not a very promising sign.

By the time the group boarded planes for Guatemala, Keegan estimated that five out of the forty-one adults actually understood the importance of prioritizing intergenerational relationships.

Five out of forty-one is far from a majority. But the intergenerational infection of those five soon became contagious, with more and more adults choosing to sit next to teenagers at meals and in the vans. By the debrief session at the end of the third service day, the leader at one of the building sites raised his hand to commend the teenagers for their amazing attitudes and hard work. The teenagers had been so amazing that he wanted more of them assigned to his group.

That construction leader was Bill.

Yes, the same Bill who had initially asked how much time he "had" to spend with teenagers.

God used this enthusiasm from Bill and the rest of the adults on the Guatemala trip to change their relationships when they returned back home. While Keegan had initially settled for a change that began on the edges, it quickly infiltrated to the core of the church and accelerated even faster than he anticipated.

At the weekly worship service "passing of the peace," the nineteen teenagers now abandoned their former practices of staring at their phones or giving other teenagers high fives. Instead, they traversed the worship center, eager to greet and update the adults with whom they had hammered and painted.

This new phenomenon of teenagers hugging adults across the worship center caught the attention of other congregants, who then asked, "Why did that kid hug you?" That question was the perfect open door for those from the trip to share how they had worked, laughed, eaten, prayed with, and come to love the next generation.

The relational momentum from the Guatemala mission trip continued to guide HOW this church moved toward God's best future. Adults wrote handwritten notes to students, sharing Scripture verses and letting them know they were praying for them. Other adults compiled and mailed care packages to graduating seniors who were headed to college or the military. Every weekend during the worship service, high fives and updates were exchanged as sixteen-year-olds and sixty-six-year-olds became not just fellow congregants but friends.

The threads of those ten days in Guatemala continued to weave their way through the relationships, culture, and programs of the congregation. What began as an out-of-the-box idea from two pastors became central to the fabric of the church.[1]

But it started as an experiment.

An experiment not on the center stage of the church but out of the limelight, involving just a few diverse folks across generations.

As we've worked with congregations like First Church of the Nazarene seeking HOW to be future-focused, we have become champions of "experiments from the edges."[2] By *experimenting from the edges*, we mean starting with initial (often smaller) changes in less public areas both to test whether they work and to gain crucial momentum before attempting higher-risk central changes.

This could be creating a pilot intergenerational group within an existing small group ministry that is typically segmented by age groups. Or it could be an intergenerational service project that invites people across age cohorts to collaborate on mission together. Or it could be a new multilingual praise night to introduce people to worshiping in different languages.

It's the rare faith community that best makes change by experimenting at the center, in the highest profile ministry areas. Generally, the most effective progress toward becoming a Future-Focused Church comes at the periphery, where the stakes are lower and mistakes can be made, learned from, and corrected with less cost.

While we usually recommend to senior leaders and church boards that they innovate at the edges, it's all the more important if you're a leader with less positional power in your church. As Keegan experienced, while he couldn't open the biggest doors of change, he could pry open smaller doors under his control. As the dominoes fell, God spurred greater future-focused change.

Thinking more big picture about societal dynamics, people who experience minoritization along race, class, and gender lines in the broader culture often experience the same patterns within churches. In the spirit of our future-focused 3 Checkpoints, it's important that our faith communities break free from the patterns of the world that keep minoritized and marginalized groups at the edges of our communities. The edges shouldn't be a place where minoritized groups are relegated to operate but spaces where you can safely and courageously test new ideas.

Based on your level of power and authority in your church, we implore you to be on the lookout for leaders who have less power and authority and feel relegated to experimenting from the edges. Identify opportunities where you can partner together to learn from those experiments and help both those individuals and the results of your experiments to move toward the center in your church.

Now, based on HOW we have seen churches journey effectively toward God's future for them, we have become strong advocates for entrepreneurial experiments from the edges that embrace three values. Let's unpack them one by one.

Value #1: Overcoming Resistance to Change

Helping your congregation know HOW to embrace and move toward God's future inevitably means change. More often than not, change brings resistance. Whether it's a greater prioritization of young people in your church budget, a fresh effort to include your ethnically diverse neighbors' music styles, or a new outreach initiative in your community, shifts of any size can be uncomfortable. When done well, pursuing experiments from the edges turns down the resistance dial, as people feel less threatened and like they have more time to adjust to smaller increments of change.

Remember Leadership Begins with Listening

As we've discussed, one of our primary Future-Focused Church principles is that leadership begins with listening. Wise leaders and Transformation Teams getting ready to launch experiments first listen in order to better understand the type of loss feared. Is it a loss of comfort or familiarity? Is it a potential loss of relationship? Or is it a more complex loss of stature or power?

In the case of the intergenerational mission trip to Guatemala, Keegan spent enough time listening to the diverse volunteers to name what each age cohort feared would change. Adults feared losing efficiency and progress if teenagers were involved in the construction; teenagers feared losing spontaneity and fun when surrounded by what could feel like more adult "chaperones."

Note that whether it's a new intergenerational mission trip or a new traffic flow in your church parking lot, HOW you best overcome resistance is *not* by explaining how great your church's experiment could be. The first step is to *listen and understand* the potential loss that is feared. Only when you have first listened can you offer the hope your people need.

Listen and ask questions first.

Cast vision and explain second.

Most of my (Kara's) worst leadership conversations happen when I reverse that order.

Ideate the Experiment

In many situations, church leaders have listened and can identify the loss but struggle to translate that loss into tangible experiments. How does a congregation or a leadership team figure out the best one or two experiments to try?

We believe you and your team have more creative wisdom than you realize; it just needs to be unleashed and channeled. To do that, we recommend an ideation exercise below that FYI has led with dozens of diverse leaders in various contexts.[3]

FIELD GUIDE:
IDEATION EXERCISE

Before beginning this exercise, we suggest you gather ten or more index cards per team member, along with pens, sticky notes, and dot stickers. Ready? Let's begin.

Step #1: Generate Ideas (Goal: develop as many ideas on separate index cards as possible in seven minutes.) Set a timer for seven minutes and have each participant simultaneously write out one idea per index card each minute (with a timekeeper announcing when each minute ends), using one to three sentences per card.

Step #2: Organize the Chaos (Goal: organize all the ideas your team developed.) Ask each team member to share their ideas out loud, and then cluster similar ideas together. Some ideas might be able to be combined for a more potent possible experiment.

Step #3: Identify Favorite Ideas (Goal: prioritize ideas for further expansion.) Through voting by raised hands or using dot stickers, the group decides which few ideas to pursue further.

If time allows, dive into another round of "generating ideas" about the few top experiments identified (perhaps through a four- or five-minute version of the seven-minute ideation in Step #1, followed by some Step #2 organizing and Step #3 prioritizing).

After a few rounds of this ideation, you'll have a few possible experiments you can consider implementing soon, as well as a handful (or more!) of ideas that might have more potential in future months and years.

Make Sure You Are Actually Working from the Edges

For most congregations, the worst place to focus your initial Future-Focused Church ideation is in your worship services.

The worship service is at the center, not at the edges.

Do we need to change our worship services to make progress in all 3 Checkpoints by prioritizing young people, elevating diversity, and tangibly loving our neighbors? Yes—but for most faith communities, that's not Step #1. That's more like Step #7. Or #17. While you can sprinkle elements of all 3 Checkpoints into worship services at any time, many leaders find fundamental shifts in worship services too great a stretch for their people.

With Keegan's ten-day intergenerational mission trip to Guatemala, Step #1 was monthly training meetings for the trip. The trip itself was Step #2. Cross-generational relational sparks that lit all sorts of fires were Steps #3–11. Eventually, more intergenerational progress was made in the worship services, but that happened slowly and after multiple steps of momentum.

As a counterexample, one church I (Jake) coached in our past training decided to focus on young adults but didn't wait for guidance on HOW to begin making shifts. Their Transformation Team got to work immediately and reasoned (without any young adults on the team) that the young adults probably wanted their own Sunday night worship service. Based on this assumption, the church invested a significant amount of time and money in launching this young adult service.

Unfortunately, very few young adults ever came. After realizing it wasn't going to get off the ground the way they hoped, their Transformation Team shared their story with us and asked, "What should we do differently?" We encouraged them to first recruit a handful of young adults to join their team, to spend time listening, and then to launch a few experiments with lower stakes than a brand-new worship service.

Very quickly, their conversations revealed that those young adults didn't want their own worship service. Instead, they wanted deeper community with older adults in the congregation who had already negotiated the challenges of having young children, launching careers, and navigating faith. The church experimented with a few intergenerational mentoring gatherings, which were wildly successful. As is often the case, given how the 3 Checkpoints are linked, not only did young adults from the church attend but they invited peers equally hungry for quality mentoring who were not yet part of the church.

Call the Change an "Experiment"

Experiment.

It's a beautiful word.

OK, we admit that, as researchers, we are positively biased toward the term.

But part of its appeal comes from its implication that an "experiment" means evaluating our progress along the way. What we're doing is not set in stone. If HOW we are attempting to move forward doesn't work, we will abandon ship or adjust course.

Every church we've interviewed had to "experiment" (often wisely labeling it as such) during the pandemic. Some of those changes worked so well that those short-term shifts became part of their post-pandemic long-term normal.

> ▶ We choose the word *experiment* because it connotes exploration and risk-taking. To experiment is to try something new for a set period of time, evaluating as you go. However, we also understand that experimentation has been used in the past against minoritized and marginalized people and communities. We are not suggesting such degrading and dehumanizing experimentation but the type of experimentation that is empowering for all involved and catalytic for Christ-centered change and transformation.

One congregation in Scotland sought to add greater relational connection to pandemic online worship services by opening up their Zoom worship services twenty minutes early for discussion and casual worship singing. That "experiment" was so well-received by the community-starved congregation that when they were able to meet in-person again, they translated that tradition to their worship services. Twenty minutes prior to the 10:30 a.m. start of the in-person service, the worship team now leads "casual worship" for anyone who wants to join.

According to the elder we interviewed, "Before COVID, if I had suggested that we would start the services with a few casual worship songs, the shutters would have gone up. . . . But this emerged through experiments that allowed us to get around what had previously seemed to be insurmountable obstacles."

So, lessen your church's resistance by publicly labeling your changes as "experiments." If the experiments work short-term, then they can become long-term changes—the kind that those initially resistant to change may be more comfortable with over time.

Value #2: Giving Freedom to Fail

Based on our interviews with church leaders, we are convinced that effective Future-Focused Church experiments not only show HOW to overcome resistance to change but also follow three key steps that grant greater freedom to fail.

Fail Fast and Fail Forward

In a test designed to ascertain whether high quality experiments were more important than high quantity, a ceramics teacher divided his class into two halves. He instructed one half that they would be judged on the quality of the single best piece they produced that semester. Those students understandably chose to work meticulously on the same pot week after week, in search of clay excellence.

He told the other half that they would be judged by the quantity of their efforts, meaning how many pots they produced. So that group of students started a new pot each class, trying to accumulate as many finished items as possible by the end of the term.

Which group produced the highest quality work? The students who kept starting over, learning, and trying new ideas.[4]

Counterintuitively, when it comes to experiments, quantity is often more important than quality. As leaders, we give more freedom to fail when we create a culture in which failures are discussed, and maybe even celebrated, as we learn from them and improve our next attempt.

Even Jesus seems to have believed in the power of experiments, sending out his disciples in pairs to preach, drive out demons, and pray for healing (Mark 6:7–12).

We recognize that we're not just creating ceramic pots; we're leading people toward the Creator God who longs to see us all become new creations (2 Cor. 5:17). The stakes are higher. One of the best paths to choose the right size and right type of experiments for your setting is to engage key stakeholders and wise community members of all ages and ethnicities as co-creators.

Whatever size and type of Future-Focused Church experiment we try, often we know pretty quickly if it is working. In one analysis of customer research to ascertain if a new product was working, 85 percent of the problems became apparent after just five customer interviews.[5] While ministry is different from product testing, and some experiments in the church may take longer to discern if they're really working, we'd encourage you to pursue what you can learn fairly rapidly.

This data confirms our experience that while some experiments from the edges take time to discern if they are working, we usually get an accurate indication quite rapidly—especially if we have identified tangible metrics of success.

Conduct Autopsies without Blame

"I'd really like to look into why we've sucked for one hundred years."

That's certainly not a typical first-day-on-the-job speech from a new, enthusiastic senior leader, is it? That phrase captures the unusual but effective posture Darwin Smith, the leader of Kimberly-Clark, took as he assumed the seat of chief executive officer.[6]

This "Why is what we're doing not working?" mindset has been described by respected leadership theorist Jim Collins as "conducting autopsies without blame."[7] The goal in these discussions isn't to point fingers or find fault but to analyze what went wrong and what can and should be done differently in the future to remedy it.

FIELD GUIDE:
AUTOPSIES WITHOUT BLAME

To help your teams and committees conduct autopsies without blame, we recommend the following.

Frame ahead of time that you're not shaming but improving for the future. From the very first email, invitation, and opening words of your autopsy discussion to the conclusion of the process, clarify that you are not finger-pointing. Rather, you are figuring out a better future.

Early on, include yourself as part of the problem. Whatever your role in a group, and especially if you are the senior leader, you lower everyone's defensiveness when you initially acknowledge that you are part of the problem. You are not the sole problem; no one is. But your actions or inactions have contributed to the problem.

Assume others' good intentions. Default to believing the best about the intent of your coworkers until you get solid evidence to the contrary.

Celebrate what went well. Don't rush past naming victories and successes. You want to repeat them in the future.

Break down the problems step-by-step. Get as granular as you can in identifying what isn't working. What steps in the process broke down or failed to accomplish what you expected, and why?

Brainstorm potential better future processes. Collaboratively dream up multiple ideas that could have worked better and can be tried next time.

As followers of Jesus, we have the freedom to be quick to admit and discuss our mistakes. The heart of Christianity, and what separates Christianity from every other religion, is grace. We are saved not by our own works but by the work of Jesus' resurrection. Whether in our churches, our families, our friendships, or our workplaces, Jesus is bigger than any mistake. If that's not true, we need a new Jesus.

Value #3: Leveraging Small Wins

In most cases, we learn HOW to be a Future-Focused Church one incremental step at a time. During the Guatemala mission trip, God used those small steps to shift Bill from seeking the bare minimum he "had" to interact with teenagers to asking for more teenagers for his construction crew.

Author John Kotter argues that such minor or moderate steps, which we call "small wins," serve four important purposes:

1. Small wins provide feedback about the validity of our visions and strategies.
2. Small wins give an emotional lift to those of us working hard to make changes.
3. Small wins build faith in, and attract new eyes to, our initiative.
4. Small wins decrease the influence of cynics.[8]

In celebrating the power of small wins, leadership experts Teresa M. Amabile and Steven J. Kramer summarize,

> Of all the things that can boost emotions, motivation, and perceptions during a workday, the single most important is making progress in meaningful work. And the more frequently people experience that sense of progress, the more likely they are to be creatively productive in the long run.[9]

Given our data, we believe churches experience the full benefits of experiments from the edges when they align with a few key principles that maximize the impact of small wins.

In a parish that is seeking greater intergenerational relationships, a small win might be greeting times during the worship service in which congregants are specifically invited to discuss a few questions with someone from a different generation.

For a church that wants greater ethnic diversity in its membership, a small win might be a prayer walk through a more ethnically or racially diverse region or neighborhood nearby.

In a faith community that's eager to sacrificially love your neighbors, a small win could be offering congregants a few hundred dollars to experiment with new initiatives that tangibly serve the local community.

Minor wins like these create momentum, which can expedite change.

Add, Not Subtract

Often the best experiments learn HOW those shifts toward THERE can feel more like additions than subtractions. That was the case for a small rural church in the upper Midwest whose volunteer youth pastor wanted the youth praise band to periodically lead worship in the main service.

That felt like too much radical change to the congregation who, like most congregations, felt worship service experiments were anything but "from the edges."

Instead of confronting this hesitation directly, the youth pastor wisely—but subtly—decided to increase the church's exposure to the youth worship team. She changed the teenagers' rehearsal time and location so they practiced right after the worship service in the basement under the worship center.

The first Sunday, the sound of the youth drums, guitar, and singers carried, and a few adults headed downstairs after the worship service to check them out. Over time, more adults strolled downstairs after worship to check out the youth team—both because they enjoyed the contemporary music and because they were pleased their young people were devoting extra time to worshiping Jesus.

After a few months, the majority of the adults in the church were heading downstairs every week for "youth worship." Soon one of the adult leaders invited the teenagers to lead worship in the main service.

That adult leader had initially been one of the loudest voices resisting the youth worship team.

Fast-forward a few years, and the church now has a mixed/blended approach to worship—with adults and young people leading together and integrating both classic hymns and more contemporary choruses.

Thanks to the volunteer youth pastor's strategy of experimenting on the edges and adding rather than subtracting, God led her church to become more intergenerational and future-focused—without a big worship fight.

This youth pastor's experiment worked as she hoped. So did Keegan's. But many experiments don't work as we envisioned.

We believe failed experiments are actually a *good* sign for your church. If some of your experiments are not failing, you might not be reaching far enough into the future. You may be playing it too safe.

But be careful that you don't experiment—and fail—so much that you lose trust. Many congregations can experience "experiment fatigue" if their church feels unstable or feels under inordinate pressure to grow better, newer, or bigger. This is another leadership area where we need to calibrate for our own context and find that synergistic balance between being innovative for the future and content in the present.

Or you might not be listening closely enough to young people or to enough diverse people, or you might not be mindful enough of those outside of your congregation. All three of those groups at the heart of the 3 Checkpoints often stretch us toward risk and adventure. They nudge us to wonder, "What if . . . ?" or "How about if we try . . . ?" With the right ongoing support, we can hand young people, diverse members of all generations, and neighbors who are newly connecting with our church the keys of change as we experiment together into God's best future for all of us.

REFLECTION QUESTIONS

For whatever change your church or team is focused on in this season, on a scale of 1–5 (with 1 being "not doing well at all" and 5 being "doing really well"), how well are you experimenting from the edges?

When and with whom can you and your Transformation Team ideate some possible experiments?

What shifts could you make to help you fail fast and fail forward?

Which of the steps to conducting autopsies without blame would help your team learn and benefit more from your experiments?

What small wins has God brought to your process that you could celebrate?

12

Fail People's Expectations at a Rate They Can Stand

"Our church has a lot of openness to change when it comes to young people, as well as to become more racially and ethnically diverse. Similarly, while we used to be very inwardly focused, we're now really intentionally and naturally outwardly focused. We've made a lot of changes recently, but people haven't resisted or sabotaged those changes, and the conflict level has been low to nonexistent."

These comments about all 3 Checkpoints aren't simply wishful thinking. Nor are they an idealized picture of a perfect church (which we do not believe exists!). They're real statements offered by Connie, the rector of St. George's Episcopal Church, a small historic church on the East Coast, as she reflected on HOW they became a more future-focused parish.

You might be wondering (like we did) if their parish always had this level of openness. Connie would be the first to answer with an ardent *no*. The church's openness didn't happen overnight, and change dynamics haven't always been so smooth.

The rector before Connie was called by God thirty years ago when the congregation was less than twenty people and nearly ready to close its doors. That pastor tried to introduce new vision and momentum, but some members felt it was more change than they were ready for, so they left the church. But the (now smaller) remaining group leaned in to transformation, and before long, the church gained the spirit and energy of a new church plant. New people joined, the church became more diverse, and the pastor led the congregation faithfully for nearly fifteen years.

Around 2006, Connie was called as the new pastor of the now healthy congregation. She could tell her leadership was also stretching for many, especially when she invited the church to increase its focus on diverse neighbors outside of the church and increase its engagement of young people and young families.

A real test for the congregation occurred when they had the opportunity to consider merging with another nearby parish. A particularly polarizing issue was that while St. George's considered themselves to be kid-friendly, the other parish had one two-year-old who was known for running around the church during worship, which some members found distressing and disruptive. Several members of St. George's expressed reservations about if the Holy Spirit was really leading them to be *that* welcoming toward young people.

This discernment process opened up a season of identity exploration for St. George's. Congregants asked themselves what it meant to reflect the diverse body of Christ and be the hospitable people of God. Once again, some people left because their expectations weren't met. But other new folks joined who infused the church with an openness to trailblaze new responses to the changing world around them (and welcome disruptive toddlers, along with more children who followed in the coming years).

Fast-forward to the past few years, and St. George's joined a Growing Young Cohort hosted by the Episcopal Diocese of Washington. While the parish was fairly healthy, they knew they needed more tools for Checkpoint #1. Leaders hungered for more widespread intergenerational ministry and deeper mentoring relationships across all ages, and they wanted younger people to have a broader voice of leadership and influence. While these future-focused changes required a disciplined level of focus, intentionality in making changes, and clear invitations to younger and older people to participate, leaders received very little pushback.

This time, no one has left the church—and it's not because the church is moving slowly or abandoning experiments when they meet any resistance. Congregants' expectations are calibrated that change will take place, and they need to change and adjust too. There's a sense of ownership that the church's future isn't just Rector Connie's responsibility but *everyone's responsibility*.

During our interview, Rector Connie offered this final advice about HOW their changes have been so successful: "The biggest challenge with change seems to be initially getting things moving. We're now hitting my favorite part where we've been pushing a big rock, it's finally starting to roll, and we're like 'Woo-hoo! We can now just run alongside it!' If you'll go into this work without too many expectations and start by listening to people and assuming you don't know everything, people will tell you where you need to go and what you're good at. Know other churches have struggled with the same things you are, and you're not in it alone."

And by the way, that formerly disruptive toddler is now a high school student who was just confirmed and made a public affirmation of faith!

Failing People's Expectations at a Rate They Can Stand

We hope you're encouraged to see that while St. George's hasn't always been open to change, they persevered over the years and eventually developed a culture supportive of (and even seeking out) healthy change. This parish doesn't always know exactly HOW they'll move forward, but their people are typically up for the journey. They share a core commitment to seeking God's direction together—especially in relationally discipling young people, modeling kingdom diversity, and tangibly loving their neighbors.

If you've been in church leadership for any period of time, you know that leading a small, medium, or large congregation involves *managing people's expectations*. This includes attending to what people like and don't like, and everything in between. You almost certainly noticed that several people left St. George's due to the changes made. But the flip side is that many new people also joined the church because of those very same shifts.

In any change, HOW you'll move forward involves failing, or shifting, some people's expectations. Ron Heifetz describes this work more directly: "Shifting their expectations is a polite way of saying *... fail their expectations at a rate they could stand.*"[1]

As a leader, part of your job is to stay in touch with the rate at which people can handle change. Since every parish and every person responds to change differently, it's both an art and a science to know how much change to make and how quickly to make it. If the transformations you seek exceed congregants' tolerance for change or clash with their vision for your church, they might emotionally (or financially) disengage or even physically exit from your community.

We previously introduced the concepts of adaptive and technical leadership. As a reminder, technical changes are those for which you can readily find the solution, or perhaps an authority figure or expert can solve the problem, and when it's solved, dynamics revert to the status quo. By contrast, adaptive changes require people to learn or adapt new attitudes, values, and behaviors. If your church needs to repaint or redecorate a classroom, that's a technical challenge. If you need congregants to become more externally focused and unconditionally love their neighbors, that's definitely more of an adaptive change.

As you're planning HOW to move forward, it's essential to understand that you cannot force an adaptive change on anyone. They need to come to the point where they feel and realize an adaptive change is needed . . . and actually participate in making the change. Hence the need to fail people's expectations at a rate they can stand.

The one caveat we'll name is when a community as a whole is misaligned with scriptural principles, and nothing short of repentance is required—often through public confession and lament. There are seasons when patiently and pastorally calling for adaptive change to address idolatry, syncretism, disobedience, or false beliefs can still lead to major divisions. While we encourage leaders to lovingly come alongside their people (and for church members to do the same with their leaders), you and your community's commitments to truth, righteousness, and justice should not be compromised. Like all leadership situations, these adaptive times require discernment and wisdom along with courage, conviction, and compassion, and we serve a sovereign God who gladly gives wisdom to those who ask for it (James 1:5).

During our research, we encountered another pastor who described their church as quite open to both technical and adaptive changes. When we asked if the church had always been this open to change, his answer was, "Definitely not!" He then proceeded to share HOW their church became open to change.

The previous pastor was more polarizing and known to be a lightning rod for conflict. Several years ago, that pastor decided he wanted the congregation to become more warm, welcoming, and open to newcomers (clearly an adaptive change). One obstacle to that potential hospitality was that the vast majority of the church had adopted "assigned seats" in their relevant pews—seats they or their family had consistently occupied for decades.

Wanting to shake up both the people and the pews, the pastor privately pursued what he thought was a brilliant idea. The next Sunday morning, as people entered the worship center, they discovered that all of the pews had been ripped out and stacked outdoors! To congregants' surprise and horror, in their place were chairs, which could be easily moved and rearranged.

In attempting to solve a complicated challenge that required shifting attitudes, values, and behaviors, the pastor had pursued the technical change of removing permanent seating. You can imagine what happened next. Infuriated members of the congregation voted out the pastor.

When the new leader accepted the pastorate, he shared with our team that he was able to make quite a lot of change rather quickly because nothing he did seemed as egregious as tearing out those pews!

Clearly, we are not encouraging you to rip out the pews at your church (if you have them). Instead, we suggest involving the right people as co-creators in any transformation.

For true and lasting change that results in a Future-Focused Church, your role as a leader is to increase the readiness for change and use the tools at your disposal to help people discover how *they can participate* in making the change a reality.

The work of leadership has been likened to the catalytic relationship of a therapist and a patient.[2] A good therapist does not simply provide people with answers. Instead, the role of a therapist is to create a *holding environment*, or a space that is comfortable enough for someone to do adaptive work but uncomfortable enough that they discover a need to change.

Another image of raising and lowering heat is more literal. In cooking, depending on the cuisine you're preparing (whether it's a casserole [Jake is Dutch], kimchee pajeon [Ray is Korean], or grilled sausages [Kara is German/Irish/Norwegian]), applying too little heat means the food will not cook. Too much heat applied too quickly will cause the food to burn. As the cook, your role is to apply the right amount of heat for the right amount of time (often monitoring what you are cooking and adjusting the temperature accordingly).

As a general principle, the type of change leadership that works best in churches is a low or medium amount of heat applied over a long period of time. In other words, most churches do best when functioning like a slow cooker.

Unfortunately, too many church leaders act more like microwaves. They want to cook something quickly without having to wait. The result? People in the church end up getting burned.

Before you proceed in your efforts in discerning HOW to lead change, we recommend discussing the following questions with your Transformation Team:

- What is the temperature around change in our church right now?
- Do we need to raise or lower the temperature? How might we do so?

As you assess whether or not you need to raise or lower the temperature and how to do so, you and your Transformation Team will want additional tools to know HOW to make needed changes and continue monitoring the heat. As we've journeyed with churches like yours, we've identified three essential insights to help you know HOW to create the right holding environment and fail people's expectations at a rate they (and you!) can stand.

Insight #1: All Change Is Loss

There's a popular myth that people in churches don't like to change.
Yes, we said *myth*.
The reality is churches change all the time. Change is not usually the challenge. It is the *loss* tied to change that people resist.
Ron Heifetz explains:

> Adaptive change stimulates resistance because it challenges people's habits, beliefs, and values. It asks them to take a loss, experience uncertainty, and even express disloyalty to people and cultures. Because adaptive change forces people to question and perhaps redefine aspects of their identity, it also challenges their sense of competence. Loss, disloyalty, and feeling incompetent: That's a lot to ask. No wonder people resist.[3]

When you're trying to introduce a change in your parish or ministry, people are not likely to resist the change. Instead, they're likely to resist the *loss or fear* behind that change.
As two of many additional researchers who highlight this principle, Robert Kegan and Lisa Laskow Lahey of Harvard University explain:

> It is not change that causes anxiety; it is the feeling that we are without defenses in the presence of what we see as danger that causes anxiety. That "change makes us uncomfortable" is now one of the most widely promoted, widely accepted, and underconsidered half-truths around.[4]

Again, people don't resist change; they resist loss.[5]
One congregation pursuing the future-focused 3 Checkpoints wanted to shift from a traditional to a more contemporary worship

style. Leaders experienced significant resistance from senior adults used to hymns, choir robes, and a more liturgical worship service. Instead of simply getting frustrated and admonishing an older generation that they needed to get on board with the changes, these leaders took time to listen. When they did, senior adults shared vulnerably that while they'd experienced many changes in the world and their own lives, those familiar hymns had remained consistent since their childhood. The dependable experience of worshiping through hymns kept them grounded and centered in the midst of so much disruption.

The leaders in this church realized that it wasn't the *change in worship style* that the senior adults opposed but the *loss of comfort and connection* to their own history.

As leaders wondered HOW to keep moving forward, they wisely recognized that senior adults' hunger for stability didn't lessen the church's need to change worship styles. But within their progress toward the future, leaders gained a greater sense of empathy for the pain behind the protest and adjusted HOW they paced their change. Instead of trying to push the changes through quickly like a microwave, the leadership took a slower and more deliberate approach akin to a slow cooker. In other words, they failed the older generation's expectations at a rate they could stand.

In the long run, the church ended up offering two different styles of worship service, one more traditional and the other more contemporary. As a coach for this congregation, I (Jake) joined a contemporary worship service and noticed a woman participating who was several decades older than the average worshipers. After the service, I introduced myself and asked why she chose this service over the more traditional option. She responded, "Don't get me wrong, I have a strong preference for the more traditional style of worship. However, my granddaughter does not connect with God through that form of worship. She connects through the contemporary service. I would much rather worship with my granddaughter and see her grow in her faith than have everything be the way I want it to be."

That grandmother's heart unlocks a powerful reality about HOW to lead change.

If people have expectations about the way things should be and experience loss and fear about change, then how might we best move forward? Instead of stalling out, how can we invite those same people to pursue uncomfortable adaptive change with us? By helping them focus on *something or someone they love that's more powerful than their loss*. This grandmother was certainly disappointed not to worship as she had during her childhood. But her love for her granddaughter and her longing for her granddaughter to experience God triumphed over the loss.

So, she changed.

Consider the changes you seek in your church. Perhaps they're related to young people, pursuing greater ethnic diversity, or tangibly loving your neighbors. Or maybe they have to do with deepening discipleship, pursuing catalytic relationships, or revamping your worship style. No matter the topic, work through these questions on your own or with your Transformation Team:

- What is the change you are seeking? Is it a technical or adaptive change?
- What is the loss or fear (some) people might associate with that change?
- How can you provide the opportunity for people to grieve or work through that loss?
- Is there something people might love more than that loss that could motivate them to work through the loss?
- What are the implications of your answers for the pace of your changes?

Insight #2: Change Requires a Sense of Urgency

One of the consistent mistakes church leaders make is failing to create enough urgency.

Based on his research and work with organizations on change, John Kotter labels this the most common first error in organizational change. In Kotter's estimation, over half of the companies he's interacted with tend to fail in this initial phase of the change effort. Often because they overestimate how easy it will be to get people on board, they underestimate how hard it will be to gain momentum. Eager to sprint forward toward the change, they miscalculate the inertia, or even opposition, they will face.[6]

Dr. Martin Luther King Jr. effectively harnessed the need for change in his "I Have a Dream" speech. In a later speech, he captured the urgency for change when he declared,

> We are now faced with the fact, my friends, that tomorrow is today. We are confronted with the fierce urgency of now. In this unfolding conundrum of life and history, there is such a thing as being too late. Procrastination is still the thief of time.[7]

For King, it was abundantly clear that addressing the disparities and devastation created by racism, greed, and militarism demanded an urgency—one we believe remains to this day.

Kurt Lewin, a pioneering psychologist who has greatly influenced organizational thinking and research, helpfully describes navigating others' expectations and resistance as "unfreezing."[8] Consider the difference between water that is frozen and water at room temperature. Ice is hard, static, and cannot be easily adapted to fit or fill any shape other than its current form. In contrast, room temperature water is fluid, movable, and can fill an infinite variety of different shapes and containers.

Applying this metaphor to your church's movement toward the 3 Checkpoints, it's best to assume that your congregation's collective way of being and doing are currently *frozen*. If you hope to introduce a new approach, you'll need to think carefully about HOW you will unfreeze that inertia and those expectations.

In the case of an ice cube, heat is required to melt the ice. The higher the heat, the faster it will melt. Consider a sense of urgency in your church as akin to introducing a significant amount of heat to an ice cube. If those in your church hold a well-established mental model of the way something *should be*, you'll have to make a compelling case that the mental model needs to change—and that it needs to change in the near future.

How might you and your Transformation Team create a sense of urgency in your church? Here are several ideas:

- Use a compelling vision or vivid description of the future to spur movement toward a preferred future.
- Share data, research, or stories about what is not going well, like data on the changing demographic realities in your neighborhood, declines in church attendance or budget, and the research and descriptions shared in this book.[9]
- Invite people to share stories, testimonies, or other direct appeals to confirm positive reasons for the change or perhaps voice their negative concerns and fears about what will happen if you don't change.
- Provide an opportunity for people to viscerally experience the problem or get tangibly involved in solving the problem themselves. For instance, if you're trying to persuade your church to serve or give financially toward global needs, you might provide opportunities for church members to participate in a justice trip and see and respond to needs firsthand.

One church in our training wanted more of their adults to understand and empathize with the challenges today's teenagers and young adults face, but they knew that shift wouldn't gain momentum without the attention of senior leaders and decision-makers. So, the youth leaders had a brilliant idea: they invited several board members in the church who were in their fifties and sixties to lead a few small groups of eleventh and twelfth graders. These board members were unlikely to stay up all night for a twenty-four-hour lock-in, but after some convincing, a few of them agreed to serve as small group leaders. Through serving as youth group volunteers, each board member experienced firsthand the hopes and challenges of being a teenager—in ways some hadn't since their own kids were teenagers up to a decade earlier. In future budget and strategy meetings, those board members advocated for an increased focus on younger people.

In this case, creating the initial sense of urgency didn't demand a presentation or sermon geared to convince the whole church. Instead, it required the attention and investment of a small group of influential decision-makers.

Insight #3: Change Leaders Manage Distress and Regulate the Temperature

Earlier, we likened leading change to being a sensitive therapist or a skilled cook. You need to understand the current temperature of your environment and know when and how to raise and lower the heat.

Church leaders typically need less coaching on how to raise the heat; we intuitively do that pretty well. Since heat increases as you move toward the future, or change can easily trigger loss or fear, your actions will often raise heat you didn't even intend or expect to receive. Ask open-ended questions to a large group, introduce a controversial idea, or challenge the status quo, and you are likely to raise the heat.

We repeat: you're likely to raise more heat than you realize and encounter resistance you didn't expect. So, when the heat gets a little too high, there are several practical steps you and your Transformation Team can take to lower it.

- Identify one or more of the most frustrated people and spend time listening to better understand their perspective and concerns.
- One simple option is to slow down the rate of change. Share with your congregation or those affected that you know things are moving too quickly and are going to slow down.
- Publicly celebrate small wins and signs of progress. If people are getting tired or wondering if the work is worth it, showcase good news you can share—even if it's somewhat modest.
- Invite congregants to share stories or testimonies about how the changes have already positively affected them.

▶ **Failing Expectations around Competing Commitments**

One big barrier to change is the existence of *competing commitments*, which researchers describe as subconscious or hidden fears or values that conflict with openly stated values.[10] An example of a competing commitment could be a leader who verbally says they want to be a team player and make consensus-based decisions, but behind the scenes they have a competing commitment to efficiency and believe that if they make decisions alone, progress will be better and faster.

In the church, competing commitments are values or decisions you and others want to support that conflict with one another. For example, if you're a lead pastor who wants to prioritize Checkpoint #1, you might support intergenerational worship and integrating young people further into the life of the church. However, you simultaneously believe in excellence in worship and hold high standards for music in your services. Or you may want to involve more young people in leading your worship service, but you know that will invariably bring some additional bumps, new mistakes, or an increased learning curve—and you want to avoid that tension.

As you surface competing commitments, the heat will inevitably rise in your church. Be prepared to identify, discuss, and resolve these competing commitments as you allow yourself to fail people's expectations (even if those expectations are your own).

Regulating the Heat in Light of Divisive Silos

Often the heat of change sheds light on silos that hinder your church's synergy and future-focused changes. Lencioni defines silos as "nothing more than the barriers that exist between departments within an organization, causing people who are supposed to be on the same team to work against one another."[11] In all of our research and nationwide training, we have not yet encountered a congregation free of silos. While it's prudent to hire or train volunteer specialists with expertise in children's ministry, student ministry, outreach ministry, and senior adult ministry, it's better for the whole faith community when these branches communicate and, as much as possible, collaborate.

When we increase the heat, people tend to return to their corners. Wise Future-Focused Churches recognize this and work intentionally to break down those walls. Prior to joining our team, one of our colleagues was a pastor who oversaw all ministries of a multiethnic, multisite church. This church was planted about a decade ago, and for a time was one of the fastest growing churches in the US. While amazing ministry was taking place, the Next Gen staff and ministry leaders who joined the team were focused on making *their own ministry areas* effective. They paid little attention to and gave no priority to coordinating with other ministry areas. In some cases, the children's, middle school, high school, and college ministries were actively competing for the same financial resources, volunteers, or meeting space.

Realizing that these siloed staff needed a shared goal, our colleague gathered them for an extended working retreat. Together they created a discipleship pathway that started with a hypothetical baby born into the church and progressed through various points of development as that baby grew into a young adult. At each age and stage, the pastors together asked, "At this particular stage, what would this young person need to learn about God and faith to eventually become a mature Christian adult?" The exercise galvanized the fragmented church staff by helping them see the important work and shared connections across the lifespan. They cemented this newfound unity by changing their job titles (which previously focused only on their age and stage of ministry responsibility) to all start with "Family Pastor of . . ." This shift served as a reminder that they were all seeking to serve and strengthen whole families, not just the primary age of responsibility under their care.

Minimizing silos can also start small—like with event calendars. (We recognize that in some churches, the event calendar is anything but "small.") One church in Southern California realized their siloed summer midweek events penalized families. Drawing from a fifteen-mile radius in every direction, this church's summer midweek pool parties and Bible studies for their preteen ministry, middle school ministry, and high school ministry all started at 6:30 p.m.—but were located fifteen to thirty minutes apart. Families whose kids straddled those three age ranges had to choose which child was going to be dropped off late, picked up early, or maybe not attend at all.

The family ministry pastor worked with the pastors who oversaw all three age ranges to end the summer siloing. They decided to move all of their Wednesday night pool parties to one area of their city with a lot of pools and stagger their start times by fifteen minutes. As a result, families were able to drop off kids with a lot less stress, traffic, and sibling squabbles.

Whether it's calendar siloing or more significant financial, relational, and programmatic divisions, God seems to help leaders know HOW to bring unity to their churches through the following three steps.[12]

Step #1: Recognize Silos Exist for a Reason

As leadership gurus Ronald Heifetz, Alexander Grashow, and Marty Linsky explain, "The reality is that any social system (including an organization or a country or a family) is the way it is because the people in that system (at least those individuals and factions with the most leverage) want it that way."[13]

Working with other wise church members, you can unearth how your church creates, reinforces, and gains from silos by discussing questions like:

- How do these silos benefit our church?
- How do these silos harm our community?
- How do each of us as leaders reinforce this siloed approach?

Step #2: Empathize with and Assume the Best of Those Who Perpetuate Silos

Odds are good that other leaders and church members create and maintain silos because of what they think is best for those they shepherd, not realizing what silos cost others. There also tends to be a lot of relational history and comfort within silos, which create rich sources of support and meaning for members but can also lead to the segregation and division we often see and wish to minimize.

To increase empathy across silos, involve a few trusted leaders or church members in discussions about:

- What would it cost other leaders or people in our church to give up this siloed approach?
- What can we do to minimize that cost, and perhaps even offer new benefits from being more integrated?

Step #3: Emphasize What You Hold in Common

While remaining committed to what is righteous, just, holy, loving, and truthful, it's important to remember that there are times when people simply disagree on nonessentials that they often feel are essential, which can lead to toxic siloing. We know silos will exist and that most people are siloed because there is deep meaning in their silos. But silos create sideways energy that hurts your ability to move forward into the future.

Instead of focusing primarily on what your area wants or needs, think about how multiple areas can make progress in the same direction by emphasizing what is shared and agreed upon across silos. You can begin by answering questions like:

- Where are we aligned? What do we hold in common?
- If or when we disagree, how can we remind ourselves of these core commitments we share?
- What mission statements, values, or Scripture verses that energize our church can provide common momentum?
- How can we frame our Future-Focused Church goals in terminology and images that resonate across our entire community?

When Raising the Heat Causes Conflict

Sometimes, no matter how diligently you seek to manage the temperature, you will encounter opposition and even significant conflict. To our delight, many of the churches in our research who had participated in an FYI Growing Young Cohort didn't face as much conflict as we (or they!) expected. To help you similarly avoid unnecessary conflict, as well as effectively navigate it when you do, we close this chapter by sharing some of the most important principles and practices that have helped our cohort churches.[14]

First, *commit that if there is no conflict, there is no honesty.* If you avoid honesty, you may be able to avoid conflict. Often in Christian communities, we are so drawn toward harmony that we quickly steer away from disagreement and settle for an artificial harmony. A false sense of agreement is not the same as authentic Christian community. The church is made up of people—people with different values, social locations, and expectations. Thus, being in community inevitably brings conflict.

> By "social location," we mean how each of us is shaped by our gender, race, ethnicity, social class, age, ability, religion, sexual orientation, and geography.

You want to avoid *toxic conflict,* but you need to pursue *productive conflict.* Toxic conflicts are disagreements that primarily tear people or communities apart and don't lead to positive growth or learning. Productive conflict occurs when two or more people view a situation differently, but their process of working through the disagreement leads to a clearer definition of the problem and tangible steps forward. The best way to true harmony is through productive conflict.

Second, *value the dissenter.* Whether that dissenter is a single individual or a group, valuing them starts by recognizing that dissenters are loved by God and you, and they share a common desire to follow Jesus. Often someone needs to know they are valued and taken seriously before they're willing to engage in substantive and meaningful conversation.

When it comes to valuing the dissenter, social psychologist Christena Cleveland muses,

> I wonder how much Christ's heart is broken when we denigrate followers of Christ who differ from us. . . . How much are the people for whom Christ died suffering because we remain paralyzed and divided by our differences when we should be working together as the hands and feet of Jesus in the world?[15]

Cleveland's work outlines how working through our different perspectives (including those fueled by cultural differences) can lead to true unity that is rooted in Christ.

Third, as you engage with a person or group who may think or live differently than you do, remember that *leadership begins with listening.* Don't start with convincing the other person you are right. Listen first to understand. Start with hearing their perspective and challenging yourself to understand where they are coming from. Try to identify the truth, even if it's just a few grains, in their concerns. As much as possible, practice a nonanxious presence and a nondefensive posture, and remain calm. Highlight the greater and more significant commitments to God, your church, and even the change you all share. For example, if you want to see your church prioritize young people and a dissenter believes that the church already places too much focus on young people, make sure to emphasize your shared commitment that all generations in the church grow and follow Jesus.

Finally, as much as possible, try to move toward *expanding the ownership of the conflict.* Don't let it simply be an "us versus them" dynamic in which you as the leader bear sole responsibility for resolving the tension. Once you've outlined elements that you agree on, discuss, "How might we solve this problem by working together?" Commit to a dialogue or process that might be productive. Along the way, stay mindful of the power dynamics and how they might impact broader group dynamics.

Through our congregational change interviews, we spoke with several pastors for whom conflict was a familiar topic, including a younger Latina/o pastor in one of the most ethnically diverse denominations in the US. When we spoke with him after the COVID-19 pandemic had begun to subside, he (like many other pastors) described 2020 as his toughest year in ministry ever. He had given serious consideration to quitting ministry altogether. Thankfully, he was in a better place nearly one year after that low point.

His church includes a K–12 school, and the church and school had been caught in the contentious culture wars of whether or not to wear masks. The community divided along political lines, with the more progressive group making the case that wearing masks was a way to love one's neighbor, and the more conservative group asserting that a commitment to masks was trampling their personal freedom. It wasn't an easy season to be the pastor . . . or the head of a religious school.

He explained that for several months, the community was defined primarily through vilifying and gossiping about those who saw things differently. As this pastor listened and discerned what his faith community needed, he and a small team of collaborators were convinced the church needed to revisit their core identity. They were overly defined by dogmatic polarization rather than what it meant to live out the good news of Jesus Christ.

While tempted to resign, instead the pastor started going to weekly counseling and prioritized self-care. He and his team met with church members in small groups to reflect on Scripture and ask, "What does it look like for us to take Jesus' message seriously in this season?" Through trial and error, he recognized that their ministry needed to be less program- or preaching-centered and more people- and relationship-centered.

Over time, the conflict and polarization began to diminish. In large part thanks to his team's perseverance through the conflict, the leadership began to develop more of a vision of church as family—with the love and grace of Jesus at the core.

In our last conversation with this pastor, he was clear that change was happening, but it was at a "snail's pace." He emphasized it as slow, intentional, and one step at a time. But he knows he's called to this church and continues (along with his team) to fail people's expectations at a rate they can stand and to take the next faithful step toward where God seems to be leading.

From Failing Expectations to a Process for Changing Church Culture

Being a Future-Focused Church and understanding HOW to move your church from HERE to THERE requires a deep understanding of what matters to your people, the potential losses they may feel, and the ability to navigate those losses carefully and fail people's expectations at a rate they can stand. We recommend that you don't tear out your church's pews overnight (or make any other major shift that will anger everyone) but instead locate the specific and intentional leverage points to raise the heat, and then carefully manage the distress people experience along the way.

At St. George's Episcopal Church, Rector Connie intuitively understood this process. At several points in their more recent history, she and other leaders helped congregants warm up to the idea that following Jesus and being a healthy church meant being open to changes. In their recent decisions around incorporating young people into the life of the overall church, they've reaped the benefits of years and years of investment and reinforcement of these principles.

Over this period of time, St. George's has been able to implement small and incremental changes that have added up to a shift in their church culture. While such culture shifts are the long-term goal of our change journey, they certainly don't happen overnight. Or within three months. It's a process, and in the next (and final) chapter, we get even more practical as we walk you through a flexible journey that will put you on the path to a more faithful and effective future.

REFLECTION QUESTIONS

On a scale of 1–5 (with 1 being "very low" and 5 being "very high"), what is the current "change temperature" in your church or ministry? Discuss your ratings as a team.

What are some of the losses or fears people might associate with the changes you seek?

How might you appropriately create an initial sense of urgency related to the changes you seek?

If needed, how might you tangibly lower the temperature around change?

If needed, how might you tangibly raise the temperature?

What conflicts might you experience related to change, and how can you best prepare for or anticipate those conflicts?

13

A Suggested 18-Month
Change Journey

Throughout this book, we've tried to provide the insights and practical tools you need to construct a map for your church's change journey. Since the path of every congregation, parish, and ministry is unique, we haven't yet offered a rough timeline to follow.

That's about to change.

As we've previously advised, you need to be sure the design and composition of both your Transformation Team and your change plan match your scope, authority, and responsibility. Try to avoid the extreme of assuming that one quick new ministry idea will solve complex challenges and thus choosing a timeline that's too short. It's also best to avoid the other extreme of assuming no real change will happen unless and until you fix every problem in your church (which will take years and likely never happen).

Here, we'll outline an eighteen-month process that your Transformation Team can consider and adapt to your context to build your best timeline. We've found a focused eighteen-month process is often the sweet spot if you're introducing adaptive changes or attempting to shift your church's culture. Eighteen months of sustained effort is long enough to bridge between multiple ministry years or seasons but short enough that you can typically invite Transformation Team members to commit for the entire duration.

We recognize many teams will not be able to commit to eighteen months, and that some of your future-focused changes are less elaborate. If that is the case for your team, we invite you to start with three, six, or twelve months, or whatever feels realistic and best for your context. After the eighteen-month process, we also outline a six-month timeframe you can use if your changes are less complex or your team wants to generate initial energy but can't commit to a longer process right now.

Calibrate Your Process with a Change Timeline Quiz

Below is a short Change Timeline Quiz to help you estimate the length of time your change effort will require.

Your first step, before taking the quiz, is to identify the change(s) you'd like to make.

Second, with your Transformation Team, score each of the following questions. (Note: because we assume you're answering the questions below as a Transformation Team, the "you" statements are meant to be plural and stand for "you and those working most closely with you." Rating these statements will likely require you to come to a consensus with others through honest discussion.)

- How much TIME do you currently have in your schedule to dedicate to this change? [1 = you're so busy you don't have time to think about anything new; 5 = you're flexible and have been waiting for a new challenge!]
- How much TRUST do you have from your supervisor or senior leadership in your church? [1 = very little; 5 = very much]
- How OPEN and READY are stakeholders in your ministry and/or church (e.g., teenagers, parents, volunteers, colleagues, key leaders) for this change? [1 = not at all open/ready; 5 = very open/ready]

- How much SUPPORT do you anticipate others in your ministry area or church (volunteers, parents) will allocate to this effort? [1 = very little; 5 = very much]
- How many of the necessary RESOURCES (finances, physical space, technology, etc.) do you have to implement this change? [1 = very few resources; 5 = abundant resources]

Your last step is to interpret your score.

If your total score is 20–25, your church or ministry may be well-positioned for change, and you can design a change journey that might be complete within six to twelve months. If your total score is 15–19, you're probably going to need more time to ready for and implement change, and you might want to design a twelve- to eighteen-month change journey. If your total score is 14 or lower, you probably have more work to do to be ready for the change and might want to envision taking eighteen or twenty-four months for your change journey.

As an example, your Transformation Team might feel God calling you to elevate intergenerational relationships and ministry as a more regular part of overall church life, or you desire to shift your culture to more significantly entrust and empower teenagers and young adults to take on meaningful leadership (what we refer to earlier in the book as "keychain leadership").

To better prioritize young people, you can certainly implement a new ministry idea within a month or two. However, one new ministry idea or program alone won't become the new norm in your culture or shift people's ongoing habits. Your new idea needs to be sustained over a longer period of time, and ideally it will catalyze additional similar initiatives. Or perhaps you face some resistance from key leaders in your congregation, lack the needed support or resources, or are short on time

▶ If you're looking for a speaker, coach, consultant, or process to guide you and your Transformation Team through lasting and transformative change, visit Fuller YouthInstitute.org to gain the support you need for your journey.

in your schedule to focus on change. All of these would be reasons to plan for a longer period of time for the initiative.

An 18-Month Step-by-Step Journey Focused on Checkpoint #1

In the example that follows, we'll envision a church or ministry that believes God is leading them toward a more intergenerational approach that hands substantive leadership keys to teenagers and young adults. The intentional steps we've mapped out already are reflected in the change journey diagram below.

FIGURE 13.1

Mapping the Journey—HOW

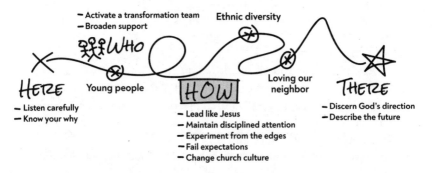

While we offer specific months and activities, these are hypothetical and contextual and are geared to illustrate a process you can—and should—modify to fit your church or ministry.

Month 1: July

For most churches and ministries, the initial dream for this future-focused shift is held by a few people, so an early step is to expand your WHO. Take time to pray for God's wisdom and guidance, and when it feels appropriate (keeping in mind that sooner is usually better than later), it's time to *Activate a Transformation Team.* Use the guidelines in chapter 3 to consider who might join the Transformation Team and how you'll invite them into the process.

Your invitations and discussions with potential team members are likely to take up much of this month as well as the next. Once your team is recruited and ready, set a regular rhythm of team meetings approximately every three weeks that will continue throughout the eighteen months (giving you twenty to twenty-four total meetings throughout the entire time period).

Month 2: August

Hopefully you're able to secure participation from all members of the Transformation Team by the end of this month (and if you can move quickly, perhaps near the start of this month). If there are people you definitely want to include on the team, but they're hard to get in touch with or want extra time to consider their involvement, it's likely worth waiting two or three additional weeks (or more) to give them the time needed.

Once you have the team recruited, schedule one or two ninety-minute meetings to pray and orient all team members to the challenges and opportunities ahead. As we outlined in chapter 3, taking sufficient time with your team to build the case for why the work is important can deepen the group's commitment. Also take time for group members to seek God together and develop relationships and an initial understanding of each other's hopes and perspectives.

Month 3: September

The next phase of your work should transition to HERE (understanding where you are now) while still keeping in mind WHO from the wider portion of your church or ministry you can involve in the creation process. We strongly recommend you take one to three months to engage in a focused listening project. Given your focus on young people, some in your church might assume you're going to implement immediate shifts that will leave older generations behind. As we've explained, taking the time to listen well reveals people's current mental models, builds empathy and trust, and provides ideas for your next steps. (The section on "How to Execute an Effective Listening Strategy" in chapter 5 can guide you through the specific scope and process.) While your main work at this stage is understanding HERE, pay attention to what you hear that might inform your church's future THERE. You might even spend one team meeting discerning a very initial picture of where God is leading you, which can begin to shape your listening and upcoming experiments.

At this stage in the process, some teams benefit from scheduling a longer planning day or off-site retreat—perhaps a Friday evening and most of the day Saturday—for a deeper exploration of the current forces that may help or hinder the desired future change. Also, begin to consider how you'll communicate the process that's underway to the wider congregation—whether that's through a town hall–type meeting or other announcements through the appropriate channels. (For ideas, see chapter 8 on communication.)

Month 4: October

As your listening process concludes, meet with your Transformation Team to consider what you've heard. (Refer back to chapter 6, which helps you pinpoint key themes emerging from your discussions.) With your focus on intergenerational ministry and keychain leadership with young people, reflect on any adaptive challenges that surfaced that might result in resistance to those changes. An example of an adaptive issue might be that many adults in the church have a strong preference for age-based programming. Shifting to more intergenerational ministry might require members of all generations to move outside their comfort zone or adopt new attitudes and actions.

You might also consider following the advice to construct and test hypotheses related to your desired shifts. Finish the statement: "_____ is happening because _____." You can also move from diagnosis to proposed action through an if-then statement, such as filling in: "If we _____, then _____."

In your Transformation Team meetings, as you reflect on your listening, also begin to ponder important insights from your church's past or feedback you received about where your church should go in the future.

Month 5: November

While you don't want to rush your listening process, you also don't need to wait too long to begin thinking about HOW you will move forward. Instead of making big changes right away, we strongly encourage you to consider conducting one or two *experiments from the edges* (chapter 11). Based on your listening, your Transformation Team might already have a few good ideas for experiments. If not, review the section on "Ideate the Experiment" and see what your team develops. For example, you might identify a quick win of an intergenerational service day or having a few teenagers assist with greeting or running the soundboard during worship services. The key is to choose something small that you can try and learn from and, if it goes well, will help you build momentum.

Month 6: December

For a change effort that will extend over a period of eighteen months, you want to be realistic about what is doable in light of the busyness of both everyday life and the church calendar. There's a good chance your team may struggle to get much done in December due to the holidays, and that's understandable.

This month might be a good time to devote a team meeting to ensure you are focused on how to *lead change like Jesus* (chapter 9) or to discuss how you will *maintain disciplined attention* (chapter 10). It's also a good time to consider if you're appropriately communicating with key stakeholders, or your entire congregation, who might appreciate an update about your work.

Month 7: January

While at this point it may feel like you're a *long way* into the change process, keep in mind that the speed of substantive church change is often glacial. Particularly when you're pursuing adaptive change or attempting to shift church culture, slow and steady tends to win the race. Also keep in mind that for most of the people in your ministry, their only exposure to the desired change might be the listening process or the smaller experiments you've conducted.

Utilize the energy of a new year to build on your listening and experiment(s) and generate momentum. This could be a good time to clarify your THERE, or where God is leading you. Review *discerning God's leading when the future is unclear* (chapter 7) and choose one or more of the exercises for imagining your church or ministry's future. As your Transformation Team engages in this work, also utilize the insights on *crafting, quantifying, and communicating a vivid description of the future* (chapter 8).

You might again consider scheduling a longer planning day or off-site retreat.

Month 8: February

In this month, continue to lean in to the goal of delineating God's best THERE for your community and those you serve. If your shift toward greater intergenerational ministry and keychain leadership is not a significant overhaul of your church's current life and ministry, you can probably move faster. If it involves big shifts for your congregation (e.g., changes to a worship service), you'll want to move more slowly. If your Transformation Team has drafted a vivid description of what the future might look like, consider sharing this with multiple stakeholders in the congregation through a church town hall meeting, or perhaps through a series of small group meetings or videos shown during worship services. It is vital that your team involves diverse people across the congregation in the creation process, so you might want to peruse the insights about how *people support what they help create* (chapter 4). Seek honest feedback and revise your direction and key statements accordingly.

Month 9: March

At this point in the change journey, it's likely time to increase your direct focus on HOW you will engage in tangible action and introduce changes. Following the advice in chapter 8, be sure you have a compelling vivid description and OKRs that call out a future vision as well as concrete actions in the short- to medium-term. While you likely want to set tangible plans for the next year or two, you also want to hold those plans somewhat loosely and be ready to adjust along the way.

Rather than make immediate and significant shifts to realize your desired change(s), we recommend you consider additional *experiments from the edges* that are likely to move you in the direction you want to go. These experiments will provide small wins and generate momentum if they succeed, while also providing you with a safe space to pilot and to learn if they don't. For example, if you want to move toward more intergenerational ministry in the church, you might experiment with new ideas related to your community's Lenten worship and Easter activities or look ahead to an intergenerational service week or mission trip during the upcoming summer.

Months 10–11: April–May

Focus on any work from previous months where you got behind and need to catch up, to finish elements of your THERE work, or to implement your experiments. Look for small wins related to how young people are honored and celebrated as they complete milestones like high school graduation or promotion from middle school.

Months 12–14: June–August

Congratulations! You're now one year into your change process! While this may sound like a long time from when you initially desired to implement your change(s), we find church and ministry leaders regularly overestimate what they can accomplish in one year and underestimate what can be done in three or five years. It's quite likely that the solid foundation you've laid for your next steps of intergenerational ministry and keychain leadership will pay off significantly and enable you to move forward more quickly than you originally anticipated.

During these months, take time in one or more Transformation Team meetings to look back and celebrate your progress. Ask if there are key lessons you've learned or shifts you'll need to make to better *maintain disciplined attention* (chapter 10). There's a chance one or two members may need to drop off the Transformation Team, and you might consider adding one or two new (and maybe more diverse) voices.

Spend most of these months making more tangible plans about HOW you will move forward and what the next year (or beyond) could hold as you polish your vision of God's THERE for your community. Survey the guidelines on how to *fail people's expectations at a rate they can stand* (chapter 12) and be sure you're calibrating the pace and scope of change as needed for your people. Often this work is best done as part of a longer planning day or off-site retreat—such as spending a Friday evening and most of Saturday together. You'll need to be realistic about what is possible with summer rhythms in your church or ministry, and you may need to adjust your regular meetings to be less frequent than normal.

Month 15: September

In many church and parish calendars, September is the start of the ministry year, which makes it a great time to implement a more substantive shift in church life or programming. The key is that you're not just guessing about what might work but have likely carefully calibrated your efforts through experimentation and listening, and your congregation is more ready for a larger change.

Months 16–17: October–November

Continue to implement your changes and make adjustments as needed. This can be a good time to engage in a second (but more abbreviated) listening process so you can receive feedback and understand how the shift is being received. Continue to look for ways to involve diverse members of your church and broader community in the creation process. If you meet too much resistance, don't be afraid to slow down the rate of change.

Month 18: December

Way to go! You are now at the end of your planned change process. Depending on the scope of your changes, you might be able to celebrate all that was accomplished and disband your team. If your changes are more substantive, you might realize it will take even more time to effectively shift your church's culture.

If your Transformation Team falls in the latter camp, it would be wise to schedule a longer meeting (or series of meetings) during this month (or perhaps the next) to consider what you'll need to do in the next six to twelve months to maintain momentum. Perhaps you don't need your team to continue to meet as frequently. Or maybe your team agrees to enact the plans you had set for the rest of the ministry year but will reconvene in May or June to evaluate. We've found many teams do well to spend a focused twelve or eighteen months of initial effort, adopt a slower pace for the next several months to let the changes sink in, and then meet again to evaluate what God might be envisioning for their church's future.

18-Month Quick Reference Chart

MONTH	ACTIVITIES
Month 1	Solidify your WHO as you begin to recruit a Transformation Team.
Month 2	Finalize Transformation Team recruitment and begin to meet regularly.
Month 3	Focus on HERE through listening and begin to discern God's THERE.
Month 4	Continue listening and begin to discern HERE and THERE themes and insights.
Month 5	Continue listening and consider experiments from the edges.
Month 6	Take the month off, consider how to lead change like Jesus, and/or discuss how to maintain disciplined attention.
Month 7	Increase your focus on THERE.
Month 8	Focus more effort on THERE through drafting a vivid description for the future.
Month 9	Lean in to HOW through making more experiments from the edges and developing tangible objectives.
Months 10–11	Catch up, refine your THERE, and continue your experiments.
Months 12–14	Celebrate the one-year mark! Revisit how you'll continue to maintain disciplined attention. Expand your WHO by adding members to the Transformation Team and make more tangible plans for HOW to move forward.
Month 15	Implement more substantive shifts based on your listening, learning, and experiments to date.
Months 16–17	Implement changes and adjust as needed.
Month 18	Celebrate and disband your Transformation Team or continue to lean in to shifting church culture.

A 6-Month Step-by-Step Journey Focused on Checkpoint #1

While we believe an extended season of effort is needed to effectively change church culture and implement adaptive changes, we recognize eighteen months isn't feasible for every ministry. If you're pursuing a less complicated change or simply need to generate some initial energy, you can consider the six-month change process outlined below. We'll continue to focus on young people but shift to a more focused goal of launching an intergenerational mentoring ministry that serves tangible needs in your community.

Month 1: July

We begin with the assumption that the desire to implement this new ministry is held by one person (likely you) or a very small group of people in your church. While your personal leadership will be essential to launch this new ministry, we nonetheless believe you'll be most effective in implementation if you spend time expanding WHO is involved and lean in to the reality that *people support what they help create* (chapter 4). You won't need to spend two months recruiting a larger Transformation Team, but you'll still invite a few people to co-create the new ministry effort with you. We'd strongly recommend involving one or more teenagers or young adults, a parent of teenagers, and an involved volunteer in your ministry.

Month 2: August

With a small team of co-creators, engage in a rapid season of listening to better understand your HERE and your THERE. You might consider drafting a short survey that asks parents in your ministry or potential volunteers to describe their interest in, or suggestions to improve, your new initiative. Gather one or two groups of teenagers (perhaps over a meal) and listen to the types of nonprofits in your community they care about, the specific adults from the church they'd want as mentors, or the ministry rhythms that would work best with their schedules. All of this feedback can inform how you design your intergenerational service concept.

Month 3: September

While you might have been ambitious about WHO you could involve in your listening or co-creation, odds are good that life and ministry got busy, and you didn't get as far as you hoped. So, take this month to continue to empathize and to develop your concept. Reflect on what you're learning (either on your own or with the small team dedicated to this work). Toward the end of the month, begin to zero in on your THERE by writing up a tangible description of the mentoring ministry. Focus on making your written summary clear and compelling, ideally one page or less.

Month 4: October

As you enter month 4, it's time to transition into the work of HOW and consider the implications of launching this mentoring ministry in a few months. While you're not trying to introduce revolutionary change, it's still worth pausing to consider how you can best *lead change like Jesus* (chapter 9). Perhaps reflect on Jesus' example of mentoring and investing in his disciples in the Gospels, and discuss with your co-creators the implications for your ministry design.

If you're able, design an initial version of the mentoring ministry you can pilot through an *experiment from the edges* (chapter 11). Perhaps consider a four-week trial in which you and another key leader or two meet regularly with a few of the teenagers who participated in your planning discussion. Launching this experiment will force you to consider who the volunteers will be, what causes or nonprofits you'll focus on, whether your church's child protection policies should be reviewed, and what (if any) curriculum or discussion questions you'll integrate. The key is to do a test run of the concept before trying to expand it so you make your inevitable mistakes in a safe space and learn how you can improve.

Month 5: November

Your experiment will likely extend into this month, and you'll realize some pieces weren't quite as well-designed as you hoped.

Take time to build on what went well and learn from what didn't go so well. Flesh out details for how you'll effectively recruit volunteers and best partner with community organizations and nonprofits, as well as secure any additional support or investment you might need from those in authority in your church.

Month 6: December

While we'd like to outline a set of tangible action steps to take this month, we're also pragmatic enough (and have served long enough in ministry settings) to know your work is likely to slow down as the realities of the holiday church calendar settle in. Carve out whatever time you can to finish plans for your ministry launch, draft communication strategies for this ministry effort in the new year, and address any other last details. Finally, be sure to celebrate with your co-creators any small wins you've been able to achieve in the past few months!

Creating Your Church's Change Journey Timeline

As we've said, there's no magical or perfect length for your ministry's change journey. While you'll want to be intentional about using the Change Timeline Quiz for an initial estimate, it will inevitably change as you dive into the work.

Further, while we've provided you with a tangible example of month-by-month activities, these are not meant to be overly prescriptive. Take the HERE, THERE, WHO, and HOW process and adapt it to *your* context and needs. The best timeline and process is one that incorporates research and ideas from others, is guided by the Holy Spirit and by Scripture, and feels achievable to your team.

The Best Days of *Your Church* Are Ahead

Remember our opening statement in this book?

The best days of the church are ahead.

Now that you've made it through the entire book (congratulations!), we hope you agree with us.

But even more, we hope you believe it is possible that the best days of *your church* are ahead.

Because we believe in a God of hope, who makes all things new.

Because we follow a Savior in Jesus, who shows us the path to follow.

Because we are empowered by the Holy Spirit.

Because we're in a season of imagination and renewal.

Because your church and wider community have people who are eager, hopeful, gifted, and full of potential waiting to be unleashed.

Because you have the tools you need to navigate your journey from HERE to THERE.

Because our world needs the hope and wholeness of the gospel.

As you lead your church through change, be encouraged that you follow the most effective change leader who ever lived. Jesus was sent into a world in need of hope, light, and joy. He challenged people's mental models. He called a group of unqualified, inexperienced people (the disciples) to join his team. He invited those disciples to journey and co-create with him. Jesus spent time listening to his team and countless others with whom he interacted. He stayed in touch with where God was leading, and he communicated a vivid description of the future through his words and parables. He gave disciplined attention to the work God had given him. He sent his disciples out to learn and grow. He failed people's expectations. And so much more.

Ultimately, Jesus taught his followers to pray the future-focused prayer, "Your kingdom come, your will be done, on earth as it is in heaven" (Matt. 6:10). As a result, his followers founded the church in Acts 2 based on the common confession that Jesus is Lord and Messiah. That early church spent time together in homes, met in the temple courts, ate and prayed together, sold property and gave to those in need, praised God together, and experienced significant growth.

That early church also experienced significant pain, division, persecution, and conflict among its leadership.

But it didn't stop there.

This Future-Focused Church leaned into the promise that there is always hope, that God is a God of resurrection who makes things new, and that we're welcomed into the process of inviting more of God's kingdom and way of life to earth here and now. This church navigated change and continued on its faithful journey.

Because of this church's foundation and witness, billions of people over the last two thousand years have come to know the gospel, or good news, of Jesus. The church has undergone countless shifts of culture and language, health and dysfunction, renewal and rebirth, decline and growth, fear and great joy. And this story of the church in Acts is *our story*.

God *has done* amazing things in the past.

God *will do* amazing things in the future.

God wants to work *through you in the present*.

You have been entrusted to discern God's direction and guide your church from HERE to THERE. It's a holy, weighty, worth-every-second-of-the-journey calling.

It has been our absolute honor and pleasure to share scriptural principles, stories, and insights with you. Our biggest prayer is that they would help you and your Transformation Team move forward in your journey and become more of the Future-Focused Church God is calling you to be.

May the best days of *your church* be ahead.

REFLECTION QUESTIONS

While the reflection questions in previous chapters have focused on that specific chapter, as we conclude our Future-Focused Church journey, these reflection questions invite you to apply insights from the entire book.

Based on your responses to the Change Timeline Quiz, what do you believe is the right anticipated length for your change journey?

On a scale of 1–5 (with 1 being "not at all well" and 5 being "very well"), rate how well your church is currently doing in each zone of the change map (WHO, HERE, THERE, and HOW).

For those zones in which you rated yourself a 1–3, what could your Transformation Team do to increase your rating to a 4 or 5? If you struggle to identify next steps, please return to the relevant chapters within that zone to identify suggestions for improvement.

As you review your notes and answers from the discussion questions in the previous chapters, what next steps could your team pursue in the next three weeks? Try to identify areas of low-hanging fruit or quick wins that help generate momentum.

What are some OKRs your Transformation Team could set for the next three months?

Given the changes you implement won't last until you've changed your church culture, what are some longer-term goals you might hope to achieve (that perhaps extend one to three years into the future)?

What are the biggest risk factors that threaten your ability to sustain your efforts over the next three weeks, three months, and three years? How might you increase your odds of maintaining your changes for the long-term?

Since we know God is the initiator and guide of all change in our churches, take time to pray as a Transformation Team that the Holy Spirit would guide your team and fill you with hope that the best days of your church are ahead. Be sure to take time to pause, listen, and consider if God has anything specific to say to you about your next steps.

APPENDIX

Research and Methodology

The content for this book emerges from three primary sources: semi-structured qualitative interviews on congregational change; Fuller Youth Institute Training Cohorts; and our combined years of scholarship and speaking, consulting, and coaching with congregations. We understand this multimethod approach as a *practical theology process*, which John Swinton, a practical theology scholar at King's College at the University of Aberdeen, describes as "critical, theological reflection on the practices of the Church as they interact with the practices of the world, with a view to ensuring and enabling faithful participation in God's redemptive practices in, to, and for the world."[1] By employing a practical theology approach, we not only report on the results of the interview research (which we will explain below) but also place these findings in conversation with our training experience, literature on organizational change, Scripture, and theology in order to hopefully and prayerfully strengthen the practices of the church in this season.

Qualitative Interviews on Congregational Change

We began our congregational change interviews in early 2020. Participants included forty-five congregational leaders from twenty-three churches that had previously participated in a one- to two-year FYI Training Cohort. During these cohorts, we walked alongside these congregations to help them discern *what* should change in their congregation as well as the initial steps for *how* to implement those shifts. Typically occurring one to five years after a church completed the cohort, interviews were especially focused on understanding how the church's change efforts developed in the year(s) following the cohort.

Tyler Greenway (FYI's research director at the time and now associate professor of psychology at Calvin University) assisted in the design of the research method. Kara Powell, Jake Mulder, and Ray Chang conducted interviews, along with Jane Hong-Guzmán de León and Patrick Jacques.

Drawing on an internal database of over one thousand congregations that had completed an FYI Training Cohort, we sought an interview sample that represented diversity of congregational race/ethnicity, church size, denomination, and geography. Once a church was contacted and agreed to participate, a church point leader nominated up to four congregational leaders to participate in separate interviews (most often two leaders with knowledge of the young people's ministries and two senior leaders with knowledge of the church's overall activities). Interview participants received a $35 Amazon.com electronic gift card as compensation for the interview.

Prior to the interview, participants completed a short survey that provided demographic and other contextual data about the church. Interviews lasted sixty to ninety minutes, were conducted by phone, and were recorded, transcribed, and coded. All interviews were completed by August 2023.

The types of questions in the interview included the following:

- What have been the top three or four goals or areas of focus for your ministry area or overall church to bring about change following the cohort? How effective have you been in those efforts?
- Reflecting on the changes that have taken place in your church, to what do you attribute these changes? What has contributed most to those changes taking place?

- What have been the biggest barriers to change in your overall church or ministry area?
- How has your church relied upon God's agency in the change process, or how has the Holy Spirit been active in your efforts?
- How would you say the unique culture of your congregation (such as denomination, race/ethnicity, or geographic location) has influenced your church's change efforts?
- To what extent would you say the changes that have taken place were planned or intentional, and to what extent have they been unplanned or more reactionary (or perhaps somewhere in between)?
- What advice might you offer to another church that is trying to make positive changes in their ministry with young people?

While we conducted a few interviews in early 2020, the research process was significantly delayed by the onset of the pandemic. We found congregational leaders were occupied with responding to the impact of the pandemic on their congregations and generally lacked the time and capacity to reflect on current or past changes. We resumed regular interviews in early 2022. While the pandemic admittedly forced leaders to respond to significant change, we were grateful for the opportunity to be immersed in leaders' stories and experiences immediately following such a disruptive season. We encouraged participants to reflect on the changes before, during, and after the pandemic in order to provide a wider view of change. Some pastors mentioned COVID-19 had accelerated positive change, and others commented that it had stalled their progress.

When we had conducted just over half of the interviews, Jake Mulder and Yulee Lee (FYI's senior director of staff and culture at the time) hosted a two-day in-person research gathering of approximately ten FYI staff members and research assistants to discuss implications emerging from the research. Each team member was assigned two or three de-identified interviews to read carefully before the gathering, noting key themes, important stories and quotes, and other observations. During the gathering, the team identified the most prominent themes that supported changes in the churches, as well as barriers to change.

We view the field of congregational change, particularly its intersection with young people, to be empirically understudied, and therefore view our research as exploratory. We utilized a *grounded theory approach*, which mixed methods researcher John W. Creswell describes as "a qualitative strategy in which the researcher derives a general, abstract theory of a process, action, or interaction grounded in the views of participants in a study."[2] Based on feedback we have received on our study design from qualitative researchers (particularly Jenny Pak of Fuller's School of Psychology & Marriage and Family Therapy), we also incorporated specific elements of narrative analysis so that the important stories of individuals and congregations were not lost in the theories developed.

While we intended to interview two participants from each congregation, in some cases (especially in smaller churches or those that had experienced significant transition) this was not possible. In the end, we interviewed forty-five church leaders from twenty-three churches.

In terms of demographics of the participating congregations, eighteen were located in the United States, two in Australia, two in Scotland, and one in Hong Kong. The ethnic diversity included four churches that identified as "Mostly Asian or Asian American," one church that identified as "Mostly Black or African American," nine churches that identified as "Mostly White," and nine churches that identified as "Multiracial or Multiethnic." Churches ranged in number of total active participants during an average week, including 100 or fewer (three churches), 101–250 (eight churches), 251–500 (three churches), 501–1,000 (two churches), 1,001–3,000 (four churches), and over 3,000 (three churches). Our sample included one church that identified from each of the following denominations: American Baptist USA, Church of Christ, Evangelical Covenant Order of Presbyterians, Evangelical Lutheran Church in America, the Church of the Nazarene, United Methodist Church, the Episcopal Church, and Presbyterian Church USA. In addition, one church had dual affiliation in the Reformed Church of America and United Church of Christ, two identified as Church of Scotland, five were Seventh-day Adventist, and seven identified as nondenominational. Finally, in terms of socioeconomic status, eight churches were primarily upper-middle class, eleven churches were primarily middle class, and four were primarily lower-middle class.

Regarding demographics of the leaders participating in the interviews, three leaders elected not to provide detailed demographic information. Ethnic diversity of the forty-two respondents who provided demographic information included eleven respondents who identified as "Asian or Asian American," five who identified as "Black or African American," one who identified as "Latina/o or Hispanic," and twenty-five who identified as "White." Twenty-seven identified as male, and fifteen identified as female. Regarding age of respondents, four were ages 18–34, seventeen were ages 35–46, ten were ages 47–54, ten were ages 55–63, and one was age 74.

We recognize one limitation of this research is the lower participation of Latina/o leaders and churches, and we are making efforts in our future research and training to involve more Latina/o leaders and churches.

Fuller Youth Institute Church Training Cohorts

For over fifteen years, FYI staff have had a front-row seat to congregational change through our cohort training. Based on the book *Sticky Faith*, we launched a Sticky Faith Cohort process that invited teams of approximately four people per church from around twenty-five churches (typically around one hundred people total) to journey through a yearlong church training process. This training process included church leaders making two three-day trips to Fuller's Pasadena, California, campus for in-person summits, along with personalized coaching, bimonthly webinars, and the creation of an action plan.

In 2016, FYI launched a second cohort process based on the book *Growing Young*. The focus of this Growing Young Cohort was shifting a church's overall culture to be more welcoming and place greater priority on teenagers and young adults. The generally yearlong Growing Young Cohort followed a similar design as the Sticky Faith Cohort, most often consisting of two in-person summits, coaching, webinars, and the development of an action plan. We conducted one to two of these cohorts annually based in Pasadena, as well as several cohorts in partnership with denominations based regionally—including in Michigan, North Carolina, Indiana, Washington State, Oregon, Texas, Washington, DC, Australia, and Scotland, as well as virtually.

The Fuller Youth Institute has also led cohort-based training on innovation, young adult ministry, and other pressing ministry topics over the past several years. In total, we have had over one thousand churches complete cohort-based training that lasts one to two years.

In their past and current roles with FYI, Kara Powell and Jake Mulder have provided key leadership for these cohort training processes, along with other FYI leaders and staff. The cohort process involves in-depth coaching, for which both Kara and Jake have served with dozens of churches, as well as spending time with the churches in-person during the summits. Cohort churches also complete an initial assessment with quantitative and qualitative responses, as well as a midway assessment survey and post-cohort survey. We have analyzed these responses for this book, as well as drawn on our experiences and interactions with these churches for our future-focused themes, stories, ideas, and examples.

Academic Experience and Other Work with Congregations

In addition to our empirical research with congregations and experience in training churches through Fuller Youth Institute Cohorts, we drew the material for this book from our other academic work and our experience speaking to, coaching, and consulting with congregations and leaders. Kara Powell's PhD is in practical theology, and she regularly speaks to tens of thousands of church leaders per year. Jake Mulder recently completed his PhD in practical theology with a focus in congregational change. Much of the literature review for Jake's doctoral dissertation, including its focus on organizational and congregational change literature, served as source material for this book. Ray Chang is pursuing a PhD in higher education with a focus on the impact of racial climate and culture on spirituality within Christian institutions, especially as it pertains to racialized minorities, and much of his literature review has also informed the source material for this book. Jake and Ray also speak regularly to Christian leaders and coach and consult with several congregations and ministry organizations per year.

While we have done our best to be faithful and rigorous in our research and the content of this book, we are aware that there is much left to learn about how to effectively guide churches through change. We're also aware that our social locations and theological commitments as authors are assets in this work but also present limitations, as we have been shaped by our various contexts—and we do not assume our perspectives should be normative or immediately applicable to all traditions and cultures. Our hope and prayer is that this book is helpful to many congregations and leaders who are dedicated yet drained and need research-based, accessible tools they can implement now.

NOTES

Chapter 1 Mapping the Journey of a Future-Focused Church

1. Exploring the Pandemic Impact on Congregations, "Back to Normal? The Mixed Messages of Congregational Recovery Coming Out of the Pandemic," August 2023, https://www.covidreligionresearch.org/wp-content/uploads/2023/09/Epic-4-2.pdf, 2.

2. Exploring the Pandemic Impact on Congregations, "I'm Exhausted All the Time: Exploring the Factors Contributing to Growing Clergy Discontentment," January 11, 2024, https://www.covidreligionresearch.org/wp-content/uploads/2024/03/Clergy_Discontentment_Patterns_Report-compressed_2.pdf. This data is similar to a 2022 survey by The Barna Group in which 42 percent of pastors expressed that they had considered quitting full-time ministry within the past year, up from 29 percent the year before. The Barna Group, "Pastors Share Top Reasons They've Considered Quitting Ministry in the Past Year," April 27, 2022, https://www.barna.com/research/pastors-quitting-ministry/.

3. Exploring the Pandemic Impact on Congregations, "Back to Normal?," 14.

4. Faith Communities Today, "Twenty Years of Congregational Change: The 2020 Faith Communities Today Overview," accessed June 18, 2024, https://faithcommunitiestoday.org/wp-content/uploads/2021/10/Faith-Communities-Today-2020-Summary-Report.pdf, 11; Mark Chaves, Joseph Roso, Anna Holleman, and Mary Hawkins, "Congregations in 21st Century America," National Congregations Study, accessed June 18, 2024, https://static1.squarespace.com/static/63e5578f1b55bd1c25cf2759/t/6459ac0a20926335c3e8fe85/1683598350842/NCSIV-report.pdf, 10. Across traditions, 70 percent of churches and parishes are now composed of less than 100 regular members, and while only 10 percent of churches have over 250 weekly attendees, those churches represent 70 percent of all US faith community attendees; see "Twenty Years of Congregational Change," 5.

So while the average church size is 65–70 people, most churchgoers actually are involved in larger congregations. The average attendee worships in a congregation of 360 regular participants; see "Congregations in 21st Century America," 10.

5. Gregory A. Smith, "About Three-in-Ten U.S. Adults Are Now Religiously Unaffiliated," Pew Research Center, December 14, 2021, https://www.pewresearch.org/re ligion/2021/12/14/about-three-in-ten-u-s-adults-are-now-religiously-unaffiliated/.

6. Pew Research Center, "Modeling the Future of Religion in America," September 13, 2022, https://www.pewresearch.org/religion/2022/09/13/modeling-the -future-of-religion-in-america/.

7. Smith, "About Three-in-Ten U.S. Adults Are Now Religiously Unaffiliated."

8. Mike Moore, "The Rise of the 'Umms,'" *Christianity Today*, March 29, 2022, https://www.christianitytoday.com/ct/2022/march-web-only/church-statistics -return-in-person-nones-dones-umms.html.

9. Nitin Nohria and Michael Beer, "Cracking the Code of Change," *Harvard Business Review*, May–June 2000, https://hbr.org/2000/05/cracking-the-code-of-change.

10. Pinetops Foundation, "The Great Opportunity," accessed December 29, 2023, https://www.greatopportunity.org/.

11. Public Religion Research Institute, "Survey: Church Attendance, Importance of Religion Declines Among Americans Overall, Yet Regular Churchgoers Largely Satisfied with Church Experiences," May 15, 2023, https://www.prri.org/press -release/survey-church-attendance-importance-of-religion-declines-among -americans-overall-yet-regular-churchgoers-largely-satisfied-with-church-experi ences/.

12. Faith Communities Today, "Twenty Years of Congregational Change," 27.

13. Practically speaking, we see so much hope, optimism, and amazing leadership gifts among all generations, especially younger people who want to see our world changed for Jesus, that we refuse to believe the best days of the church are only behind us. For example, while many young people are leaving institutional aspects of faith, others are retaining elements of spirituality, belief, and religious practice—often starting new or creative faith communities.

For a nuanced treatment on religious disaffiliation, see Ryan P. Burge, *The Nones: Where They Came From, Who They Are, and Where They Are Going* (Minneapolis: Fortress Press, 2023).

Further, while many capable and optimistic young leaders are in the US, they are also shaping churches in other countries and contributing to the reality that Christianity is growing globally. Many scholars are even suggesting that the centers of Christianity are shifting to Africa, Asia, and Central/South America.

14. Michael Tushman and Charles O'Reilly, *Winning Through Innovation: A Practical Guide to Leading Organizational Change and Renewal* (Boston: Harvard Business School Press, 1997), 184.

15. Our approach to congregational change as constructing a map consisting of these four zones is inspired by Richard Osmer's book *Practical Theology: An Introduction* (Grand Rapids: Eerdmans, 2008). Osmer conceives of practical theology as an interpretive process for making sense of situations that consists of descriptive-empirical tasks, interpretive tasks, normative tasks, and pragmatic tasks. While our four zones do not exactly replicate Osmer's tasks, we find his way of thinking about

congregational leadership to be essential for today's churches, and we've drawn some aspects of our framework from his writing and research.

16. We credit the phrase *the next faithful step* to our Fuller colleague Scott Cormode. For more on this topic, see Scott Cormode, *The Innovative Church* (Grand Rapids: Baker Academic, 2020), 203–28.

17. See Ronald A. Heifetz and Marty Linsky, "Part Three: Body and Soul," in *Leadership on the Line: Staying Alive through the Dangers of Leading* (Boston: Harvard Business School Press, 2002), 163–236.

18. If you're eager to see how the whole process fits together in a tangible timeline, you might consider doing a brief scan of chapter 13, where we suggest an eighteen-month and a six-month change timeline.

Chapter 2 3 Checkpoints That Shape Your Church's Culture

1. This quote is most commonly attributed to management guru Peter Drucker.

2. Scholar Edgar Schein offers a more detailed description that the culture of organizations (including churches) is "a pattern of shared basic assumptions learned by a group as it solves its problems . . . which has worked well enough to be considered valid and, therefore, to be taught to new members as the correct way to perceive, think, and feel in relation to those problems." See Edgar H. Schein, *Organizational Culture and Leadership* (San Francisco: Jossey-Bass, 2010), 33.

3. Please see our commentary on these phrases in chapter 9.

4. Pinetops Foundation, "The Great Opportunity."

5. Faith Communities Today, "Twenty Years of Congregational Change," 17–18.

6. Jean M. Twenge, *Generations* (New York: Atria Books, 2023), 396, 398.

7. See Kara Powell and Brad M. Griffin, *3 Big Questions That Change Every Teenager: Making the Most of Your Conversations and Connections* (Grand Rapids: Baker Books, 2021), 35; and Kara Powell, Jen Bradbury, and Brad M. Griffin, *Faith Beyond Youth Group: Five Ways to Form Character and Cultivate Lifelong Discipleship* (Grand Rapids: Baker Books, 2023), 34–47.

8. Powell and Griffin, *3 Big Questions That Change Every Teenager*, 35; Powell, Bradbury, and Griffin, *Faith Beyond Youth Group*, 34–47.

9. Springtide Research Institute, *The State of Religion & Young People 2021: Navigating Uncertainty* (Farmington, MN: Springtide Research Institute, 2021), 26.

10. The Barna Group, "How Teenagers Around the World Relate to Jesus," *The Open Generation* vol. 1 (2022): 22, https://www.barna.com/the-open-generation/open-to-jesus/.

Young people's openness to Jesus is strongly reflected in previous FYI research, which found one of the core commitments of churches that are thriving with teenagers and young adults is that those churches *take Jesus' message seriously*. Many of today's young people bemoan that too many churches water down the teaching or focus too much on hyper-entertaining programming.

11. Kara Powell, Jake Mulder, and Brad M. Griffin, *Growing Young: 6 Essential Strategies to Help Young People Discover and Love Your Church* (Grand Rapids: Baker Books, 2016), 203.

12. We chose not to use the term "BIPOC," or "Black, Indigenous, and People of Color," because while it rightly emphasizes the unique racial injustices of Black and

Indigenous communities, it simultaneously clumps Asians and Latina/os together in a way that overlooks their unique experiences of discrimination and racism.

13. Nicholas Jones et al., "2020 Census Illuminates Racial and Ethnic Composition of the Country," U.S. Census Bureau, August 12, 2021, https://www.census.gov /library/stories/2021/08/improved-race-ethnicity-measures-reveal-united-states -population-much-more-multiracial.html.

14. D'Vera Cohn and Andrea Caumont, "10 Demographic Trends Shaping the US and the World in 2016," Pew Research Center, March 31, 2016, https://www .pewresearch.org/short-reads/2016/03/31/10-demographic-trends-that-are-shaping -the-u-s-and-the-world/.

15. Sabrina Tavernise and Robert Gebeloff, "Census Shows Sharply Growing Numbers of Hispanic, Asian and Multiracial Americans," *New York Times*, August 12, 2021, https://www.nytimes.com/2021/08/12/us/us-census-population-growth -diversity.html.

16. Faith Communities Today, "Twenty Years of Congregational Change," 20.

17. Faith Communities Today, "Twenty Years of Congregational Change," 21.

18. Tom Gjelten, "Multiracial Congregations May Not Bridge Racial Divide," *All Things Considered*, July 17, 2020, https://www.npr.org/2020/07/17/891600067 /multiracial-congregations-may-not-bridge-racial-divide.

For a more nuanced academic treatment of Michael Emerson's work on the topic, see Kevin D. Dougherty, Michael O. Emerson, and Mark Chaves, "Racial Diversity in U.S. Congregations, 1998–2019," *Journal for the Scientific Study of Religion* 59, no. 4 (2020): 651–62.

19. Gary Orfield and Danielle Jarvie, "Black Segregation Matters: School Resegregation and Black Educational Opportunity," December 17, 2020, The Civil Rights Project UCLA, https://www.civilrightsproject.ucla.edu/.

20. Gjelten, "Multiracial Congregations May Not Bridge Racial Divide."

21. Gjelten, "Multiracial Congregations May Not Bridge Racial Divide."

22. As is the case in many settings in which one culture or group is dominant and shapes what is considered to be the norm, we believe it's best when the primary responsibility for catalyzing cultural change in faith communities is carried by the dominant group. So while all churches certainly need to be thoughtful and intentional in moving toward greater ethnic diversity, we believe predominantly White churches and White Christians (including Kara and Jake) bear special responsibility to step outside of comfort zones as well as share and release power.

23. Soong-Chan Rah, *The Next Evangelicalism: Freeing the Church from Western Cultural Captivity* (Downers Grove, IL: InterVarsity Press, 2009), 12.

24. The Annie E. Casey Foundation, "Social Issues that Matter to Generation Z," February 14, 2021, https://www.aecf.org/blog/generation-z-social-issues.

25. "What Kids Think: Junior Voices Survey," *The Week Junior*, November 10, 2023.

26. Exploring the Pandemic Impact on Congregations, "Congregational Response to the Pandemic: Extraordinary Social Outreach in a Time of Crisis," December 2021, https://www.covidreligionresearch.org/wp-content/uploads/2021/12 /Congregational-Response-to-the-Pandemic_Extraordinary-Social-Outreach-in -a-Time-of-Crisis_Dec-2021.pdf, 1.

27. Change expert John Kotter writes, "Culture changes only after you have successfully altered people's actions, after the new behavior produces some group benefit for a period of time, and after people see the connection between the new actions and the performance improvement." See John P. Kotter, *Leading Change* (Boston: Harvard Business School Press, 1996), 156.

28. Kim S. Cameron and Robert E. Quinn, *Diagnosing and Changing Organizational Culture* (San Francisco: Jossey-Bass, 2011), 109.

Zone I   WHO—Partners for the Journey

1. Scott Cormode has made the case that Christian leaders do not have followers but rather people who are entrusted to their care. See Scott Cormode, *The Innovative Church: How Christian Leaders and Their Congregations Can Adapt in an Ever-Changing World* (Grand Rapids: Baker Academic, 2020), 8.

Chapter 3   Activate a Transformation Team

1. Kotter Inc., "The 8 Steps for Leading Change," December 28, 2023, https://www.kotterinc.com/methodology/8-steps/.

2. Alexia Salvatierra and Peter Heltzel, *Faith-Rooted Organizing: Mobilizing the Church in Service to the World* (Downers Grove, IL: InterVarsity Press, 2014), 145.

3. Salvatierra and Heltzel, *Faith-Rooted Organizing*, 8.

4. Justo L. Gonzalez, *Santa Biblia: The Bible Through Hispanic Eyes* (Nashville: Abingdon Press, 1996), 17.

5. Rocío Lorenzo et al., "How Diverse Leadership Teams Boost Innovation," Boston Consulting Group, January 23, 2018, https://www.bcg.com/publications/2018/how-diverse-leadership-teams-boost-innovation.

6. David Rock and Heidi Grant, "Why Diverse Teams Are Smarter," *Harvard Business Review*, November 4, 2016, https://hbr.org/2016/11/why-diverse-teams-are-smarter.

7. Alison Reynolds and David Lewis, "Teams Solve Problems Faster When They're More Cognitively Diverse," *Harvard Business Review*, March 30, 2017, https://hbr.org/2017/03/teams-solve-problems-faster-when-theyre-more-cognitively-diverse.

8. Salvatierra and Heltzel, *Faith-Rooted Organizing*, 55.

9. Henrik Bresman and Amy C. Edmondson, "Research: To Excel, Diverse Teams Need Psychological Safety," *Harvard Business Review*, March 17, 2022, https://hbr.org/2022/03/research-to-excel-diverse-teams-need-psychological-safety.

10. Jim Collins, *Good to Great: Why Some Companies Make the Leap . . . and Others Don't* (New York: HarperCollins Publishers, 2001), 41.

Chapter 4   People Support What They Help Create

1. John P. Kotter and Dan S. Cohen, *The Heart of Change: Real-Life Stories of How People Change Their Organizations* (New York: Harvard Business School Press, 2002), 1.

2. Makoto Fujimura, *Culture Care: Reconnecting with Beauty for Our Common Life* (Downers Grove, IL: InterVarsity Press, 2017), 25.

3. Søren Kierkegaard, "Purity of Heart," in *Parables of Kierkegaard*, ed. Thomas Oden (New Jersey: Princeton University Press, 1989), 180–81.

4. See the Robloxian Christians Youth-Led Online Ministry, accessed June 24, 2024, https://www.therobloxianchristians.org/.

5. For more on online approaches to church, see Dave Adamson, *MetaChurch: How to Use Digital Ministry to Reach People and Make Disciples* (Cumming, GA: Orange/The reThink Group, Inc., 2022).

6. Stephen M. R. Covey, *The Speed of Trust* (New York: Free Press, 2018), 2.

7. Springtide Research Institute, *State of Religion & Young People 2021*, 33.

8. Martin B. Copenhaver, *Jesus Is the Question: The 307 Questions Jesus Asked and the 3 He Answered* (Nashville: Abingdon Press, 2014).

Chapter 5 Leadership Begins with Listening

1. Wollongong Church is an Australian congregation that has participated in a previous two-year Growing Young Cohort through the Fuller Youth Institute.

2. Cormode, *The Innovative Church*, 39.

3. Adam Bryant and Kevin Sharer, "Are You Really Listening?," *Harvard Business Review*, March-April 2021, https://hbr.org/2021/03/are-you-really-listening.

4. Yulee Lee, *Leading Change While Loving People: Change Management Insights from the Non-Profit Sector* (New York: Routledge, 2023), 1.

5. Peter M. Senge, *The Fifth Discipline: The Art & Practice of the Learning Organization* (New York: Currency Books, 2006), 8.

6. Guy Itzchakov and Avraham N. (Avi) Kluger, "The Power of Listening in Helping People Change," *Harvard Business Review*, May 17, 2018, https://hbr.org/2018/05/the-power-of-listening-in-helping-people-change.

7. Jeffrey M. Jones, "LGBT Identification in the US Ticks Up to 7.1%," Gallup, February 17, 2022, https://news.gallup.com/poll/389792/lgbt-identification-ticks-up.aspx.

8. A more technical description of Appreciative Inquiry is "a collaborative and highly participative, system-wide approach to seeking, identifying, and enhancing the 'life-giving forces' that are present when a system is performing optimally in human, economic and organizational terms. It is a journey during which profound knowledge . . . is uncovered and used to co-construct the best and highest future of that system." For more, see Jane Magruder Waktins et al., *Appreciative Inquiry: Change at the Speed of Imagination*, second ed. (San Francisco: Wiley, 2011), 22.

9. If you're interested in understanding more about Appreciative Inquiry, you can find many free resources and tools online. We would also highly recommend the book *Memories, Hopes, and Conversations: Appreciative Inquiry, Missional Engagement, and Congregational Change* from our Fuller colleague Mark Lau Branson. For those engaging in intercultural communication or ministering in multicultural contexts, we also strongly suggest *Churches, Cultures & Leadership: A Practical Theology of Congregations & Ethnicities* by Juan F. Martinez and Mark Lau Branson.

10. A resource we've found especially helpful is *Studying Congregations: A New Handbook*, edited by Nancy T. Ammerman, Jackson W. Caroll, Carl S. Dudley, and William McKinney. If you want to go deeper in your own listening, this book

provides chapters on understanding the context of a congregation, understanding congregational culture and identity, and methods for congregational study.

Chapter 6 Know Your *Why*

1. Simon Sinek, *Start with Why: How Great Leaders Inspire Everyone to Take Action* (New York: Portfolio/Penguin, 2009), 39.
2. Ronald A. Heifetz and Marty Linsky, *Leadership on the Line: Staying Alive Through the Dangers of Leading* (Boston: Harvard Business School Press, 2002), 13.
3. Heifetz and Linsky, *Leadership on the Line*, 13.
4. Ronald Heifetz and Marty Linsky, "A Survival Guide for Leaders," *Harvard Business Review*, June 2002, https://hbr.org/2002/06/a-survival-guide-for-leaders.
5. Osmer, *Practical Theology*, 1–7.
6. Ronald A. Heifetz, Marty Linsky, and Alexander Grashow, *The Practice of Adaptive Leadership: Tools and Tactics for Changing Your Organization and the World* (Boston: Harvard Business Press, 2009), 7.

Chapter 7 Discerning God's Leading When the Future Is Unclear

1. United States Census Bureau, "Median Age at First Marriage: 1890 to Present," accessed December 28, 2023, https://www.census.gov/content/dam/Census/library/visualizations/time-series/demo/families-and-households/ms-2.pdf.
2. Centers for Disease Control and Prevention, "American Women Are Waiting to Begin Families," December 11, 2002, National Center for Health Statistics, https://www.cdc.gov/nchs/pressroom/02news/ameriwomen.htm.
3. Anne Morse, "Stable Fertility Rates 1990–2019 Mask Distinct Variations by Age," United States Census Bureau, April 6, 2022, https://www.census.gov/library/stories/2022/04/fertility-rates-declined-for-younger-women-increased-for-older-women.html.
4. For example, Peter Senge's *The Fifth Discipline* focuses on creating a learning organization, *Harvard Business Review* has a set of feature articles on "10 Must Reads on Design Thinking," and Tim Shapiro has written a book on application for churches called *How Your Congregation Learns*.
5. Jim Collins and Jerry I. Porras, "Building Your Company's Vision," *Harvard Business Review*, September–October 1996, https://hbr.org/1996/09/building-your-companys-vision.
6. Collins and Porras, "Building Your Company's Vision."
7. Collins and Porras, "Building Your Company's Vision."
8. Craig Dykstra, "Imagination and the Pastoral Life," *Christian Century*, March 8, 2008, 26–31.
9. Dykstra, "Imagination and the Pastoral Life."
10. Dykstra, "Imagination and the Pastoral Life."
11. Walter Brueggemann, *The Prophetic Imagination* (Minneapolis: Fortress Press, 2018), 3.
12. Esau McCaulley, *Reading While Black: African American Biblical Interpretation as an Exercise in Hope* (Downers Grove, IL: InterVarsity Press, 2020), 91.

13. Jennings's writing on imagination is well worth reading for those interested in better understanding topics of race and faith. As a brief sample of his insights, tracing the historical and theological reasons for current challenges, he writes,

> Christianity in the Western world lives and moves within a diseased social imagination. I think most Christians sense that something about Christians' social imaginations is ill, but the analyses of this condition often don't get to the heart of the constellation of generative forces that have rendered people's social performances of the Christian light collectively anemic.

See Willie James Jennings, *The Christian Imagination: Theology and the Origins of Race* (New Haven: Yale University Press, 2010), 3–5. We've also already highlighted Justo Gonzalez's book *Santa Biblia: The Bible Through Hispanic Eyes*, and would commend it as another book to help you and your team interpret Scripture from another perspective. One additional book we would recommend for deeper work on Checkpoint #2 is Jemar Tisby, *The Color of Compromise: The Truth about the American Church's Complicity in Racism* (Grand Rapids: Zondervan, 2019).

Chapter 8 Crafting, Quantifying, and Communicating a Vivid Description of the Future

1. In this chapter we continue to draw on the work and research of Jim Collins and Jerry Porras in their book *Built to Last*. They recommend organizations create a vivid description of the future, which they describe as "a vibrant, engaging, and specific description" of what it will look like to achieve the future you imagine. For a helpful article version of the book, see Collins and Porras, "Building Your Company's Vision."

2. Cormode, *The Innovative Church*, 14–15.

3. For more on the Beloved Community, see "The King Philosophy—Nonviolence 365," The King Center, accessed July 9, 2024, https://thekingcenter.org/about-tkc/the-king-philosophy/.

4. Martin Luther King Jr., *Where Do We Go from Here: Chaos or Community?* (Boston: Beacon Press, 1968), 9.

5. Martin Luther King Jr., "Honoring Dr. Du Bois," *Freedomways* 8 (Spring 1968): 110–11.

6. Wartburg Seminary, "Master of Divinity Student Emily Norris' Story," accessed December 28, 2023, https://www.wartburgseminary.edu/student-story/emily-norris/.

7. Ryan Panchadsaram, "What Is an OKR? Definition and Examples," What Matters, accessed July 1, 2024, https://www.whatmatters.com/faqs/okr-meaning-definition-example.

8. Collins and Porras, "Building Your Company's Vision."

9. Collins and Porras, "Building Your Company's Vision."

10. Panchadsaram, "What Is an OKR?"

11. Panchadsaram, "What Is an OKR?"

12. John P. Kotter, "Leading Change: Why Transformation Efforts Fail," *Harvard Business Review*, May–June 1995, https://hbr.org/1995/05/leading-change-why-transformation-efforts-fail-2.

13. John Kotter, "Think You're Communicating Enough? Think Again," *Forbes*, June 14, 2011, https://www.forbes.com/sites/johnkotter/2011/06/14/think-youre -communicating-enough-think-again/?sh=1e6b287a6275.

14. Lee, *Leading Change While Loving People*, 117.

Chapter 9 Lead Change like Jesus

1. Jurgen Moltmann, *The Church in the Power of the Spirit* (Minneapolis: Fortress Press, 1993), xvii.

2. Christian Smith and Melinda Lunquist Denton, *Soul Searching: The Religious and Spiritual Lives of American Teenagers* (Oxford: Oxford University Press, 2005), 129.

3. Kenda Creasy Dean, *Almost Christian: What the Faith of Our Teenagers Is Telling the American Church* (New York: Oxford University Press, 2010), 3.

4. Dean, *Almost Christian*, 12.

5. Dallas Willard, *The Divine Conspiracy: Rediscovering Our Hidden Life in God* (San Francisco: HarperSanFrancisco, 1998), 301.

Chapter 10 Maintain Disciplined Attention

1. Ronald Heifetz and Donald L. Lurie, "The Work of Leadership," *Harvard Business Review*, December 2001, https://hbr.org/2001/12/the-work-of-leadership.

2. Angela Duckworth, *Grit: The Power of Passion and Perseverance* (New York: Scribner, 2016), 7–8.

3. Chip Heath and Dan Heath, *Switch* (New York: Broadway Books, 2010), 7.

4. John P. Kotter and Dan S. Cohen, *The Heart of Change* (Boston: Harvard Business School Press, 2002), x.

5. Pete Scazzero, *The Emotionally Healthy Leader: How Transforming Your Inner Life Will Deeply Transform Your Church, Team, and World* (Grand Rapids: Zondervan, 2015), 16–17.

6. Brené Brown, *Dare to Lead* (New York: Random House, 2018), 211.

7. There are other variations on "RACI" or "RASCI." We are sharing the version we have created, adapting from other versions, that we think works best.

8. Motivated by other studies' findings that, in most organizations, two out of three change initiatives fail, Harold L. Sirkin, Perry Keenan, and Alan Jackson studied 225 companies to identify the "common denominators of change." One of the four denominators that emerged was "Duration," meaning both the length of the project and the rhythms of systemic review. Interestingly, the length of the project wasn't nearly as important as the ongoing evaluations and subsequent enhancements. They summarize, "The time between reviews is more critical for success than a project's life span." Harold L. Sirkin, Perry Keenan, and Alan Jackson, "The Hard Side of Change Management," *Harvard Business Review*, October 2005, https://hbr .org/2005/10/the-hard-side-of-change-management.

9. Sirkin, Keenan, and Jackson, "The Hard Side of Change Management," 8.

Chapter 11 Experiment from the Edges

1. Kara Powell and Brad M. Griffin, *Sticky Faith Service Guide: Moving from Mission Trips to Missional Living* (Grand Rapids: Zondervan, 2016), 56–57.

2. Adapted from the phrase "experiments on the margins" from Scott Cormode, *Innovative Church* (Grand Rapids: Baker Academic, 2020), 207.

3. Steven Argue and Caleb Roose, *Sticky Faith Innovation: How Your Compassion, Creativity, and Courage Can Support Teenagers' Lasting Faith* (Pasadena, CA: Fuller Youth Institute, 2021), 135–40; Chauncey Wilson, "Using Brainwriting for Rapid Idea Generation," *Smashing Magazine* (blog), December 16, 2013, https://www.smashingmagazine.com/2013/12/using-brainwriting-for-rapid-idea-generation.

4. Tom Kelley and David Kelley, *Creative Confidence* (New York: Random House, 2013), 123.

5. Jake Knapp, *Sprint* (New York: Simon & Schuster, 2016), 198.

6. Jim Collins, "Autopsies without Blame," Jim Collins, accessed July 1, 2024, https://www.jimcollins.com/media_topics/AutopsiesWithoutBlame.html.

7. Jim Collins, *Good to Great* (New York: Harper Collins, 2001), 77.

8. Kotter and Cohen, *The Heart of Change*, 127.

9. Teresa M. Amabile and Steven J. Kramer, "The Power of Small Wins," *Harvard Business Review*, May 2011, https://hbr.org/2011/05/the-power-of-small-wins.

Chapter 12 Fail People's Expectations at a Rate They Can Stand

1. Ronald A. Heifetz, *Leadership without Easy Answers* (Cambridge: Harvard University Press, 1994), 83. Emphasis added.

2. Heifetz, *Leadership without Easy Answers*, 104.

3. Heifetz and Linksy, *Leadership on the Line*, 30.

4. Robert Kegan and Lisa Laskow Lahey, *Immunity to Change: How to Overcome it and Unlock the Potential in Yourself and Your Organization* (Boston: Harvard Business Press, 2009), 49.

5. We learned this phrase from Scott Cormode, who teaches for the Fuller Youth Institute. He has adapted an idea originally coined by Ronald Heifetz in *Leadership without Easy Answers*.

6. Kotter, *Leading Change*, 1995.

7. Martin Luther King Jr., *Beyond Vietnam: A Time to Break the Silence*, ebook ed. (New York: HarperCollins, 2024), 146.

8. Kurt Lewin, "Quasi-Stationary Social Equilibria and the Problem of Permanent Change," in *Organization Change: A Comprehensive Reader*, edited by W. Warner Burke, Dale G. Lake, and Jill Waymire Paine (San Francisco: Jossey-Bass, 2009), 73.

9. If you'd like to find data on the change in the size of your denomination or tradition, please visit the Association of Religious Data Archives, "U.S. Membership Report (2020)," ARDA, accessed July 2, 2024, https://thearda.com/us-religion/census/congregational-membership?y=2020&t=4&c=99.

10. Robert Kegan and Lisa Lahey, "The Real Reason People Won't Change," *Harvard Business Review*, November 2001, https://hbr.org/2001/11/the-real-reason-people-wont-change.

11. Patrick Lencioni, *Silos, Politics, and Turf Wars* (San Francisco: Jossey-Bass, 2006), 175.

12. Adapted from Jake Mulder, "3 Steps Toward Breaking Down Ministry Silos," Fuller Youth Institute, July 21, 2017, https://fulleryouthinstitute.org/blog/silos#_ftn2.

13. Heifetz, Grashow, and Linsky, *Practice of Adaptive Leadership*, 17.

14. Much of the Growing Young Cohort teaching on conflict is given by our colleague Scott Cormode, who weaves together his own insights with those from William Ury, *Getting Past No: Negotiating In Difficult Situations* (New York: Bantam Books, 1991).

15. Christena Cleveland, *Disunity in Christ: Uncovering the Hidden Forces That Keep Us Apart* (Downers Grove, IL: InterVarsity Press, 2013), 20.

Appendix

1. John Swinton and Harriet Mowat, *Practical Theology and Qualitative Research*, second edition (London: SCM Press, 2016), 7.

2. John W. Creswell, *Research Design: Qualitative, Quantitative, and Mixed Methods Approaches* (London: Sage Publications, 2015), 243.

KARA POWELL, PhD, is the chief of leadership formation at Fuller Theological Seminary, the executive director of the Fuller Youth Institute, and the founder of the TENx10 Collaboration. Named by *Christianity Today* as one of "50 Women to Watch," Kara also speaks regularly at national parenting and leadership conferences and has authored or coauthored numerous books, including *Faith Beyond Youth Group, 3 Big Questions That Shape Your Future, 3 Big Questions That Change Every Teenager, Growing With, Growing Young, The Sticky Faith Guide for Your Family*, and the entire Sticky Faith series. Kara and her husband, Dave, are regularly inspired by the learning and laughter that come from their three young adult children.

CONNECT WITH KARA:

KaraPowell.com

 Kara.Powell.Author

 @kpowellfyi

✗ @kpowellfyi

JAKE MULDER, PhD, is the assistant chief of leadership formation at Fuller Seminary, executive director for the non-degreed online Christian leader training platform FULLER Equip, and senior adviser for the Fuller Youth Institute and the TENx10 Collaboration. He is the coauthor of *Growing Young* and frequently speaks, coaches, and consults on congregational leadership and change. Passionate about helping individuals and churches achieve their full potential, Jake has a wide-ranging background of business and ministry roles. He lives in Grand Rapids, Michigan, with his wife, Lauren, and sons Will and Theodore.

CONNECT WITH JAKE:

Jake Mulder

@jakermulder

@jmulderFYI

RAYMOND CHANG is the executive director of the TENx10 Collaboration (part of Fuller Seminary), which is a collaborative movement that is geared toward reaching ten million young people over ten years with the gospel. He is also the president of the Asian American Christian Collaborative, which seeks to see Asian American Christians and churches established in their spiritual and cultural heritage. A writer, consultant, and speaker, he has contributed chapters to several books on preaching, leadership, culture, race, and Christianity. He and his wife, Jessica Min Chang, are proud parents of Sophia, and they reside in Chicago.

CONNECT WITH RAYMOND:

raymondchang.org

🅕 raychang502

🅘 @raychang502

🅧 @tweetraychang